SPIRIT, SOUL, BODY

Stillpoint at Beckside Retreat Center
1625 Huntley Road
Bellingham, WA 98226
www.stillpointatbeckside.com

Stillpoint at Beckside Retreat Center
1625 Huntley Road
Bellingham, WA 98226
www.stillpointbeckside.com

Spirit, Soul, Body

Toward an Integral Christian Spirituality

Cyprian Consiglio

LITURGICAL PRESS

Collegeville, Minnesota

www.litpress.org

Contents

Introduction

In 1992 I heard Fr. Bede Griffiths speak in the chapter room of the monastic community I was just joining, New Camaldoli Hermitage in Big Sur, California. It was his last trip to the United States; he died the following spring at his beloved Saccidananda Ashram, Shantivanam, on the banks of the River Kauvery in South India. There were two themes from that one-hour talk that struck me then and have stayed with me ever since, indeed, that set the course for the whole of my monastic life, spirituality, study, and work. The first theme, "The Universal Call to Contemplation," was the topic and subtitle of my first book, *Prayer in the Cave of the Heart*. The second theme is the topic of this book: the spirit, soul, and body anthropology. I have been called upon and fortunate enough to lead many retreats these past years, and almost every one of them has had one of these two themes or both as its title.

This second theme has been particularly fascinating to me for years. As the famous dictum has it, *lex orandi lex credendi*—the law of praying is the law of believing. How we understand ourselves is going to affect how we approach God (or Ultimate Reality, if you will). What we understand our goal and our end to be is going to affect how we live our lives. I have explored this from many angles and from the perspective of many traditions.

In some sense this has always been the easier of the two themes since it is so eminently practical. Thus, the second part of this book, in which I lay out a practical approach to spirituality, almost wrote itself from the numerous talks, articles, and conferences I have given on it. But the first chapters of this book, in which I attempt to lay out the philosophical framework and background—be forewarned!—are denser and will require some dedication on the part of the reader. I have been tempted to say one could skip right to the later chapters, but I think that the journey there will be much richer if you wade through the river of wisdom that flows from the great spiritual traditions and human history in the evolution of consciousness, presented in the first part of the book. Besides which, I didn't think I could put this all in writing without laying out the philosophical framework and background upon which this anthropology is based, what problem it is addressing, and particularly how Fr. Bede came to his way of thinking. As with many other things contained in his writing, Bede often alluded to and assumed readers' fore-knowledge of broad concepts. I have taken it upon myself to explore some of those broader concepts in detail, particularly the work of Sri Aurobindo Ghose (1872–1950) and Pierre Teilhard de Chardin (1881–1955), as much for myself as for my reader, to assure myself that my own conclusions were justified. If I have succeeded, these initial chapters should provide a good vocabulary with which to discuss the practical applications suggested in the second part of the book.

All of this philosophical framework and background comes down to practical application. That is, the "why" is immediately followed by the "what." The subtitle of this present book carries the weight of that: *Toward an Integral Christian Spirituality.* Anyone familiar with the work of Sri Aurobindo or the American philosopher Ken Wilber (b. 1949) will recognize the use of the word "integral." In Sanskrit, Aurobindo calls his Integral Yoga *purna yoga*, which could be translated as "full yoga." Like Ken Wilber after him, Aurobindo thought that the whole person needed to be involved in the spiritual life, the whole person is what/who is meant to be transformed in the spiritual life, so that no aspect of one's being is left behind. This is the conclusion that Fr. Bede came to as well, and that is the purpose of this book, to encourage a new spirituality that honors and incorporates every aspect of being human. As well, I want to bring a Christian voice to an exciting conversation about spirituality that is going on beyond the walls of our churches, believing not only that we have a lot to learn but that we also have something remarkable to offer the conversation as well, if we could shift our focus ever so slightly.

It almost goes without saying that I will quote Fr. Bede often in the pages ahead, with deep respect and gratitude, as our wisdom guide on this journey. But I especially dedicate and address this work to the young folks with whom I have been surrounded these past years, who gave me such hope and inspired me to continue my work as well as my own inner journey.

I end this brief introduction and begin this book with the phrase from St. Paul's letter to the Corinthians that was so enticing to Teilhard, and sums up our end as well: *God will be all in all* (1 Cor 15:28).

Part 1

Honor your body as much as the world,
then you can be trusted to care for all things.
Love the world as your very self,
then you can truly care for all things.

—Tao te Ching (no. 13)

1

The Problem of Dualism

As we study theology and spirituality, we find out along the way that for the most part all of our theological and philosophical questions, including and maybe especially our questions about spirituality and the spiritual life, are usually also (or really) anthropological questions. For example, we are not just asking who God is, or what Absolute Reality is; we are also asking, "Who am I?" and wondering how those two things go together: "What is Absolute Reality, and how should I live my life?" Who we think we are and where we think we are heading (Absolute Reality) is going to determine very practically the way we live each day, and the praxis of our spiritual life.

As we begin this text, we have to put right out front the issue of, or the *problem* of, dualism. Or shall I say "dualisms"? Because I note that there are two different though related ways that the term "dualism" is used. The first concerns the relationship of the individual to the whole, the Absolute to the relative, the One to the many, the Creator to the created, God to creation, the Subject to the object, the *aham* (I or Self) to the *idam* (the objective world of "this"). These "dualists" maintain that there is an abiding distinction between the two (hence, "dual"), while others say that God and creation are "not two." "Non-duality" is the best

7

translation of *advaita*, the Sanskrit word that has worked its way into the lexicon of many a modern Western spiritual seeker. The prophetic traditions—Judaism, Christianity and Islam—tend toward this dualism, always maintaining a distinction and distance between the Creator and the created. There are plentiful examples of this dualism in the so-called mystical traditions of Asia as well. We shall wrestle with (and not even dare to try to solve) this tension at length.The second dualism is that of flesh versus spirit-soul-consciousness. There are some (many, even) who are very comfortable stating a firm belief in the nonduality of individual self and the Divine, and yet still fall into the trap of this other, insidious dualism, that may have far more serious negative implications for our practical lives on earth than the first more ephemeral one. Stated simply, the problem I see is that having overcome the first dualism in having discovered and claimed our identity-union-communion with the Divine (Self/ self, Spirit/spirit, God/individual soul), our religious traditions and tendencies often still fall into the trap of the second dualism—thinking that the soul or spirit is good and real, whereas the body and matter are bad, or at least illusory. The practical, often subtle and insidious ramifications of this dualism are everywhere. We will begin by grappling with this second dualism.

Mistrust of the Body

Cultures in the West have inherited a kind of mistrust of the body, and by extension, matter in general, that we can never quite shake no matter how far we try to distance ourselves from Christianity. Of course, there are countless anecdotes about Christians (is it especially Catholics?) being so uptight about anything dealing with the body and bodily functions, and especially a deadly silence around anything dealing with sexuality. Such reticence could be viewed as a kind of "noble shame," but practically speaking, it has led to an enormous amount of oppression, suppression, and repression, instead of a healthy sublimation. And what we learn from psychology is that any kind of oppression, suppression, or repression ultimately leads to some kind of obsession; and obsession leads to compulsivity, and compulsivity leads to shame, and shame leads to oppression, suppression, repression, and the cycle goes on and on, the gift that keeps on giving.

As the Italian philosopher Marco Vannini explains, "It is essential for us human beings to have an experience of sexuality," for example—and I want to expand that to say that we need to have an experience of our erotic-physical self or simply of our corporeal existence—in its deepest reality, because without such an experience our physical self remains something unclear. And whatever is not brought to the light actually becomes a tie, a bond. As a matter of fact, there could really be no better place to talk about the human body than in the context of spirituality because, quoting Vannini again, "One also does not, indeed cannot, even have true knowledge of soul and body without experience of the spirit."[1]

We only have to remember the pessimism of Greek philosophy regarding the body to understand where we come from. According to the Greeks, "Life is destined to death; since the body (*soma*) is a tomb (*sema*), salvation can only consist in being freed of it through evasion. One thinks of the contrast between the Greek belief in the immortality of the soul and the Christian faith in the resurrection of bodies."[2]

Unfortunately, it is the pessimistic "body-as-tomb" view that finds its way immediately into the anthropology that most of us have inherited instead of the "Christian optimism," even (especially!) among the early Christian writers. The late theologian of Eastern Christianity Tomas Spidlik gives a list of the most famous Greek invectives. It starts out with the ancient Orphic formula *soma–sema*: "The body (*soma*) is a tomb (*sema*) for the soul." And from that the earliest writers of Christianity riff on: Clement of Alexandria says that we must "free the soul from the fetters of the flesh," or as Gregory Nazianzen writes, "from its bond (*desmos*) with a corpse," because the body is like mire where the soul can only befoul and defile itself. Gregory of Nyssa taught that "the body is a stranger to the soul" and an ugly mask, so we should "free ourself from the body" and "lay down this burden." Basil wrote that we should "take care of the soul" and never mind about the rest. The monks are just as pessimistic. Palladius, the great monastic chronicler, records the sayings of Macarius the Great that we should *despise, mistreat, and kill the body*: "It kills me I kill it." Antony the Great likewise says of the body, "It flays me I flay it." And John Climacus says that the body is an ungrateful and insidious friend of whom we should be suspicious.[3]

In this light we can understand why someone like American philosopher Sam Keen would write in his book *To a Dancing God* that neither the Christian culture nor the secular culture, in which he had been jointly nurtured, ever gave him adequate categories to interpret the warmth and grace which pervade his body. Nor did secularism or Christianity ever teach him how to interpret the sacred in the voice of the body and the language of the senses. "In the same measure that Christian theology has failed to help me realize the *carnality* of grace," he wrote, "secular ideology has failed to provide me categories for understanding the *grace* of carnality. . . ." In spite of the denials of sophisticated theologians, Christianity has never been able to escape "that ancient and perennial dualism," which he says is equally manifest in Platonism, Gnosticism, and schizophrenia, which speaks of the flesh as being of lesser dignity than the spirit and the senses inferior to the mind. In recent times there has been a resurgence of the Hebrew idea of the psychosomatic unity of the human person, and gradually "a modicum of celebration of the senses has infiltrated the church." However, as Keen reminds us, "in spite of these minor steps forward there remains a deep-seated suspicion of the carnal enthroned in the Christian understanding of history and salvation. Nothing less than a major theological revolution will allow Christianity to escape from the heresy of Gnosticism."[4]

A contemporary Catholic theologian, Louis-Marie Chauvet, expresses it in similar terms. In spite of a more positive view of matter, because it was created by God, and in spite of a more positive view of the bodily condition of human beings because it has been assumed by the Word of God itself in Jesus, even Christianity "has never fully cast away this suspicion of the sensible."[5] But it is not just Christianity. On a practical level, I have found that this issue—what we call "dualism"—comes up in almost every tradition I have studied, all the way from the ascetical overexuberance of Hindu devotees to the teachings of great Advaitin saints, such as Ramana Maharshi. At first glance, it seems right to many people who are trying to be "more spiritual"—body bad, soul good! Cast off the body to free the soul. Here is an example from the Dhammapada, the early Pali text of Buddhism.

> Look at the body adorned,
> A mass of wounds, draped upon a heap of bones,
> A sickly thing, this subject of sensual thoughts!
> Neither permanent nor enduring!
> The body wears out,
> A news of disease,
> Fragile, disintegrating,
> Ending in death.[6]

Bernie Clark put it very plainly in his book on Yin Yoga, saying that very few Yoga teachers realize that Samkhya philosophy and thus the Classical Yoga of Patanjali's Yoga Sutras are also dualistic philosophies. In them the dynamic is between *purusha* and *prakriti*, with purusha as the soul, pure consciousness, and prakriti as that which is created. Purusha does not create prakriti, although it is responsible for prakriti becoming animated and alive. But, according to Samkhya, this union of the two was a horrible mistake, an unfortunate marriage that never should have happened. So, as Clark explains, "Samkhya and Classical Yoga are *not* about union. The yoga of the Yoga Sutra is about getting a divorce, as quickly as possible."[7] (He does not eschew Yoga altogether, of course. It is for this reason that he espouses a return to a type of Tantric Yoga that he and others refer to as "Yin Yoga.") This is also one of the major themes of Sri Aurobindo's Integral Yoga. Warning about an incipient dualism, he wrote that in the past the body was regarded by spiritual seekers as an obstacle, "as something to be overcome and discarded" rather "than as an instrument of spiritual perfection and a field of the spiritual change." But, he writes, "if a divine life is possible on earth, then this self-exceeding (i.e., perfection of the body) must also be possible."[8]

Enlightened Dualism

I have noticed how often people around me flippantly say that "we are not our bodies." I am not sure that that is completely accurate, or at least it presents us with a slippery slope toward a whole new kind of dualism. Sam Keen writes that we have to be careful of being seduced by the dualism implicit in the language that encourages us to speak of "having a body," as if the possessor and the possessed were different entities, what I've come to call an "enlightened dualism." All human knowledge, all human value and aspiration are stamped with the mark of the body. Keen says that the insight we gain from existential philosophy into the incarnate nature of human existence could be stated like this: "Our body is our bridge to and model of the world; therefore, *how we are in our body so will we be in the world.*"[9] This is very important! Keen further states, "As I trust or mistrust the rhythm of my body, so I trust or mistrust my total world. If we lose the self we lose the other; if we lose the body we lose the world. Thus the danger of not loving one's body. Love of both neighbor and cosmos rests upon love of self."[10] He also explains that as we are in the world, so will we be in that mystery that founds, sustains, and engulfs the known world: "But even more, the sacred rests upon the carnal."[11] There is a correlation between our attitudes toward our body, our social and material context, and our absolute context.

The great monk, theologian, and scholar Cipriano Vagaggini (1909–99) writes that the root of the defect is to be found in a contemporary anthropology that is unwittingly faulty. "Without our realizing it," he says, "there is a survival in us of a kind of dualism resulting from an exaggeratedly spiritualistic idea" of the human person, in which "the body and its functions in human nature are scorned in favor of the soul."[12] Ken Wilber, in one of his early books, says it this way: "Biologically there is not the least foundation for this dissociation or radical split between the mind and the body, the psyche and the soma, the ego and the flesh, but psychologically it is epidemic." The mind–body split and the dualism that follows from it are a fundamental perspective of Western civilization. "Even St. Francis referred to his body as 'poor brother ass,' " Wilber writes, "and most of us do indeed feel as if we just sort of ride around on our bodies like we would on a donkey or an ass."[13]

He goes on to point out that this strange boundary line between the mind and the body is not at all present at birth. But as individuals grow in years and we begin to draw up and fortify all kinds of boundaries between "self" and "not-self," we also start to look at the body with mixed emotions. And by the time we have matured the body becomes foreign territory, almost (but never quite) as foreign as the external world itself. The boundary line is drawn between the mind and the body, and the person identifies squarely with the mind, and we come to live in our heads as if we were a miniature person in our skull, giving directions and commands to the body, which may or may not obey.[14] And unfortunately, as Keen reminds us, how we are in our bodies is also how we will be in the world.

Let's add one more voice to this, that of Wendell Berry, the great novelist, poet, farmer, and social critic. Berry uses similar language when he refers to "the isolation of the body." He says that at some point "we began to assume that the life of the body should be the business of grocers and medical doctors who don't have to take any interest in the spirit; and the life of the spirit should be the domain of churches who would have at best only a negative interest in the body." But this isolation of the body puts it into direct conflict with everything else in creation, and "gives it a value that is destructive of every other value." Of course, speaking of Christianity, "Nothing could be more absurd than to despise the body and yet yearn for resurrection!"[15] Worse, what follows on this way of thinking is that we can also make the body—usually someone else's body—do things that both insult the mind and degrade the spirit. And then when the soul is set against the body—the soul thriving at the body's expense—a whole spiritual economy of competition is set up. The soul lives by denying the body, and as a consequence its relation to the world is too superficial to cope with the world in any meaningful way, and suddenly we are surprised to find out that spiritual values have ceased to carry any weight, or any authority, that our spiritual values lack vigor or power or purpose in the world. Of course, *it's not possible to devalue the body and value the soul*! If the body is "devalued and cast out of the temple," it does not "sulk off like a sick dog to die in the bushes." It sets up a whole counterpart economy of its own based on a law of competition that devalues and exploits the spirit in turn. Then these two faulty economies "maintain themselves at each other's expense, living upon each other's losses, collaborating without cease in mutual futility and absurdity."[16]

The prototype of this is forcing people into slavery and then converting them, or any attempt at spreading religion by the sword or violence of any kind, which is a destruction of the body. Contempt for our own bodies inevitably leads to contempt for others' bodies as well—of women, of laborers, of the infirm or weak, of animals and plants—and finally of the earth itself. As Keen stated, *how we are in our bodies is how we will be in the world*! If the body is set in conflict with creation itself, of which all bodies are members, then ultimately the body stressing its autonomy is at war against itself.

If this is indeed faulty, as I am suggesting, or at least only partial, how can we adjust our vision? Where do we look to find a healthy holistic spiritual anthropology and a practical spirituality that reverences the whole person? The antidote in seed form may be found in each of our traditions as they evolve and as our own consciousness evolves, and as these traditions engage in dialogue with one another. This is what we shall explore in the chapters that follow.

In what lies ahead, we shall be looking at different spiritual traditions and seeing not only if Christianity shares any common ground with them but also what they may have to teach us, some aspect of the treasure map that they have figured out in a way Christianity has not yet articulated.

Before proceeding with our discussion, I find it useful to distinguish between three concepts: the end, what theology calls the *telos*; the goal, or the *scopos*, the proximate aim; and finally the *praxis*, the Greek word for practice, from the ascetical tradition. I have found that, while I believe there is a core of wisdom that the authentic spiritual traditions share (as we shall discuss below), we do have different ways of describing the end, the *telos*. Yet it is fascinating to me that we often have a similar vocabulary for the *scopos*, the proximate goal, and because of that we can often learn from one another's practice—the *praxis*—because we share a common goal as well as a common humanity. This shall be important for the pages ahead.

*The various worlds of cosmic existence
and the various planes of our being
are as if a ladder plunging down into
Matter and perhaps below it, rising up
into the heights of the Spirit.*[1]

—Sri Aurobindo

2

Axial Consciousness and the Darshanas

For the most part, the later chapters of this book will be very practical, as my aim is toward an integral spiritual practice. But in order to show how we get from what I have just explained as the problem of dualism to a new vision of reality that could give us a new understanding of our place in the universe and a new understanding of the universe's place in our individual practical spiritual lives, I first need to lay out some of the threads that make up the philosophical matrix upon which I am suggesting we build this new way of practicing our spirituality. As mentioned earlier, I came to this new way of thinking through my immersion in the thought of Bede Griffiths. However, delving into his teaching did not just change my way of thinking; it had a profound impact on the way I live my daily life, my spiritual life, my monastic life. In order to show the "method behind the madness," I will explain here the various elements that influenced Fr. Bede, some of which offered mostly positive contributions and some that served as a partner in dialogue with which to compare and contrast.

The Axial Period and Axial Consciousness

Our first thread is the theory of the Axial Period and Axial Consciousness. The word "axial" comes from the geometric and mathematical term "axis," which refers to a reference line of some sort that marks a division. According to the German philosopher Karl Jaspers (1883–1969), an axial moment that was especially pivotal to humanity's spiritual development started to emerge in human consciousness around 500 BCE.[2] This is the period when the great religions emerged, began to separate themselves from their primal antecedents, and took shape in more or less the classical form that we know them today. The main movements, for example, were Hinduism moving from the sacrificial, ritualistic Vedas to the inward focused Upanishads, and Buddhism leaving Hinduism behind almost completely; and Confucianism and then Taoism arising in China; the period of the late prophets arising in Judaism (and then the Hellenistic-inspired Wisdom tradition, which does not get mentioned often) as contrasted to the historical/mythological narratives and the establishment of the covenant through the Law; and finally the rise of the philosophy of Greece.

What is Axial Consciousness? To understand that, let's look at consciousness before the so-called Axial Period, pre-Axial Consciousness. We are assuming here that not only is there a collective consciousness but that that collective consciousness is evolving, not unlike material reality. The ancient consciousness before the Axial Period was essentially tribal; it was at least *more* feminine (though the extent of matriarchal cultures and deities is still debated); it was rooted in the earth because it grew out of agrarian cultures. It also included a greater preponderance of female deities, which tend to be fertility deities. It was primal consciousness, mythic consciousness, and ritualistic consciousness. In this period human beings perceived truth in a different way than we "moderns" do. This is in no way meant as a value judgment. Some cultures have not grown much out of this consciousness, and every individual human being has to evolve through this same consciousness.

Whereas primal consciousness was tribal, one of the main features of the Axial Period is the emergence of individual consciousness that is self-reflexive and analytic. "Know thyself" became the watchword of Greek philosophy; the Upanishads identified the *atman*, the transcendent center of the self; the Buddha charted the way of individual enlightenment; the Jewish prophets awakened individual moral responsibility. This sense of individual identity naturally distinguishes itself (for the first time?) from tribe and from nature. And although it applies especially to religion in the form of mapping an individual spiritual journey, it also refers to nature in the form of scientific theories, to society in the form of social critique, and to knowledge in the form of philosophy. In sharp contrast to *mythic* consciousness, this new consciousness is the self-reflexive *logos*, which we will simply translate for now as the rational mind as contrasted to the mythical mind. Mythic and ritualistic *mythos* consciousness survives, but is more submerged, and surfaces from here on out mainly in dreams, in literature, and in art. There was a great benefit of this bursting forth of the logos in that it released enormous spiritual energy and allowed an understanding of the deeper self as a way to the transcendent.

In this Axial Period there is also a move away from earth to "spirit," and perhaps the celibacy and chastity of the monastic life can serve as a concrete embodiment of this movement, even away from the natural fertility cycles. (Indeed, it is in this period that monasticism is born, the ultimate expression of the individual spiritual journey, removed from tribe and fertility.[3]) Many people point out that this is the time of the shift from female deities to male deities, which is also a shift from earth goddesses to sky gods. Further, whereas for the primal peoples sin would have been separating oneself from the earth, for the emerging Axial consciousness more and more sin would be being too rooted in the earth! And then there is also a concomitant shift away from the female and the emergence of the male, because the female is more tied to fertility and symbols of earth. And so there is also the emergence of dualism, the second dualism we addressed in Chapter 1, the relationship of matter to spirit, especially from the Greeks, in Plato's famous soma–sema schema —the body as a tomb for the soul. Now, matter is bad; spirit/soul is good, and the object of the spiritual life is to escape this "veil of tears."

The Perennial Philosophy

What also came out of this Axial Period, important for our purposes and very important to Fr. Bede, was an awakening to, and various articulations of, what came to be known as the perennial philosophy. The term "perennial philosophy" goes back to the Sanskrit term *sanatana dharma*, the "eternal teaching" that Hinduism considers itself to be. But the phrase was first coined in the West by a German philosopher and mathematician, Gottfried Leibniz (1646–1716), and then made more popular again by Karl Jaspers, as mentioned earlier. The following is my favorite articulation of the perennial philosophy, put forth by Aldous Huxley, himself being the popularizer of the term with his book of the same name in the mid-twentieth century.

1. "The phenomenal world of matter and of individualized consciousness—the world of things and animals and [human beings] and even gods—is a manifestation of a Divine Ground within which all partial realities have their being."
2. Human beings are capable of realizing the existence of the Divine Ground "by a direct intuition [that is] superior to discursive reasoning" or rational knowledge; this intuition is a knowledge that unites the knower with that which is known.
3. Human beings possess a double nature, "a phenomenal ego and an eternal Self, which is the inner person, the spirit, the spark of divinity within the soul." Our phenomenal ego itself is a manifestation of the Divine Ground.
4. The end and purpose of human life is to identify oneself with this eternal Self and "so to come to unitive knowledge of the Divine Ground."[4]

We are now in the area of the first dualism mentioned in Chapter 1, related to the issue of the relationship of matter to spirit, but specifically concerning itself with the relationship of the individual self to the Divine.

The Darshanas of India

Four of the darshanas (philosophies) of India that came out of this Axial Period were particularly influential on Bede: Samkhya, Advaita Vedanta, Buddhism, and Tantra.[5] So let me offer a thumbnail sketch of each of their respective general teachings. These will serve both as our dialogue partners as well as building blocks, both in relation to Fr. Bede's thought and as regards the conversation going on in spiritual circles—for the most part outside of Christianity—in the modern West, because these philosophies have been very influential, at least inchoately as transmitted through the practices associated with them.

Samkhya

Samkhya is arguably the oldest of the Indian philosophies or darshanas. It is generally thought to have provided the philosophical foundation not only for Yoga but for Buddhist cosmology as well.[6] The legendary father of Samkhya is the sage Kapila of the late seventh/early sixth centuries BCE. Samkhya teaches that there are two eternal principles, matter (prakriti) and spirit or consciousness (purusha), and so it is immediately forced into a kind of dualism. The world evolves out of the womb of prakriti and is left to the domain of prakriti. Purusha is merely a witness, an enjoyer of all that prakriti manifests or presents before him. As such, purusha has no part to play in the creative process of the evolution of the world. As a matter of fact, the entanglement of purusha with prakriti has been an "unfortunate marriage." Liberation then means being freed from prakriti. This freedom is called *kaivalya*, which is usually translated as "isolation": purusha must be isolated from prakriti. This isolation is achieved through renunciation and the discriminatory knowledge (samkhya). This is not intellectual, rational knowledge, because even the intellect is still in the realm of prakriti. Samkhya is a deeper way of knowing, an "inner knowing" that can discern the ephemeral from the actual, the apparent nature of the world from its underlying reality, the true from the false, the permanent from the impermanent. In other words, it can distinguish purusha from prakriti! This discriminatory knowledge is gained through reasoning, but one must also develop the will to renounce everything that is unreal. Basically it is the realization that the world is impermanent and perishable and that the true self (purusha) alone is real.[7]

We will see this tension at play in other philosophies: as this applies to all created things, so it applies to us as individuals. We aim toward isolating consciousness from prakriti, which includes all things in the realm of manifestation, including thoughts as well as material objects such as our very flesh.

Classical Yoga

By Classical Yoga we mean the Yoga of Patanjali, whose Yoga Sutras were composed between the second and third centuries, although other sources spread the date of origin from the fourth century BCE to the fourth century CE.[8] Patanjali synthesized various ancient Yoga traditions, molding them into one system based on Samkhya philosophy and then developing the *ashtanga*, or eight-limbed practical approach, also known as *raja yoga*, the "king of Yogas." As Patanjali lays it out, there are eight very practical limbs: First the *yamas,* the five moral restraints, followed by the *niyamas,* five observances. Then come the practical physical disciplines: *asana*—the postures for which Yoga is mostly known; *pranayama*—energy control and expansion mainly through breathing exercises; and *pratyahara*—sense withdrawal, an immediate preparation for meditation. The last three limbs are sometimes grouped together and called the *samyama,* that is, the fullness of discipline: *dharana*—concentration; *dhyana*—meditation; and *samadhi*—absorption in the Divine.

The major difference between Samkhya and Classical Yoga is that whereas Samkhya was nontheistic and aimed at renunciation and discrimination, the Yoga Sutras do mention a divine being, *Ishvara* (as a matter of fact, one of the *niyamas* or observances of the eight limbs is *Ishvara Pranidhana*—that is, surrender to the Divine), and aim toward renunciation and absorption in the Divine—*samadhi*—rather than discriminative knowledge.

Advaita Vedanta

Advaita Vedanta has no founder per se because its roots are found in the oldest scriptures of India, known as the Vedas, and particularly the Upanishads, which were attached to the Vedas (hence, they are *veda-anta*, "the end of the Vedas"). However, Advaita is generally associated with the eighth-century wandering ascetic Shankara, who was its greatest exponent.[9] The central teaching of Advaita is that the individual soul (*jiva*) is one with the Absolute ground of being, *Brahman*, and that there is ultimately no difference between the individual soul and Brahman. Four great sayings, or *mahavakyas,* derived from the Upanishads serve as a summary of Advaita Vedanta:

> *Prajnanam Brahma*: Consciousness is Brahman.
> *Aham Brahmasmi:* I am Brahman.
> *Tat Tvam Asi*: You are That! Meaning, "You, the individual, are That—Brahman."
> *Ayam Atma Brahma*: The Self is Brahman.

One easy way to understand the terms *Brahman* and *atman* in this context, especially as applied to this last *mahavakya*, is that Brahman is the ground or source of being, and atman (usually translated as "self" or "Self") is the ground or source of consciousness—hence, the real self. And if one were to take the interior journey through meditation and arrive at an awareness of the very ground of one's own consciousness, one would discover that the ground of our individual consciousness is none other than the very source of being. My consciousness and the source of all being are "not two"! Hence, *ayam atma brahma*—the self is Brahman. This is the essential teaching of the Upanishads, that Reality is one and the individual is essentially identical with it. And here we have a quintessential response to the first duality we spoke of in Chapter One, the relationship of the individual to the whole, the Absolute to the Relative, and so forth.

However, Advaita also holds that the empirical world that we experience is not real. Whereas Samkhya accepts the reality of creation and the objective world, the language of Vedanta keeps the Absolute unsullied and pure by emphasizing that all creation is *maya,* or an illusion, and therefore unreal. Thus, the quintessence of the doctrine of Advaita Vedanta as expounded by Shankara can be summed up in the famous verse:

Brahma satyam / jagan mithya
jivo Brahmaiva na aparah—

That is:
Brahman is alone real, / this world is unreal;
the *jiva* [individual self] is nondifferent from Brahman.

To explain this further, the world is relatively real, while only Brahman is absolutely real. The unchanging Brahman appears as the changing world because of a superimposition of non-Self on Self, the superimposition of objects onto the subject, who is Brahman. But this superimposition is *avidya*—ignorance! Here is a classic formulation from the Panchadasi, the standard text on Vedanta.

Before the matter is thoroughly investigated,
Brahman appears to be identical with the world (*jagat*).
But by thorough study of the Vedas,
the phenomenal world is recognized as an illusion,
and Brahman is known to be its basis.[10]

And yet, Shankara is a pure monist, believing that whatever exists is Brahman and that it is really difference and plurality that are illusory. In other words, if Brahman is nondual, one without a second, if nothing is different from Brahman, then Brahman is the world! So, you might say, ultimately the world is not actually an illusion according to Shankara.[11] So the variation on Shankara's teaching attributed to the great twentieth-century Indian sage Ramanamaharshi: "The world is an illusion. Brahman alone is real. Brahman is the world."

The individual soul (*jiva*) too is also only relatively real; its individuality lasts only so long as it is mistaken for the limiting conditions, when the jiva identifies itself with the body, the mind, and the senses. But just as a drop of water becomes one with the ocean when it drops into the ocean, so also does the jiva become one with Brahman when the jiva acquires knowledge of Brahman (*brahmavidya*). It is then freed from its individuality and finitude, and realizes its essential nature as *satchitananda*—Being, Knowledge, and Bliss. It merges itself in the ocean of bliss.

Because duality exists due to ignorance, knowledge (*jnana*) alone can reveal our true nature. Jnana, like samkhya, is not about acquiring any external knowledge; instead, it is simply removing the *avidya* (ignorance) and *maya* (illusion).[12] What Samkhya (and Classical Yoga) and Advaita Vedanta share is a common goal, the ideal of isolation (*kaivalya*) total separation from the world, since all activity in the world is *maya*, an illusion due to ignorance. Wisdom on the other hand is the bliss (*ananda*) of being (*sat*) in pure consciousness (*chit*)—*satchitananda*, a Hindu term for the divine that will appear again later.

Buddhism

We will now turn briefly to Buddhism, that other child of India. The other Indian traditions are what we might call "essentialist"; they teach that there is an unchanging essence, a Self or a Ground of being, an underlying real something that does not change. The Buddha's teaching is a radical departure specifically because it breaks from this essentialist thinking. The Buddha's view was that there is no essence; instead, *everything changes!* Even the "self" and the "Self." One of the three marks of existence is *an-atta*, or no self![13] Our everyday world, "the Wheel of Life," is characterized by "dependent coorigination" or "codependent arising": all things arise together, connected to one other. So instead of trying to describe what the Self or the soul was, the Buddha concentrated instead on how the soul works, how it functions, because for him what we call the "self" is a process, not some kind of fixed immutable unchanging essence. The ultimate end for the Buddha was for this sense of self, separate or otherwise, of people, things or the Divine, to be extinguished, achieving nirvana.

I am most familiar with the Buddhist teaching of Eihei Dôgen Zenji. Dôgen lived in the thirteenth century, hundreds of years after the Buddha, and is known as the patriarch of the Japanese Soto Zen tradition. Usually Buddhism teaches that all sentient beings *have* Buddha nature. Dôgen, on the other hand, emphasizes that every creature *is* Buddha nature, and that all things *are* Buddha nature, not just sentient beings but all things—animals and plants as well as rocks and human beings, gods and angels. What is important here is that instead of saying "have" Buddha nature, Dôgen says "are." "Have" could be taken to mean that there is some kind of eternal self, some hidden unchanging nature, a "hidden potential like a seed that when it is nourished blossoms into a Buddha"![14]

Some traditional Buddhists tend to suggest that we can seek liberation from the ever-changing by finding the permanence of Buddha nature. However, for Dôgen even that is a kind of Buddhist heresy, "sneaking atman in the back door."[15] *There are no eternal substances* either within us or within the world; all there is, is impermanence. Thus Dôgen coined a compound word in Japanese: *mujo-bussho*—"impermanence-Buddha nature." Buddha nature is impermanence.

Fr. Bede was mainly interested in this, what is called the Mahayana tradition of Buddhism, which is mainly associated with China, Japan, and Korea, which gave birth to Zen. He pointed out in his book *New Vision of Reality* that this school of Buddhism does not dismiss form and matter and the whole of life as unreal. This is a subtle but very important difference from other Indian darshanas. From the so-called "void" in Mahayana Buddhism, the universe issues forth through the principle of differentiation, but in the very moment it does so it also returns to unity, "an eternal movement outwards and an eternal movement of return, all within the Ultimate."[16] So the great phrase from the foundational text of Mahayana Buddhism, the great Heart Sutra—"Form is empty (*shunyata*), emptiness is form"—lets us know that *shunyata* (emptiness) is also "a reservoir of infinite possibilities" and not just a state of vacuity.[17]

Antiworld Bias

Fr. Bede had a great appreciation of what India refers to as the *sanatana dharma*, the Eternal Teaching, the belief in a perennial philosophy, a "Universal Wisdom." So Bede does not dispute any of these articulations of the nature of Absolute Reality. As a matter of fact, he states that there is a profound truth here, "an experience of pure consciousness which gives lasting peace to the soul."

> It is an experience of the Ground or Depth of being in the Center of the soul, an awareness of the mystery of being beyond sense and thought, which gives a sense of fulfillment, of finality,

of absolute truth. And indeed there is a sense in which this experience is ultimate. It is an experience of the undifferentiated Ground of being, the Abyss of being beyond thought, the one without a second."[18]

However, this is not the *end* of the story for Bede; rather, it is just the beginning.

The problem is, there is still a tendency in these traditions that we have discussed (is it particularly when Westerners get a hold of them?) to fall into a kind of "enlightened dualism," seeing material reality and/or the body as somehow "less than." In his marvelous book *Evolutionaries,* Carter Phipps calls this problematic tendency by a different name: *antiworld bias.* And this bias can subtly militate against any kind of development or progress, and against any kind of evolution in the broadest sense of the word, not just biological evolution, but psychological and cultural evolution as well. This antiworld bias, he writes, has been part and parcel of religion for millennia, and is alive and well, in East and West, in the afterlife promises of Christianity and Islam as well as in the Eastern promises of *nirvana* or *moksha* (liberation), the freedom from the shackles of time and the bondage of birth and death. Phipps states:

> There are many ancient and contemporary spiritual and religious teachings that present themselves differently—nondual mystical paths that claim no fundamental difference between form and emptiness, between spirit and matter, between heaven and earth. But dig a little deeper and more often than not the subtle antiworld bias will reveal itself.[19]

Phipps turns to the same two figures to whom Bede Griffiths turns, whom Phipps calls the patron saints, East and West, of evolutionary thinking: Aurobindo in the East and Teilhard de Chardin in the West. But before we get to these two great men, we need a look at another strain of Indian thought, the Tantric tradition. There are three reasons why we turn to Tantra and spend a little more time on it than on the other systems: first, to understand Aurobindo better; second, because Fr. Bede was particularly fascinated with Tantra the last years of his life; and finally, because of all the darshanas we are discussing, all of which have been explored as possible alternate ways of expressing Christianity, it may be that the Tantric tradition, as controversial as it has been in its application and misunderstanding, may come the closest to a Christian understanding of the place of matter and the body.

The Tantric Movement

Although the birth of the Tantric movement is generally thought to have been in the first centuries of the Common Era, Tantra's roots are deep in the history of ancient India. The religious tradition that we know now as Hinduism, indeed Indian civilization itself, is a synthesis of at least two different spiritual traditions and cultures coming together. The semi-nomadic Indo-European Aryans migrated to the subcontinent of India around 2000 BCE, perhaps by way of the Khyber Pass. However, when the Aryans descended into the subcontinent of India, they fused with the indigenous peoples of that region, especially the Harappan culture of the Indus Valley (modern-day Pakistan), who already had a thousand-year-old civilization that was thriving in technology and trade. Even though the Harappan culture was no match for the warlike Aryan invaders, some elements of the pre-Aryan culture and spiritual tradition remained.[20] There is some conjecture that the Yogic tradition in general may have derived from this Harappan culture. Many sources, for instance, point to a pre-Aryan "proto-Shiva" statue of a man in lotus position. There is a little more certainty yet that the specifically Tantric approach to Yoga is a remnant of this ancient tradition that was able to survive and then reemerge, especially in border areas that were able to resist complete Aryanization.

One important pre-Aryan element that was able to survive was devotion to the Divine Feminine. A strong element of worship of the Great Mother was prevalent especially among the Dravidian people of South India, as it still is to this day. When the Aryan invaders and settlers came down from the north, along with the Vedic mythology and philosophy, worship of male gods came into prominence and the indigenous goddesses were assigned lesser importance. Nevertheless, goddess worship was assimilated into the Vedic tradition in a way that ought to sound familiar to us—the Great Goddess became prakriti, the active principle that we saw in Samkhya philosophy. Similarly, Shiva, the god who was often represented by the image of the *lingam* or phallus, became the Vedic purusha, the inactive, conscious witnessing principle.[21] The survival and assimilation of the feminine principle alongside Shiva, the masculine principle, will be an important element in the rise of Tantra.

It is almost impossible to assign much specificity to the beginning of the Tantric movement in India because of the anonymity of most of its texts except to say that it was sometime in the beginning of the Common Era. Its golden age was undoubtedly the tenth to twelfth centuries, the age of Abhinavagupta, the great chronicler of the Trika school of Hindu Tantrism, and Naropa, one of the founders of the Kagyupa school of Tibetan Buddhist Tantrism. Both of these men were from the region of Kashmir. It is also an open question if the movement began first in Hinduism or in Buddhism, although many sources speculate that the Buddhist texts are older.[22] It is safe to say that there was mutual influence between the two. What is widely held is that Tantra arose at least in a large part as a reaction against both the Vedic Hindu tradition of Brahminism, with its priesthood and sacrifices and rituals, and in reaction to the ascetical monasticism of Buddhist orders, specifically "the dualistic and renunciate practices taught in the Vedas and Upanishads and further codified in the Yoga Sutras," traditions "that would put the devoted yogi in an isolated cave and insist that normal human experiences such as desire or sexuality prevent or at least limit true happiness or enlightened being."[23]

The Tantric tradition builds on—but, adherents will say, surpasses—the foundations of Samkhya, Classical Yoga, the Upanishads, as well as the Puranas and the Bhagavad Gita and early Buddhism. Where the Tantric elements remain especially strong is in the theistic traditions known as Shaivism and Shaktism.[24] As we saw, both Samkhya and Vedanta concede that the world has an empirical reality, a reality that can be observed and experienced. But the question is whether or not there is a greater reality than that to the world, and if so, what kind of reality it is. Tantra offers the doctrine of "duality in unity," a middle course in which the reality of the world is affirmed, at least in a certain sense, without compromising the truth of the unity of Brahman. The Tantras teach that it is only the products of prakriti (known as *vikrti*) that are not real in the Indian sense of the term "real"—in other words, they are not "that which was, is, and will be forever"; the products of prakriti themselves are not that which never changes and never ceases to be. And so the world as a product of prakriti is not real but a mere appearance. But Tantra is distinct from Advaita Vedanta in that it recognizes the reality of prakriti itself. In this way it follows Samkhya. But it differs from Samkhya in that it believes that prakriti is not a separate principle from Brahman, but exists *in* Brahman and as a principle of the substance of Brahman. Here is what is important: even if the products of prakriti, the world, for example, are not really real, the ground principle of that appearance—prakriti itself—is real, and furthermore is a part of Brahman! And so there is a reality behind all the apparent transformations.[25]

The other philosophical doctrine common to Hindu and Buddhist Tantra is that although reality is one, it is grasped through a process of polarization, both conceptually and intuitively. The two poles are activity and passivity (the feminine and masculine), and the universe "works" through the interaction of these two poles. The pole of passivity is the static principle, and is essentially cognitive—"encompassing wisdom, realization, beatitude, and spiritual illumination" similar to the concept of purusha in Samkhya. The pole of activity, on the other hand, the dynamic principle, is conative—that is, it is directed toward action or behavior, impulse, desire, striving, "movement, energy, activity,"[26] similar to Samkhya's concept of prakriti. In the Hindu Tantric tradition, the passive, static principle is masculine; it is the mind—*chit*—and it is identified with Shiva. The active, dynamic power and primordial energy is feminine, identified as Shakti. This unusual attribution of the active principle with the feminine (in Hindu thought) is seen by some as a direct inheritance from the worship of the Divine Feminine in India, as was noted earlier. (Note that Buddhist Tantra reverses this: The male principle is activity and the female one is passivity.)

Normally, pure consciousness or awareness would be called by the Sanskrit term *chit*. However, in the Tantra it is called *chit-shakti*—"consciousness-power"—to indicate that we are speaking not just of static consciousness, or even divine consciousness or self-consciousness, but of the *power* of Self-consciousness, the *power* of Self-revelation by which the Supreme shines by itself, the dynamism of the Absolute that manifests the world, *the divine energy that is always inherent in consciousness*. Again, this energy in the divine is Shakti, God as universal Mother, the feminine creative aspect of God. On the other hand, in its practical manifestation in the human person, it is referred to as *kundalini*.[27]

The universe reaches a state of absolute oneness and quiescence in the practitioner when these two poles of activity and passivity, the masculine and the feminine, consciousness and matter, merge. The Tantric practitioner seeks the reunification of these two opposite principles—Shiva and Shakti, the masculine and the feminine, the passive and the active—in his or her own person, through experience in spiritual practice, or *sadhana*. Note that in Samkhya the union of purusha and prakriti had been an "unfortunate marriage," whereas Tantra seeks the union of the two! They merge when the body—and with it all of creation—is experienced as an instrument of spiritual perfection. But again, this insight is filtered through and is only gained by experience, by *sadhana* (spiritual practice). With the emphasis on *sadhana*, we see that the body is of central importance: even though the body seems to bind the individual soul (jiva), it can also be the means of human perfection. Fr. Bede often quoted the adage, "That by which you fall is that by which you rise."

So here we have a corrective to Axial Consciousness and its tendency to leave behind the world, the body, the feminine, and creation due to an at least implicit dualism. Instead, we have these important elements of Tantra: Where the earlier schools were patriarchal and tended toward a kind of dualism, Tantra arose in reaction to the denial of the body and the denial of the feminine that we saw in the First Axial Consciousness.[28] As opposed to the hierarchical priestly and caste based brahminism, Tantra was egalitarian, and ignored class structure, and "opened up the fullness of spiritual practice to anyone."[29] In Tantra, the idea "that the world is an illusion from which one must escape is itself a delusive mental construct that must be given up."[30] The fundamental intention of Tantra is instead "to pass from the gross to the subtle"; that is, from the material phenomenal world to the absolute spiritual one, "but then to permeate the gross with the value and meaning of the subtle."[31] Further, in Tantric philosophy "Every upward process of realization of pure subjectivity is . . . equally a downward free construction in knowledge and creation in action."[32] The philosophy of Tantra "identifies the path of freedom not through renunciation of human desire and experience, but indeed largely through it."[33] "For this reason, the Tantras emphasize the value of the body and of all human experience."[34] "Instead of suppressing the sense pleasures, the joy and the suffering of the phenomenal world, these should be approached more and more directly and openly, without fear or hesitation."[35] Finally, and in summary, Tantra teaches that liberation "is possible while we are in the body. This is known as *jivanmukta*—that is, "living liberation." In fact, the body is a necessary tool to reaching this liberated state since "only incarnate beings can become enlightened and liberated."[36]

Bernie Clark says it well and clearly: Society's unfortunate but understandable disgust for some of Tantra's extreme and aberrant forms happily resulted in the evolution of a new school of yoga, Hatha Yoga, the Yoga of the sun and the moon (*ha–tha*), the masculine and feminine, and his own school of Yin Yoga.[37]

With all this in mind, we can speak of two great thinkers of the twentieth century, Sri Aurobindo Ghose and Pierre Teilhard de Chardin, on whom we will focus in the next chapter.

Are we not at every instant living the experience of a universe whose immensity, by the play of our senses and our reason, is gathered up more and more simply in each one of us? Are we not experiencing the first symptoms of an aggregation of a still higher order, the birth of some single center from the convergent beams of millions of centers dispersed over the surface of the thinking earth?[1]

—Pierre Teilhard de Chardin

3

Aurobindo, Teilhard, and the Second Axial Consciousness

Fr. Bede speaks of Aurobindo and Teilhard almost in the same breath, as we saw Carter Phipps do as well: "Teilhard presented an evolutionary view of matter evolving into life and into consciousness," he wrote in *New Vision of Reality*. And Bede says that what Teilhard did for Christianity, "Aurobindo did for Hinduism. He developed a system of Vedanta which incorporates the concept of evolution into the Hindu vision of the universe." To summarize the output of these two intellectual giants is a rather daunting task, and to cherry-pick certain of their teachings for our use here seems a huge disservice, but for the scope of this book, the following is what strikes me as most important.

Aurobindo: The Instrument and the Field

Aurobindo Goshe was an English-educated Indian from Calcutta. He was a political revolutionary, journalist, and social critic before immersing himself in the language and philosophies of India. He was sent to prison for trying to overthrow British rule, and it was there that he had his first spiritual experiences.

When he was threatened with further arrest, he took refuge in the French Indian colony of Pondicherry in 1910, and remained there in the ashram that established around him for the rest of his life. He became known as a great yogi and spiritual teacher. Employing the language of Advaita, Samkhya, and Tantra, he developed what could almost be considered his own new darshana, what he called *purna yoga*, or "Integral Yoga," which aimed at integrating spiritual practice into life rather than raising the practitioner to the heights of spiritual attainment and remaining there.

In his teaching, Aurobindo stresses a different, gentler interpretation of *maya*, normally understood to mean "illusion" as we saw in Shankara's Advaita. Aurobindo insists that the Vedic meaning of maya is not really "illusion," but "wisdom, knowledge, capacity, wide extension in consciousness."[2] Aurobindo thought that Shankara overstressed the notion of maya, "because it was most vivid to his own experience," whereas he himself preferred to stress the idea of *lila*, "the divine play." And so he writes to a student, "For yourself, leave the word [maya] for subordinate use and fix rather on the idea of Lila, a deeper and more penetrating word than Maya. Lila includes the idea of Maya and exceeds it."[3] He further explains that the crowning realization of Yoga will be "when you become aware of the whole world as the expression, play or Lila of an infinite divine personality."[4]

Aurobindo also espoused a belief in evolution, a forward trajectory of time, as opposed to most Asian philosophies that see time as something to be escaped. But he understands evolution in a very specific way that has to do with what he calls the "supramental transformation." Evolution actually starts out with a term that is fundamental to understanding Sri Aurobindo's thought: "involution." He writes that the manifestation of the Divine Being in our universe "takes the shape of an involution," a descent into seven gradations of manifesting consciousness, a sort of ladder of consciousness of, we might say, God involving Godself in creation and matter.

Going down the ladder, first there is the Divine Existence, Consciousness, and Bliss—the famous *satchitananda* of the Indian tradition. This is arguably the most famous name or description for the Godhead: Being (*sat*), Knowledge (*chit*), and Bliss

(*ananda*), three attributes that make up this one level. Satchitananda is God's perfection before any manifestation.

Then, just one degree below satchitananda comes the Over-
mind or Supermind, which is perfection *in* manifestation. Here
there are the first glimmers of difference and diversity, even
the first hints of an approaching unconsciousness,[5] but it is still
"unity in infinite multiplicity," differentiation without conflict.

Continuing the descent, after the level of Supermind comes
the mind; that is, the ordinary mind, or *manas*. In the ordinary
mind "ignorance, conflict, violence, and dissension" first appear. Then follows "life, with all its vital instincts, passions and
impulses." Then beneath life is physical matter, "with its rigid
laws and restrictions."[6]

To repeat, the seven gradations of consciousness as it manifests: Being, Knowledge, Bliss, then Supermind followed by
mind, life, and unconscious matter.[7]

But that far point of involution, the manifestation of the Being
in our universe, is also "the starting point of an evolution, with
matter the nethermost stage, spirit the summit." The Supreme
Self has involuted ("involved" itself) all the way down to the
level of matter and now is evolving back to satchitananda. And
what is happening in the universe at large, in matter in general,
is happening in the individual as well, each individual evolves
all the way through matter to life to mind, all the way to satchitananda. The descent culminated in a "total [unconsciousness]
out of which the involved Being and Consciousness have to
emerge by a gradual evolution," which is an ascent of the ladder of consciousness, "reaching upwards from the very depths
of matter" and unconsciousness, through life and mind, to the
regions above the mind and on to Divine Perfection.[8]

Aurobindo lamented that the body is often regarded as an
obstacle by spiritual seekers, as something to be overcome and
discarded. Even in Tantra the body is still called *sariram*, a Sanskrit word that comes from the root *sri*, meaning "to decay."
However real they may seem to us, if they are subject to decay
the body and the world are still deemed unreal in the sense that
they are not eternal. The body and nature may be the *instruments*
of this realization, but they are not necessarily seen as that which

is transformed. What Aurobindo teaches instead is that the body, "the nature," our physical being, is not only the instrument, the vehicle, and the means; the body (the nature, our physical being) is also that which can be transformed, and with it matter itself! (Note that nature and the body, the earth and the human person, are spoken of in the same vein.) What has to be overcome, he writes, is the ignorance that does not long for, await, and expect the transformation of the nature: "Evolution takes place on earth and therefore the earth is the proper field for progression."[9] The body is not just the instrument, but the field of transformation! The earth, and with it matter and the body, are all that which gets transformed! In fact, Aurobindo thought and taught that if the transformation of the body were complete, it would mean that we would no longer be subject to death. He believed that the body—indeed all of nature—was able to undergo a transformation by the evolution toward Spirit.

> Let the whole dynamic nature led by the psychic make itself full of the dynamic spiritual light, peace, purity, knowledge, force; let it afterwards get the experience of the intermediate spiritual planes and know, feel and act in their sense; then it will be possible to speak at last of supramental transformation.[10]

Teilhard: The *Within* of Things

Pierre Teilhard de Chardin will be more familiar to contemporary Christian readers. He was a twentieth-century French Jesuit priest, paleontologist (credited with discovering the *Sinanthropus*, the so-called "Peking Man"), theologian, and author whose influence on contemporary thought can hardly be overestimated, although he was not allowed to publish theological writings in his own time. What of Teilhard's thought serves best for our discussion is his theory of *cosmic embryogenesis*.[11] We start out following a phenomenon in planetary, cosmic evolution. Teilhard first distinguished the *geosphere*, the realm of minerals and chemicals, from the *biosphere*, which is the realm of life itself. A first stage in evolution has been for the geosphere to evolve into the biosphere. This "transit to life," as Teilhard calls it, has taken place because chemicals and minerals, and, at a deeper level, atoms, molecules, and cells have synthesized, come together. That coming together has caused something new to evolve. The biosphere then grows more complex all the way up a "tree of life," beginning with bacteria through plant life, to one branch that leads to crustaceans, scorpions, and insects, and another branch that leads to fish, amphibians, reptiles. That second branch splits into two other branches, one that ends in birds, and another that leads to mammals, then primates, and eventually human beings.[12]

What Teilhard notes is a double phenomenon that happens in this biosphere. The more complex a being becomes externally, the more aware of itself it becomes, "centered upon itself" inwardly. It is in animals first that we can observe an awareness of what is going on around them. This awareness is accompanied by a certain spontaneity of action and an ability to adapt more and more readily to the surrounding environment, and even dominate it. So actually three things come together: the more complex the creature becomes exteriorly with its sophisticated nervous sytem, the more highly centrated a creature is interiorly, and the more highly centrated a creature is interiorly, the greater the awareness the creature has of its surroundings and its place in it. Another way to think about this is the greater the reach *without*, the deeper the awareness is *within*, and the greater the involvement can be with the environment (again, without). But in the human being the growth in awareness reaches an even higher level of awareness, an awareness of *self* and an awareness of awareness itself.

Teilhard suggests that at this point there is a certain *discontinuity* in the steady movement of evolution, a *leap* into thought.[13] "Outwardly, almost nothing in the organs had changed. But in depth, a great evolution had taken place: consciousness was now leaping and boiling in a space of super-sensory relationships and representations, and simultaneously consciousness was capable of perceiving itself in the concentrated simplicity of its faculties."[14] This is what Teilhard calls the *noosphere*, the realm of thought, "a new era in evolution,"[15] and, a phrase I like very much, another realm in which creation is "wrapped."

Teilhard also calls this "hominization," the humanizing stage of evolution. The human being has—or, better, *is*—a reflective psychic center able to access the realm of abstraction, logic, invention, art, emotions, and love. Often Teilhard calls this interiority "the *within*" of things, but actually "the *within*, *consciousness*, and then *spontaneity*" are three expressions for this same phenomenon "to indicate every kind of psychism, from the most rudimentary forms of interior perception imaginable to the human phenomenon of reflective thought."[16] But it is important for our purposes to note that this phenomenon did not come from nowhere! It had actually been there from the beginning! If this reflective consciousness emerged in the higher animals, Teilhard says, that's because it was already present in some, perhaps inchoate, manner in lower forms of life and matter, but somehow "needed," was dependent on, this greater complexity to call it forth and develop it. He believed that there always was this inner lining—the *within* of things—to all matter.

This is the theory of *cosmic embryogenesis* and the basis of Teilhard's understanding of evolution.[17] According to Teilhard, there is nothing that comes to light at some stage of evolution that was not present in some form from the very beginning. And so for the *within*, or consciousness: It is a dimension that informs *all* cosmic matter, even if at different intensities. As Joseph Kopp puts it, "The whole physical world contains a psyche but in differing concentrations."[18] So we should not limit the origin of the *within* of consciousness only to the place where it is most evident, in more evolved creatures. As we also saw in Aurobindo's thought, so Teilhard posits that there is a *within* of inanimate material too. Throughout the whole cosmos material externals are accompanied by conscious spirit, even though their consciousness is not yet a coherent structure or a self-reflexive consciousness.[19]

This consciousness resembles a spectrum: At the bottom of the scale in inanimate objects it is dark and obscure, but in the human being at the top of the scale it is bright and unmistakable.[20] We could also imagine consciousness as a cone that is actually a spiral, with the cosmos rising in a spiral toward an ever denser inwardness—an ascent to the depths.[21] What Teilhard also adds to this is that instead of this cone resting on its base, it is actually hanging from its apex, and its apex is unity. Its apex is the Omega point; its apex is Christ, the total Christ, which is consummated by this universal evolution. As the Franciscan theologian Ilia Delio writes, with this way of thinking we can now "locate Christ at the heart of the whole evolutionary process: from cosmic evolution to biological evolution to evolution of human consciousness and culture."[22] And that which lies ahead—that is, unity, the unifying force—is also the energy that is animating this whole movement; the unity ahead is drawing all creation to itself. This is a kind of legitimate Christian "pantheism": God is all in every being in the universe because God is the ultimate principle of differentiating unification.[23] But there is a significant element in the Christian understanding that separates us from other types of monism: in that unity the *individual is not lost, nor is multiplicity suppressed*. Instead, all the individual elements are *fulfilled* in their individual qualities by entering this centered and organized unity.

Another term that Teilhard uses (in a different way from Aurobindo) is "involution," literally, from the Latin *involvere*, a "folding in on itself," as opposed to "evolution," which is a rolling out of itself. According to Teilhard, involution is when matter no longer merely spreads itself out in diffuse indefinable layers but begins to coil in on itself and around itself in a closed volume or system. Involution is what happens when elements converge to form a collective. The greater the complexity outside, on the surface of the element, the more each element closes in on itself and is self-contained, and the deeper its consciousness, until it finally breaks through to the very center of its being, the ground, the core, the fount of being itself. And when it breaks through to the center of its being another realm bursts forth: the Theosphere, the realm of God and the realm of divinization.[24] Teilhard insists that the Omega point is not only the association or relationship with all other centers around us; the ultimate Omega is also the core, the center, the source. This Theosphere/Omega point is both the source *and* the summit. That is why we can say that these realms are wrapped in each other: the geosphere in the biosphere in the Noosphere in the Theosphere. And if we follow the theory of cosmic embryogenesis we suspect that this too has been there all along, and it pushes us from within as much as it pulls us from ahead. This Omega point, the Theosphere, has been "already in existence and operative at the very core of the thinking mass."[25]

Thus, and this is perhaps the main point, for Teilhard, God is not structurally detached from creation as merely an "efficient cause" working in an *interventionist* way; God is more a "formal cause," meaning God is immanent in the world, dynamically interior to creation, bringing all things to their full being by the act of unification, "creative union." As Delio explains, "God is not the supernatural being above but the *supranatural* center of everything that exists."[26]

One last point: for Teilhard there is nothing impersonal about any of this. Teilhard suggests that it is and must be love, or at least a kind of love, that forms the material of human energy in its pure state. It is the attraction that is "exercised on each unit of consciousness by the center of the Universe in course of taking shape."[27] As everything is evolving, it is also at the same time being drawn back to its source, tethered by a bond of love, if you will. Love is what we call that which "calls us to the great union," and ultimately this is what is taking place in all of nature, a realization of the great union. Teilhard says we may also define this love as "the primal and universal psychic energy." Even clearer, he says, "Love is a sacred reserve of energy; it is like the blood of spiritual evolution."[28] Or we can invert this for the skeptics: The spiritual energy of evolution is what we call "love." The radial energy at the center of our being, that which is driving us onward, is what we call "love." The stuff of the *within* of things is love. And more specifically, as Delio points out, for Teilhard this orientation toward and yearning for wholeness is "the creative role of erotic attraction." This love can be called *eros*.[29] This will be an important point for the discussion that follows.

Aurobindo and Teilhard: A Shared Perspective

So both of these men believed in an evolutionary trajectory, both saw matter as containing consciousness, impelled forward by Spirit, and both of them taught that "matter will reveal Spirit's face." In addition, and important for our purposes, this overarching understanding of reality led both of them to teach that we do not have to escape the world, but rather to reinvolve in the world through our labor and action. Hence, in this way, both offer an antidote to any antiworld bias. Aurobindo says that for the spiritual seeker departure from the world and its activity, a supreme release and quietude, cannot be the sole aim. One must take into account the world and its activities. What at first seemed to be dark and incomprehensible *maya* (illusion), "was all the time no other than the Consciousness-Puissance"—*puissance* is French for "power"—the *chitshakti* of the Eternal behind the *lila*, "the divine play," the gratuitous unfolding of the universe.[30] As Fr. Bede explained, contrasting Auribondo to the pure Advaita of Ramana Maharshi, Aurobindo "filled it in, as it were."

Teilhard too filled it in. He refers to his own early experiences of nature mysticism as "communion with earth," which he suspected was a kind of pantheistic monism. His later suspicion of pantheistic monism, specifically as he related it to the inward journey of Eastern mysticism, is that it is *too* inward, *too* immanent. At the same time "communion with God" conjures up for him another excess, that of being excessively other-worldly, an understanding of God and religion as separate from the world (or "antiworld," as Carter Phipps laments), an exclusive concern for the transcendent, which is often regarded and stated as the main goal of the religious quest. To Teilhard, this is a spirituality that does not place enough importance on the value of human effort and the development of the world, a theme he developed extensively in *The Divine Milieu*. As British theologian Ursula King, a leading voice in evolutionary Christianity, describes it, both of these attitudes are incomplete. What we are looking for is "communion with God *through* earth," through flesh, through matter, through creation. This reflects Teilhard's lifelong attempt "to relate God and the world in the most intimate manner," as shown through his efforts at seeing science and religion as part of the same quest for ultimate unity, and also in relating mystical spirituality to effort and action.[31]

The Second Axial Period

Many thinkers, among them Christians such as Ewert Cousins and Bruno Barnhart, have suggested, and I have come to believe, that in our present age we are on the brink of a Second Axial Period with the birth of a new Axial Consciousness, and one can see in the massive cultural shifts taking place the possibility of the emergence of the same. And Aurobindo and Teilhard de Chardin are the patron saints of this Second Axial Period, as well as the patron saints of "evolutionaries" of all stripes.

One characteristic of this new Axial Consciousness is the move now *from individual consciousness to the birth of global consciousness*, and at the same time recovering a sense of tribe. We are actually recapturing the unity of the tribe, but this time we are realizing it on a global scale. What globalization in this sense (not in the commercial sense!) could provide us with is a sense of the human race as one tribe.[32] At the same time—drawing on Teilhard's theory that *union differentiates*—global consciousness and recovery of a sense of tribe does not mean that all differences will be eliminated, but actually intensified. Just like subatomic particles, by touching each other at the creative core of our being we release new energy, which leads to more and more complex unions, and that greater complexity leads to greater interiority, which then leads to more and more creative unions. In other words, we do not lose our identity, but deepen and fulfill our identity through creative union. This applies to individual people as much as it does to religions and cultures. But it must be deep calling on deep; that is, it is dependent on *greater interiority*, when we meet at the center.

A second concomitant feature of the consciousness in the Second Axial Period, however, and a prerequisite for it, is *a rediscovery of our roots in the earth*, and along with that *a recovery of the feminine and of our bodies*. In a sense it is a rediscovery of the spirituality of the primal peoples of the pre-Axial Period, but not a romantic attempt to live in the past (what Ken Wilber calls the "pre/trans fallacy"). We come at this rediscovery with our self-reflexive consciousness intact, and with our analytic and critical intellect, and we integrate what has been lost into them, and vice versa: we integrate our analytic and critical intellect into the earth and our bodies. As the American philosopher Jacob Needleman writes, this revolutionary way of understanding creation "requires that we seek to inhabit the physical with more, not less, of our psyche."[33] As we evolve, we do not merely transcend, we include. The higher states and stages contain all that has come before. We still need to overcome our dualism, our thinking that the earth is something separate from us, from our real selves, and so can be abused or ignored or simply subjugated. It too is a manifestation of the Divine Ground. And remember Sam Keen's great maxim as a warning: How we are in our bodies is how we will be in the earth. Needleman agrees, and emphasizes this point: *"Humanity's relationship to the Earth mirrors our own essential relationship to our own physical body."*[34]

So there are both a horizontal and a vertical dimension, horizontal, in that cultures and peoples meet and share riches, creative unions giving birth to deeper interiority and more creative unions, with vertical roots deep in the earth and deep in the person. Both of these dimensions combined then become avenues toward the transcendent. Notice that we are abutting Teilhard's notion of centreity here, where three movements come together: the more complex the creature with its sophisticated nervous system becomes *exteriorly* (globalization), the more highly centrated a creature is *interiorly* (contemplation); and the more highly centrated a creature is interiorly, the greater the awareness the creature has of its surroundings and its place in it (the environment, the earth)—the horizontal dimension again. Put another way, the greater the reach *without*, the deeper the awareness is *within*, and the greater the involvement can be with its environment (again, without).

A New Spirituality

The late Jesuit mystic William Johnston writes about the four characteristics of what he calls the "new mysticism" for a new era, and each is somehow very rooted in the body and in earth. First, the new mysticism will be a *kataphatic* mysticism of light, a mysticism that gives full weight to symbols and imagery; then a more feminine mysticism that emphasizes the earth; then a mystical theology like that of Teilhard de Chardin that sees God in all things, not a flight from matter but entering more deeply into matter; and finally a mysticism that is inspired by the movements of social justice and care for the poor. (Even this is rooted in created reality and the body.)[35] The late theolgian Ewert Cousins explained it this way: As the First Axial Period tended to *disengage* spirituality from matter, so the Second Axial Period "faces the challenge of discovering a new spirituality of matter—or, more precisely, a new holistic spirituality that integrates in an organic way matter, the human, and the divine."[36]

To this thinking I would like to add what my monastic confrere Bruno Barnhart calls for as well in his prophetic book *The Future of Wisdom*: The dawning of this new consciousness demands the dawning of a *new anthropology*, a renewed understanding of the human person, "a depth anthropology which integrates the post-modern attainments of radical critical rationality and unconditioned creativity together with the Enlightenment values of human dignity and rights into a view of the human person grounded beneath human consciousness in the nondual divine mystery."[37] I would add that this new anthropology must be *incarnate* as well, both rooted in the earth and celebrative of the body and corporeality. This is what I'm after in my quest for an *integral* spiritual practice. What will aid us in finding this new spirituality for this new consciousness? What would this depth anthropology look like? We'll find answers to these and other questions in the next chapter.

*When we have come to know the true God, both our bodies
and our souls will be immortal and incorruptible. . . .
when we have been deified and made immortal, God has
promised us a share in his own attributes.
The saying "Know yourself" means therefore that we
should recognize in ourselves the God who made us in his
own image.*[1]

—St. Hippolytus

4

Incarnational Theology

It is specifically in addressing the dualism that came about
from the *ascending* movement of First Axial Period consciousness,
away from the body and away from the earth, that the *descending* movement of the incarnational theology and spirituality of
Christianity, properly understood or, perhaps, understood in a
new light, might just have an invaluable contribution to offer.
With all due respect to the genius of the patristic era, the (afore-
mentioned) invectives against the flesh could not possibly be
the final word on Christian anthropology.

In Ursula King's study of Teilhard de Chardin and Eastern
religions, in *Towards a New Mysticism*, she offers a beautiful sum-
mation of the great Jesuit mystic's thought that will also serve
as an introduction to a discussion of Christianity's specific contribution to the discussion: Christianity's specific contribution
lies in its belief in the Incarnation of God.

> Through this belief [Christianity] has the extraordinary ability
> to engender an all-transforming dynamic love which embraces
> both God and the world. The interpenetration of the material
> and the spiritual given through the Incarnation lends Christi-
> anity a singular force of attraction of adoration, of worship, of

[our] access to God via the world. Here is a universal presence, a living God, whose energy animates all life and levels of life, an ultimate centre where everything finds its consummation.[2]

The event around which Christianity centers itself is Jesus as the Word-made-flesh. Part of the scandal of the myth of Christianity is first of all that the Divine Word could have become flesh at all. It's helpful to recall exactly what this Greek philosophical concept *logos* (word) had come to mean to Jesus' contemporaries. For example, for Philo (who was a Hellenized Jewish philosopher who lived from 20 BCE to 50 CE, therefore a contemporary of Jesus) the logos was both the creative principle and divine wisdom, or (as Origen would describe it later) primal reason, primal spirit, primal life. But Philo, like all the ancient Greeks, always felt it was necessary to maintain a distinction between the perfect idea and imperfect matter. And that's why the logos was necessary, he taught, because God cannot come into contact with matter. This is exactly what Christianity challenges in claiming, as in the Prologue to John's Gospel, that the Word was not only *with* God, but that the Word *was* God and that "the Word was made flesh and dwelt among us." God has come into contact with matter! Worse yet, God has become matter. "The Word became flesh and lived among us" (John 1:14). God becomes a baby with dirty diapers. In contrast to the ascending movement of the Axial Period, Christianity interjects the descent of the Divine.

So, first of all, the flesh—and, with it, matter—could not be bad or, as Christianity claims in its foundational myth language,[3] the Word would not have taken it on. And according to Origen, what the Christian tradition calls the "image of God" in the human soul is in reality the very image of this Logos. "The Logos is primal reason, primal spirit, primal life," and the Father has created all things in this Word, and formed all other images according to its ideal.[4]

Further, one constantly runs into admonitions not to impose a Greek dualism onto even the Hebrew mentality. The body–soul (*soma–sema*) dualism of Greek thought has very little in common with biblical anthropology. To the Hebrew mind there was no separation of body and consciousness or soul. As a matter of fact, Judaism only began to allow for survival of a soul after death when it came into contact with foreign religions and philosophies—perhaps some influence of Persian Zoroatrianism, but certainly the form of Greek Platonism that allowed for this separation of body and soul. And so, for example, Catholic Scripture scholar Jerome Murphy-O'Connor wrote that this is what Paul had to face when confronted with the belief of the followers of Jesus after the Resurrection, that it was not just a metaphorical way of speaking of Jesus' survival. Paul like other Pharisees did not believe that the body and soul were distinguishable, let alone separable. He held to the "Jewish monistic anthropology in which a person had to be spoken of as 'an animated body' or 'an embodied soul,'" or some other way of speaking that made it clear that there was no such thing as a body without a soul or vice versa, no such thing as a soul without some kind of body.[5]

Three Events in the Life of Jesus

I want to approach this mystery of Jesus now largely from a scriptural and ritual language drawn from the Catholic liturgical tradition (in which I have been steeped both as a practitioner and a professional, student and teacher, for decades). In this way we can tell the story again in a manner that lies closer to the brackish waters where the *logos* of the rational mind is not yet completely extricated from the *mythos* of symbolic language. From this standpoint let's look again at the marvelous stories told about three events in Jesus' own life: the transfiguration, the resurrection, and the ascension.

Having been raised in the theological environment of the historical critical method and liberal exegesis, at an earlier time in my life I had gotten pretty comfortable with accepting the notion that perhaps all three of these stories were, at the least, exaggerations with no basis in historical fact, or descriptions of feelings that those surrounding Jesus had, trying to make sense out of the phenomenal presence he had been. I've grown comfortable now, however, in saying to almost any group of people, "I don't care if you believe that these events happened exactly as they are recorded in the Scriptures. Please don't miss the point of the story!" I happen to have been convinced that they could have happened exactly as they are recorded, but even those who do not believe that should not miss the point of the story! In a very real sense these accounts are myths—not meaning that they are not true, but that they are trying to convey a deeper truth. And all three of these accounts are trying to convey a deeper truth that we keep missing: that the flesh, and with it all matter, shares in spiritual glory, that even the body and matter itself are meant to undergo a spiritual transformation.

Let's begin by looking at the transfiguration, as recorded in the Gospels: Jesus climbed up a mountain with Peter, James, and John and "was transfigured before them, and his face shone like the sun, and his clothes became dazzling white" (Matt 17:1-2), "such as no one on earth could bleach them" (Mark 9:3; see also Luke 9:28-35). By tradition this event takes place on Mount Tabor, just outside of Nazareth in the Galilee; hence, the light that emanates from Jesus' body is known as the "Taboric light." This inner glory was permeating Jesus' very body, even his clothes. Matter was not being cast off; rather, it was being affected by the power of spiritual transformation. Or, as Aurobindo might say, the body itself was the field of transformation.

The account of the resurrection, the story of Jesus' actual rising from the dead, is the greatest story in Christianity. Yet it too gets dismissed as simply a pious myth trying to convey how the disciples still felt the presence of Jesus in their lives even after he died. But at some point I came to realize that if we lose the empty tomb, if we demythologize the actual risen body of Jesus away, we lose the fact that the resurrection is *all about the body*—not only Jesus' body, but the flesh in general, all bodies. The point is that Jesus' body was not annihilated by the death experience, the story tells us; matter was transmuted in some marvelous mysterious way into something else. This is why we sing from Psalm 16 at Easter time: "For you will not leave my soul among the dead, nor let your beloved know decay" (Ps 16:10, Grail Psalter). When and if we lose that empty tomb we are not actually making more sense out of the story; we may in fact be in danger of overspiritualizing it, no doubt the very opposite of the effect intended.

The gospels are not teaching that the soul of the risen Jesus simply stripped off his corporality, nor do the followers of Jesus understand the resurrection simply as the survival of his immortal soul, which is how the Greek mind might think of it in the soma–sema construct—that is, the "body is a tomb for the soul." The body–soul dualism of Greek, specifically Platonic, philosophy has little in common with biblical anthropology. To the Hebrew mind, and to the mind of Paul and other New Testament writers (as well as for Aristotelian metaphysics), there is no such thing as a body without a soul, or a soul without a body; body and soul are always a substantial unity, albeit a unity that can be approached from different angles, either from the viewpoint of corporeality or from the viewpoint of psychology. From this perspective, the body cannot be "at war" with the soul.[6] Jesus' first followers are Hebrews, and for Jesus, Paul and any other Jew of the time, "body" does not mean just the physical, material aspect of our being abstracted from the spiritual aspect. These early Christians do not have that kind of dualism operative in their mindset. For them the "body" is the whole person, with his or her rootedness in the world, with relationships, with a history. As the Spanish scripture scholar José Pagola wrote, "They cannot imagine Jesus without a body; he would be something else, not a human being."[7] But at the same time nor are they thinking simply of a physical body, merely flesh and blood that would be once again subject to death. Rather, they are imagining some kind of glorious body. And so the writers of the gospels describe the post-resurrection appearances where the disciples do not recognize him, even when they are walking down the road next to him. He can eat fish and yet walks through walls. The physical body has not been left behind but nor is it unchanged. Something marvelous has happened to it in the process; even the physical nature of Jesus has shared in the spiritual transformation.

The same applies to the ascension, a story told to us only by Luke. Jesus, body and soul, transformed in some marvelous way, disappears into the great mysterious cloud, goes to the right hand of the Father. In some ways, the ascension is the most mysterious event of all.

Over time, I have found it interesting how many people who are more comfortable with Asian philosophies and metaphysics easily defend all of these events, as well as the Assumption of Mary, even literally. Using the language of Yoga instead, Fr. Bede explained that Jesus' body, like all human bodies, was first of all a "gross body," a temporary structure of condensed energy that anyone could recognize. But at the resurrection, that gross body became a psychic or "subtle body," a glorified body we might call it. The Scriptures tell us that he can walk through walls and yet eat fish; he walks and talks with his disciples and yet they do not recognize him. And then at the ascension he transcends matter at both the gross and subtle level and enters the spiritual level.[8]

What This Has to Do with Us

If we demythologize these stories too much we also lose what they are trying to teach us about ourselves and about all of creation, the anthropological and teleological lessons, if you will. What is all this telling us about our end, what theology would call our *telos*? First of all, let us recognize that Jesus' mission was not solely a question of assuring his listeners of a better life in the afterlife: a significant part of his ministry was healing peoples' bodies, for which he was notoriously famous, not to mention feeding them and ridding them of demons. As Pagola wrote, what moved Jesus was "his love for those who suffer, and his will that they should experience now, *in their bodies* [emphasis mine], God's mercy which liberates from evil." I also like how Pagola writes that Jesus rebuilt sick people "from the bottom up," first their bodies and then their souls; and that Jesus' "power to awaken unrecognized energies in people created the conditions that made the recovery of health possible." How often is Jesus reported saying, "Your faith has saved you"?[9] Pagola suggests that Jesus and the sick person "were fused into a single faith."[10] What was this energy? What was this faith?[11]

Aside from that, while it has never been fully accepted in Western Christianity, in Eastern Orthodox theology the Taboric light of the transfiguration came to be seen as something very tangible and even accessible, identified also with the light that Paul experienced during his conversion experience on the road to Damascus (Acts 9:1-9), and even further back with the burning bush of God's self-revelation (Exod 3:1-6). It is related to the theory of the "uncreated energies of God" expounded by a fourteenth-century monk of Mount Athos named Gregory Palamas of the hesychast mystical tradition. According to the hesychasts, a saint who is completely pure, someone who has reached divine union, experiences a vision of divine radiance that is the same light that was manifested to Paul and Jesus' disciples. This experience is known as *theoria*.[12] The way Gregory explains it, this divine, uncreated light is the light where God makes himself manifest to those who enter into union with God. And those who receive this spiritual light, first of all, can perceive that which is beyond all intellect. But they also may participate in the divine energies and become themselves a kind of light.

What Gregory presents is a step further than *seeing* the light; he suggests that we can *participate* in the divine energies and become light ourselves. In the same way, he borrows the language of Maximus the Confessor, stating that God and the saints, even though they do not have the same essence, have one and the same energy: "since in all birth that which is begotten is identical with the begetter; that which is born of the flesh is flesh, and that which is born of the Spirit is Spirit."[13] This language of deification, a kind of identity with God, shocked Gregory's theological adversaries. Deification is also suggested by the scripture passages and prayers with which the Roman Church surrounds the liturgical celebration of the transfiguration. Examples include the beautiful passage from the First Epistle of John, in which the church teaches us that "we will be like him, for we will see him as he is" (1 John 3:2). Similarly, in Paul's letter to the Philippians, used for funerals, we hear: "He will transform the body of our humiliation so that it may be conformed to the body of his glory" (Phil 3:21). The prayer after communion on the feast of the Transfiguration also suggests as much:

> Lord, you revealed the true radiance of Christ
> in the glory of the resurrection.
> May the food we receive from heaven
> change us into his image.

As we are told again and again, we shall be like Christ. He will transfigure our lowly bodies into glorious copies of his own.

There are many monasteries named after the Transfiguration (or Mount Tabor) because the Christian monastic tradition, especially that of Eastern Christianity, has a special love for this image going back to the Fathers of the Desert, perhaps because of monasticism's emphasis on the practical spiritual life and asceticism. Here is one of my all-time favorite stories.

> Abba Lot went to see Abba Joseph and said to him, "Abba, as far as I can I say my little office, I fast a little, I pray and meditate, I live in peace, and as far as I can, I purify my thoughts. What else can I do?"
>
> Then the old man stood up and stretched his hands towards heaven. His fingers became like ten lamps of fire and he said to him, "If you will, you can become all flame."

Life in Christ is a life permeated by the power and energy of the Holy Spirit. Life with Jesus is to be fused into a single faith with him. "I am the vine; you are the branches" (John 15:5). And the sap running through us is the fire, the power and energy of the Holy Spirit. And so Maximus the Confessor writes, "The Saints participate in God; not only do they participate, but they also communicate him."[14]

Our share in the resurrection should be the most obvious. Paul tells us over and over again in different words: "If the Spirit who raised Jesus from the dead dwells in you, then the one who raised Jesus from the dead will give life to your mortal bodies also through his Spirit that dwells in you" (Rom 8:11). It's that simple. That's what we lose if we lose the empty tomb.

As for the ascension, my favorite explanation of our share in it comes from the French liturgist Jean Corbon, in what he calls "the continual ascension,"[15] meaning that the ascension is not simply one static moment in history, but rather a dynamic event. The ascension of Jesus is the first movement of a progressive event. As Paul notes over and over again, Jesus is the head of a Body, and the fullness of that Body is in the church. Where the head has gone, so will go the rest of the body. "So that where I am, you also may be" (John 14:3). I have a quite literal image in my mind of this: the head of the body is there, but for all of history that head, Jesus, will be dragging, sometimes kicking and screaming, the rest of the body behind him, to follow him, to be with him at the right hand of the throne of God in glory. We are his body! We are, our flesh is, the work of this continual ascension.

Let us now focus on our discussion of the *telos*, the ultimate end. What is the ultimate end according to the Christian tradition?

Eschatological Integration

We now turn to the renowned Anglican scripture scholar N. T. Wright, who gave me a whole new vocabulary for something toward which I had been sneaking for some time. Rather shockingly, Wright says that "the traditional preaching about everyone having a 'soul' which needs saving" is "almost hopelessly misleading." Ultimate salvation according to the Christian scriptural tradition, he states, rather controversially, "is not in heaven"! Ultimate salvation is "in the resurrection into the combined reality of a new heaven and a new earth."[16] The end, the telos, according to Christian scriptures, is a new heaven and a new earth; the end is eschatological integration.

According to Wright, if we take Paul's anthropology and mystical intuition seriously, we learn that "God's ultimate future for the cosmos is the joining together in the Messiah [that is, in Christ] of all things in heaven and earth," and so for the human being the ultimate future also is "the full integration of all that we are made to be." Wright describes Christian anthropology this way: "God, says Paul, will be 'all in all'; and for Paul it is the body, not just the soul, the mind or spirit, which is the temple of the living God. The body is meant for the Lord, he says, and the Lord for the body" (1 Cor 15:28).

Hence, Wright continues, we have the shocking belief in bodily resurrection. "The story of all four gospels is not the story of how God came in Jesus to rescue souls for a disembodied, other-worldly heaven." Therefore, the central message of the New Testament is not that we are supposed to escape the world and go to heaven, but rather that God's sovereign saving rule will come to the world, as Jesus prayed and taught us to pray, "on earth as it is in heaven."[17]

What is important about this is that this way of thinking was actually Fr. Bede's bridge to the Yoga tradition. As he understood it, the work of Yoga is the transformation of the body and the soul by the Spirit, and the leap to a Christian Yoga, though it may sound odd to us, is based in Scripture, and it is no leap at all: the goal of a Christian Yoga is that "body and soul are to be transformed by the divine life and to participate in the divine consciousness. There is a descent of Spirit into matter"—both the breath being blown into the clay at creation and the descent of the Holy Spirit at Pentecost—"by which matter is transformed by the indwelling power of the Spirit and the body is transfigured." Now the belief in the possibility of understanding a real, actual, historical, literal resurrection from the dead seems within reach, because, "This is the cosmic drama, this transformation of nature, of matter and the body, as to become the outward form of the divine Spirit, the body of the Lord. And this transformation is taking place in our own bodies. In every human being matter is being transformed daily into Spirit."[18]

Now, we all know that most bodies do not literally come out of the grave and resuscitate. I've always struggled with how to explain the fact that we know that most bodies do decompose in the grave, even the bodies of great saints (though some have been found to be "incorrupt"). How can this be, if we believe in resurrection? Fr. Bede gives this beautiful, humble explanation. He wrote that for most of us the process of transformation remains incomplete. Matter, meaning the flesh, is never fully assimilated by the Spirit, and at death the matter that has not been assimilated by the Spirit is returned to the earth. But in the body of Jesus, "we can see that transformation of matter by Spirit taking place, which is the destiny of all of us at the end of time." Bede points out that the body of Mary too "is said to have been transformed in the same way, and doubtless there are other saints and yogis of whom this is true."[19]

And so we see a rather conservative Christian scripture scholar (Wright) and a progressive monk and mystic (Griffiths) immersed in the genius of Indian spirituality, in agreement. The Scriptures literally mean that Jesus rose from the dead; Paul bases his whole argument on this and claims that our salvation too is integral. As the best of the ancient Christian tradition teaches, in the famous phrase of Tertullian (*c.* 160-*c.* 225), *Carne cardo salutis es*—"The flesh is the hinge of salvation." But we may go a step further and say that the flesh, and with it all of matter, is also that which is saved. Yet the wildest part of this vision is that it doesn't stop there. Paul applies it to all creation as well.

All Creation Is Groaning

In Gerald Vann's book *The Water and the Fire*, he has an explanation of the Assumption of Mary that beautifully explicates what we have been exploring concerning the Christian view of flesh and matter. He wrote, in a beautifully poetic way, that the reason the doctrine of the Assumption is of supreme importance is because it means that

> there is still in the world, there will always be in the world, a voice to affirm and a power to defend the dignity and the ultimate glory of matter, of material things, of human flesh and blood, of the lovely mystery of human love, of the beauty which is the work of [human] hands. There is a voice which affirms, there is a power which defends, all the material things which make life worth while; and they bid us be of good heart because we can hope in the end to achieve our own lives, full, rich, unified, free, not by escaping from the flesh and material things, but by the healing and sanctifying of the flesh and material things.[20]

So these are not just moments for Jesus alone, nor are any of these events only about Jesus and his body. This is what is meant for all flesh, for all humanity. Nor is this meant for human flesh alone. We sometimes refer to the human person as the priest of creation. St. Paul's mystical theology explains what that means: "We know the whole creation has been groaning in labor pains until now; and not only the creation, but we ourselves, who have the first fruits of the Spirit, groan inwardly while we wait for adoption, the redemption of our bodies" (Rom 8:22-23). These two things—redemption of our bodies and the destiny of creation—are intimately connected in the Christian vision of the cosmos. All of creation is groaning and in agony while we work this out. The rest of creation is not left behind in this economy, because in some marvelous way, as Paul writes several times, God will be "all in all" (1 Cor 15:28)—or, as we pray in the old doxology, "world without end, Amen!" The world in some way is not going to end. It is merely going to be brought into right relationship with God again, through us first, the priests of creation. And that is why the Christ event is itself an axial moment, a pivotal moment, because in Jesus' body "the matter of this universe is taken up into the Godhead." And we Christians believe that this was an important event for all of creation: as Fr. Bede wrote, the matter which exploded in the Big Bang fifteen or twenty billion years ago "at that point was finally transfigured." Rather than consciousness separating itself from matter, "in Jesus consciousness finally took possession of matter"; the marriage was consummated. In Jesus, the matter of the universe was made totally conscious and became one with God, the ultimate nonduality.[21]

It is easy to look around our concrete physical universe and see right now just how badly we have exercised our priestly "dominion" over creation. But that is no surprise since, as we noted earlier, as Sam Keen says, "how we are in our bodies is how we are going to be in the world." And the Earth is groaning and in agony while we work this out, groaning under the weight of pollution and exploitation, overfishing, deforestation and strip-mining, gas-guzzling SUVs and mountains of single-use disposable products, islands of plastic rubbish in the middle of the ocean, and entire species being eliminated because of our lack of good stewardship of that over which we have been given "dominion." And all this is because we are out of right relationship with our own bodies, and that because our physical beings are out of right relationship with the deepest spiritual part of our existence.

We need to remember that these transformative events in the life of Jesus, indeed the very event that was the life of Jesus, are also all about the triumph of the flesh, not just Jesus' flesh; and that the triumph of that one body—Jesus' body—and flesh in general is also a triumph for all of creation that has been groaning and in agony while we await the redemption of our bodies. Bede traces this process all the way back to the Big Bang, saying that the matter that exploded fifteen or twenty billion years ago, and has been in the process of transfiguration all throughout history and evolution as consciousness works on matter, is finally transfigured in Jesus. In Jesus, rather than there being a great divorce of consciousness and matter, consciousness takes full possession of matter, "and this means that matter was spiritualized . . . in other words, made totally conscious and became one with God, in the Godhead."[22] As Teilhard and Aurobindo would have us believe, matter reveals Spirit's face. This, I believe, is the ultimate nondual experience.

Pentecost: Some Lessons from the Liturgy

Let's now look at one more event, one that occurs after the earthly life of Jesus, but is the birthday, you might say, of the Body of Christ, the Church. This event, Pentecost, is another foundational Christian myth, because it is when we celebrate who we are.

I think we could safely say that the operative image of Pentecost for most Christians is that of the Holy Spirit coming down upon the heads of the apostles, and therefore by extension pouring over the whole church. And so we read from the book of Joel, "I will pour out my spirit on all flesh" (Joel 3:1-5) and the story from the Acts of the Apostles about the "sound like the rush of a violent wind" and the tongues of fire that came to rest on the apostles (Acts 2:1-11). But there are two different liturgies for the feast of Pentecost, the vigil (celebrated the evening before) and the Mass during the day.[23] At the vigil Mass the gospel that is used is from the seventh chapter of the Gospel of John, when Jesus cries out: "As the scripture has said, 'Out of the believer's heart shall flow rivers of living water.'" To which John adds (I like to think, whispering off to the side as if revealing a secret), "he said this about the Spirit" (John 7:37-39). And so the church teaches that Spirit does not just cover over us but actually dwells in the deepest part of our being and courses through our veins. That gospel reading is coupled with the incredible reading from the Letter to the Romans (Rom 8:22-27), arguably the most important scriptural passage about prayer, which teaches about how we groan inwardly, and how the Spirit likewise groans inside of us: "Likewise the Spirit helps us in our weakness; for we do not know how to pray as we ought, but that very Spirit intercedes with sighs too deep for words" (Rom 8:26). So Pentecost is also about the fact that our prayer is actually the prayer of the Spirit praying *in* us; our prayer is actually all about lining ourselves up with that prayer that is already humming inside of us. But best of all, the entrance antiphon that is offered as an opening chant for the feast of Pentecost (out of every text about the Holy Spirit that could have been offered that day) is *Caritas Deus diffusa est in cordibus nostris per inhabitantem Spiritum eius in nobis*: "The love of God is poured into our hearts by the Spirit living in us" (Rom 5:5). (This is not an exact translation of the scripture passage from Romans, and for that reason it is even more important, as if the church were wresting a new meaning out of the text.) This also is what Pentecost is all about—that is, the Holy Spirit living in us, and that same Spirit pouring out of us like a stream of life-giving water. This is a very exciting idea. Especially in Luke's Gospel the Holy Spirit is always associated with *dynamis* (power). This is what dwells in us, the power, the energy of God. And the liturgy of the church knows this and is trying to convey it. All of Easter—indeed the life, passion, death, resurrection, and ascension of Jesus—have been pointing toward this.

Streams of Living Water

There is a song that I myself composed some years ago called "Streams of Living Water." I chose to use that above-mentioned passage from John 7 as a refrain that could convey what I thought to be the heart of the Christian spiritual life. It's an *ostinato* refrain in which the assembly sings that line over and over again, while superimposed on it the cantor sings another text. The text I chose to add was a verse from Ezekiel: "I saw water flowing from the right side of the temple; the water brought God's life and his salvation" (Ezek 47:1). That Ezekiel passage is the preferred text for the Sprinkling Rite during the season of Easter, the rite that reminds the assembly of their Baptism, and indeed is also recommended to be sung immediately after the renewal of Baptismal promises at the Easter Vigil. In the original context, the prophet Ezekiel is having a vision of the life-giving power pouring from the new temple, and of course here we mean the original temple of Jerusalem. The prophet describes a river of fresh water that flows from out of the east side and slightly south through the Kidron Valley, which is incidentally where John in his Gospel tells us Jesus went with his disciples that fateful Thursday night before he was arrested and put to death. Ezekiel's vision is of a miracle that attests to the life-giving power of God dwelling in the sanctuary. But under Jesus everything gets "relocated,"[24] including the temple.

At the beginning of the Gospel of John, Jesus has come up to Jerusalem for the Passover and found people selling cattle, sheep, and doves there, and moneychangers seated at their tables. And Jesus is not very nice; he takes a whip of cords and drives everybody out. "Take these things out of here!" he says. "Stop making my Father's house a marketplace!" When the Jews challenge him—"What sign can you show us for doing this?"—he says, "Destroy this temple, and in three days I will raise it up." Of course, they take him literally, as if he were speaking about the building, but John lets us in on the secret and whispers to us again off to the side, somewhat parenthetically, "he was speaking about the temple of his body" (John 2:13-22).[25] So the temple has been relocated. It was a building, which had already been destroyed once. But according to Christianity, the vision that Ezekiel has of the new temple was not another one of brick and mortar, but a person in whom the fullness of the godhead dwelt bodily (Col 3:3). The life-giving power of God now dwells in *that* sanctuary, the sanctuary of Jesus' body. So, of course, when we sing "I saw water flowing from the right side of the temple" at Easter, we are supposed to remember that the temple is now Jesus' own body, as we are still remembering and are supposed to call to mind that two days before we had just heard the story, again from the Gospel of John, of how one of the soldiers "thrust a lance into his side and immediately blood and water flowed out" (John 19:34). This blood and water symbolize, among other things, the sacramental life of the church, most specifically Bap-

tism and Eucharist, but most of all the blood and water symbolize the very energy of life.

But we cannot stop there. St. Paul understood the implications of all this and never tires of reminding his readers that the
temple was relocated yet again, from the body of Jesus, to *our*
bodies. And so the words of the First Letter to the Corinthians:
"Do you not know that you are God's temple and that God's
Spirit dwells in you?" I can almost hear Paul shouting this last
line: "God's temple is holy, and you are that temple!" (1 Cor
3:16-17). The great psychotherapist Carl Jung himself wrote that
life seemed to have gone out of the churches in the West, and as
its next dwelling place the Holy Spirit appears to have selected
the human individual. This comes as no surprise to Christians.
"Destroy this temple," said Jesus, "and in three days I will raise
it up again" (John 2:21). John tells us that Jesus was talking about
the temple of his own body, but by extension he was also speaking about the temples of our bodies. As St. Paul says, "Do you
not know that you are God's temple by the Holy Spirit who
dwells within you?" (1 Cor 3:16-17). What Jung was articulating,
of course, is authentic Christianity: "The love of God has been
poured into our hearts by the Spirit living in us" (Rom 5:5), into
the deepest part of our beings.

The Real Church

These Scriptures come together again liturgically on the feast
of the Dedication of the Lateran Basilica in Rome. The Lateran
Basilica is the cathedral of Rome, built during the reign of Con-
stantine and consecrated in 324 by Pope St. Sylvester. Over time
the feast became a universal celebration, the liturgical books
tell us, in honor of the basilica, which is called *omnium urbis et
orbis ecclesiarum mater et caput*—"the mother and mistress of all
churches of Rome and the world," and a "sign of love for and
union with the See of Peter." But what the readings for the feast
tell us is something different.

The first reading is that same one from the prophet Ezekiel: "I
saw water flowing from the right side of the temple." The second
is the one from the First Letter to the Corinthians: "God's temple

is holy, and you are that temple!" The gospel is the same one from John about which we wrote: "Streams of life giving water shall flow from out of the believer's heart. . . . He was talking about the Holy Spirit." This is what Jesus came to establish, that the love of God would be poured into our hearts by his Spirit living in us; that the human person, the human body, would be the dwelling place of God. And this then, in the words of St. Peter, is what it means to be church: "like living stones let yourself be built into a spiritual house" (1 Pet 2:5), stones and a house, a temple out of which the love of God, the Holy Spirit, would pour like a stream of life-giving water, pour out like love, like charity, as creativity and participation, full active and conscious participation, not just in the liturgy and life of the church, but, as St. Peter says, "participants in the divine nature" (2 Pet 1:4). These words are echoed in the words whispered by the priest in the Roman Rite as a drop of water is symbolically poured into the wine at the preparation of the gifts: "By the mystery of this water and wine may we come to share in the divinity of Christ who humbled himself to share in our humanity." We think we are ascending to God but God in Christ descends, "humbles himself," and becomes one of us. And so, we will learn, we too only ascend by descending.[26]

The Full Stature of Christ

Let me recap with the words of Ursula King again: when understood properly, or in a new light, Christianity has the extraordinary ability to engender an all-transforming dynamic love that embraces both God and the world. Christianity sings of an interpenetration of the material and the spiritual given through the Incarnation, and this could lend it a singular force of attraction, adoration, and worship as well as access to God through the world—not merely communion with the world, nor mere communion with God, but communion with God *through* the world. Christianity sings of a God who is a universal presence, a living God whose energy animates all life and levels of life, God as an ultimate center where everything finds its consummation.[27]

In conclusion, let me go back one more time to this mysterious event of the ascension and rearticulate it using some of the vocabulary we have gleaned thus far. Here is Paul writing about the ascension in the Letter to the Ephesians.

> When it says, "He ascended," what does it mean but that he had also descended into the lower parts of the earth. He who descended is the same one who ascended far above the heavens, so that he might fill all things . . . until all of us come to the unity of faith and of the knowledge of the Son of God, to maturity, to the measure of the full stature of Christ . . . we must grow up in every way into him who is the head, into Christ. (Eph 4:9-10, 13, 15)

Paul is speaking here about the unity of the Body of Christ, but note the dynamic going on in terms of what we have studied so far. Christ, the Word, our name for the self-consciousness power of *chitshakti*—the "first-born of all creation" (Col 1:15) descended into the lower parts of the earth, into dark and muddy depths of unconscious matter. This is the incarnation. The Word—the creative principle and divine wisdom, primal reason, spirit, life, the Tao—did not maintain the amnesiac distance that involution had wrought. At the appointed time, according to "the plan of the mystery hidden for ages in God who created all things" (Eph 3:9)—the plan of evolution—"the fullness of deity dwelt bodily" (Col 3:9) in this human being Jesus. We might say that Christians see this "Christ event" as the high point, what Bruno Barnhart calls the "noonday," the turning point in the history of creation, from the death and abandonment of Friday's cross and darkness, and the *asat*, or nonbeing, of Saturday's tomb, to the triumph of Easter, the ascension, and then Pentecost, which could be seen as an image of the descent of Shiva–Shakti. At this point, in this man, the realms of heaven and earth, the spiritual and the material—what Hinduism calls purusha and prakriti, or consciousness and matter, and Buddhism calls *samsara* and *nirvana*—we believe, are reconciled; the marriage is consummated. And what that event has set off is a continuous movement for all created matter, "so that he might fill all things." Where the head has gone the rest of the body will follow, with the human person first as the priest of creation, so that we may "come to fullness in him" (Eph 3:10), "until all of us come to maturity, until all of us come to the measure of the full stature of Christ, until all of us grow up in every way into him who is the head, until all of us grow into Christ" (Eph 4:9-10, 13, 15). If we go with Spirit into our own humanity and indeed into the lower depths of all of creation, which we somehow hold in our muddy depths, the root of our own beings, and descend to the ground of our own consciousness, which is until now unconscious of itself, if we descend to the extreme involution where Spirit all but forgets Herself, we will reascend together, "the Spirit and the Bride," that very Spirit bearing witness with our spirit (Rom 8:15).

But even that is not the end; instead, it is the *beginning* of the life in Christ. This understanding leads us to two things contained in our preceding argument. First is participatory consciousness—that is, being conscious of our participation, or participating consciously—in the divine nature. Second is the realization that the ultimate goal is not the ascent away from matter, earth, society, and the body, but about a descent in a deeper consecratory way.

Part 2

.arely realize that there is Something/Someone beyond name and form that is not simply extrinsic to material reality but is also both the Source and the Summit of all reality. Put another way, the holy darkness that is the fount of Being that/who we call God is not only outside of us, working like a superimposed reality, but is deep within us, welling up, or wanting to well up, like a stream of life-giving water, a transforming power. And it is for this reason, in my opinion, that so many of us have turned to Asian spirituality, practice, and mysticism. What we often have found there is a way that roots itself more healthily and wholly in material reality but also stretches beyond all name and form into the holy darkness that is the Divine.

That is not to say that these aspects are not in Christianity. Hopefully, what I have shown throughout the preceding chapters is that these aspects are present to an eminent degree in Christianity, but are simply often unrealized. Jesuit mystic William Johnston wrote beautifully about how certain Asian traditions and Eastern mysticism in general can reveal new aspects of the gospel to Western Christians, aspects that have been there all along but that we simply have not noticed; and these other ways might be able to help us to understand the depth of our own kerygma and tradition, as well as help us find a new vocabulary to understand and express Jesus' experience for ourselves and to a new age. Or as Ewert Cousins explained in a similar way, often the partners in dialogue with another tradition discover in that other tradition "values which are submerged or only inchoate in their own."[2] Obviously, this does not only apply to Asian spirituality. Bruno Barnhart wrote beautifully that not only is the mystery present in a different way in other traditions, but we are to learn from all of them, "from the primal, tribal religions as well as the highly developed traditions of Hinduism and Christianity." Furthermore, he says, the only reason external religion exists—and as the poet David Whyte might say, this is an "only" that you could say over and over again; an "only" that contains multitudes—with its rites, dogmas, and institutional structures, is "to bring people to the personal experience of this mystery." Toward that end, "all external forms, all the 'language' of religion, has to be continually revised if it is to communicate the mystery to people of a new age."

At the same time—and this is equally vital—the mystery actually "already dwells in the heart of every human being, and the church must awaken to this 'universal revelation.' "[3] As Thomas Aquinas taught, grace builds on nature, God builds on what is already there in the heart of every human person.

For me, this is where holistic spirituality, integral spirituality, what Sri Aurobindo would call *purna yoga* (literally, "full or complete Yoga"), comes in. It is a new articulation of a depth anthropology, along with its practical application, learned from and shared with the great traditions of the world, which we shall be exploring in the remaining chapters.

Bede Griffiths' New Vision

For me, the most significant contribution that Bede Griffiths left us was a new understanding of spiritual anthropology, an understanding of the human person wrapped inside an ancient cosmology. As evidenced by the quote above, however, it was actually the recovery of an ancient understanding of reality: the recognition of the spiritual, psychological, and physical aspects of all created reality and, following on that, a realization that the human person is at once spirit, soul, and body. So in a sense to speak of a "new vision of reality" (the title of his last major publication) is ironic. This was the one topic I heard Fr. Bede speak on in 1992 and it permanently changed my way of thinking about and seeing reality, and gave me a whole new approach to the practicalities of the spiritual life.

Father Bede was convinced that as we entered this new age, Western science was slowly recovering, rediscovering, the perennial philosophy, the wisdom that had prevailed throughout the world from about 500 BCE through 1500 CE. It's almost as if Western science is slowly catching up with mysticism and "discovering" what especially the Asian spiritualities and philosophies had never doubted: that the material universe is pervaded by and finds its explanation in a transcendent reality. That discovery was precisely what had already taken place in India in the fifth century before Christ, during the First Axial Period when, as Bede put it, there was a breakthrough beyond mental consciousness to the discovery of the Ultimate Reality sustaining the whole universe.

Let's start with Aldous Huxley's articulation of the perennial philosophy, which was highly influential on Bede.[4] This is from Huxley's introduction to Christopher Isherwood's translation of the Bhagavad Gita, where he insists that the focus of Indian religion is "one of the clearest and most comprehensive summaries of the Perennial Philosophy ever to have been made."[5] He states it in four points. First, that the phenomenal world of matter and of individualized consciousness—the world of things and animals and human beings and even "gods"—is actually a manifestation of a Divine Ground "within which all partial realities have their being." This calls to mind the words of St. Paul in the Acts of the Apostles, in which he tells the Athenians that God is the one "in whom we live and move and have our being" (Acts 17:28). Second, the perennial philosophy teaches that human beings are capable of realizing the existence of this Divine Ground by a direct intuition, and that this direct intuition is superior to discursive reasoning and the rational mind. As Christian mystical writers would surely concur, particularly the anonymous author of *The Cloud of Unknowing*, there is, and this is, a knowledge that unites the knower with that which is known, a "unitive" knowledge. Third, human beings possess a double nature, a phenomenal ego and, beyond that phenomenal ego, what Huxley refers to as "an eternal Self, which is the inner person, the spirit, the spark of divinity within the soul." The two Christian scriptural images that immediately come to mind are St. Paul's writing about our life "hidden with Christ in God" (Col 3:3) and, perhaps better, St. Peter's reference to the "inner self with the lasting beauty of a gentle and quiet spirit" (1 Pet 3:4). And finally, the perennial philosophy states that the end and purpose of human life, the telos, is to identify oneself with this eternal Self and "so to come to unitive knowledge of the Divine Ground."[6]

The Threefold Nature of Reality

Similarly, Fr. Bede taught that the great insight the Vedic philosophers had come to was an understanding of the threefold nature of reality, that the world is at once physical, psychological, spiritual. In the so-called primitive mind, which Bede thought ...us probably a lot closer to being the natural mind, there is no such thing as a merely physical object. The world is at once physical, psychological, and spiritual, and these three realms of reality are always interdependent and interwoven. "Every material thing has a psychological aspect, a relation to human consciousness, and this in turn is related to the supreme spirit which pervades both the physical world and human consciousness."[7] In other words, all of physical reality has a psychological aspect, and both the psychological and physical realms have an underlying reality—a spiritual reality—that is the source of both other realms. And these three levels of reality should never be separated. Bede wrote that this cosmology was "typical of the whole ancient world which had emerged out of the mythological world of more ancient times," and "the Oriental view of the universe, which is in fact, the view of the 'perennial philosophy', the cosmic vision which is common to all religious traditions from the most primitive tribal religions to the great world religions, Hinduism, Buddhism, Islam, and Christianity."[8] I hope the reader will also see here Teilhard's geo-sphere and biosphere, noosphere, and theosphere.

One could validly divide reality into countless other strata or realms and name them many different ways, as many have done. There is, for instance, the beautiful teaching of Hinduism about the *koshas*, the five coverings of the atman or Brahman, especially as articulated in the Taittiriya Upanishad.[9] Buddhism has the teaching of the five *skandhas*, the five aggregates that compose human appearance.[10] In modern times the great scholar of world religions Huston Smith, among other perennialists, has revived the ancient notion of the Great Chain of Being, body–mind–soul–spirit, which Smith associates with respective realms: the terrestrial realm, the intermediate realm, celestial and infinite realms. Ken Wilber expands that to include matter as well, and called it instead "the Great Nest of Being," adding the great stress that this is both hierarchy and a holarchy (hence the word "nest" rather than "chain").[11]

As beautiful and comprehensive as these other articula-tions are, I have stayed with and continue to be satisfied by this tripartite understanding for its simplicity and its resonance with so many traditions. But I think that Wilber's vocabulary about the nest and the holarchy is especially helpful in stressing that these are *interpenetrating* realms of reality. Even if we present reality as a hierarchy, such as in the scale of evolutionary theory, we are actually regarding each element according to its holistic capacity, its ability to integrate what has gone before: What is whole at one stage becomes part of a larger whole at the next stage. Hence, the notion of interpenetrating or, even better, enveloping levels of reality. This is very much in keeping with the thought of Teilhard as well. We might have a tendency to see spiritual reality or the soul or consciousness as something distinct or apart from material reality, either intervening in material reality or trapped in corporeality like some forms of Gnosticism or the Greek notion of the soul that escapes the body at death, or even Descartes's idea of the mind as an alternate substance operating completely independently of the physical universe. This ancient view would have us understand instead that these three realms of reality—the physical, the psychological, and the spiritual—are always interdependent and interwoven. The hierarchy is also a holarchy; the chain is actually a nest.

"Every material thing has a psychological aspect," Bede writes, "a relation to human consciousness, and this in turn is related to the supreme spirit which pervades both the physical world and human consciousness."[12] The word "psychological" may strike us as strange and clinical, but it helps to recall that it comes from the word *psyche*, whose translation is really more accurately "soul." The psychological realm is the realm of the soul, and the soul as Bede understands it contains a broad spectrum of subtle dimensions. But just as every physical reality has a psychological aspect, what is equally important is that both the psychological and physical realms have an underlying reality, one that is beyond the realm of soul, that is the source and summit of both other realms—spiritual reality. The Vedic philosophers never separated these aspects.[13]

Perhaps rather idealistically, Fr. Bede thought that up until the Middle Ages, in China, India, and the Islamic world, as well as in Europe, a creative synthesis had been achieved and was maintained in which the physical, psychic, and spiritual worlds were integrated. Economic, social, political, and cultural orders were all conceived as a harmonious unity in which each human being was related to nature, to one's fellows and to the Divine. But then, as he often lamented, Bede thought that the Western mind gradually came to be dominated by a philosophy of materialism, whether implicit or explicit. And thus the unitive vision began to be lost, and after the Middle Ages this creative synthesis began to disintegrate. He thought that the Renaissance and the Reformation, the Enlightenment, and the French Revolution, the Russian and Chinese Revolutions were all stages in this process of its disintegration. (Note the less hopeful view of this Bede has than Bruno Barnhart's notion of Western civilization in some way continuing the incarnational trajectory of the Christ event through these movements.[14])

In *New Vision of Reality*, beginning with Descartes's separation of mind and matter (everybody blames Descartes!), through Francis Bacon, Galileo, and Isaac Newton, Bede shows how by the eighteenth century all aspects of a divine reality governing the universe had been gradually eliminated, and a mechanistic system alone remained. He goes on to accuse rationalism of setting the human mind free from the divine, and Communism of depriving human beings of their basic liberty and enslaving them to the material world, all as a result, he says, of this mechanistic, materialistic philosophy.[15] Consequently, in modern times we have inherited a mindset that separates matter from mind, and separates matter and mind from the Supreme Reality, from God.[16] Especially in the West we suffer from the disease of the merely rational mind that causes us to see matter, mind, and spirit "as separate from one another, to imagine a world extended outside of us in space and time, and the mind as something separate from the external world."[17] This eventually has an effect on all aspects of science from social theory like Marxist dialectical materialism all the way through Freudian psychology. Just as the existence of a divine Ultimate (spiritual) Reality was no longer needed in cosmology and the natural sciences, so in Freud's initial mechanistic model, which Bede thought Freud never fully transcended, the existence of a soul was gradually deemed unnecessary in psychology.

Bede wrote *New Vision of Reality* in the last years of his life. He had had such a mistrust of modern science and the technological age from his young adult years on, but here at the end of his life, due partially to friendship and conversation with wonderful modern thinkers such as Rupert Sheldrake, he immersed himself in the works of modern science and began to rejoice that "the elements of the more universal and profound vision" were being recovered in the context of modern scientific thought.[18] He saw far-reaching consequences for the West slowly regaining this original and ancient vision, this perennial philosophy, not just through modern physics but through depth psychology as well. He then explicates in his own words, through his own filter as mystic and monk, the work of "the new physics" of Fritjof Capra, David Bohm, Rupert Sheldrake, and Ilya Prigogine, as well as the new psychology, first of all of Carl Jung, but more contemporary thinkers such as Karl Pribram and Ken Wilbur as well, and the emergence of transpersonal and depth psychology.

Spirit, Soul, and Body

So, now we finally come to the main topic of this book!

What I find especially helpful and practical about Fr. Bede's teaching is that it starts out with a broad cosmological view and then resolves in a fresh view of the human person in all our glorious transcendent capacity. From this perennial philosophy he comes to understand that just as all created reality has a spiritual, psychological, and material dimension, so each human being is not just body and soul, but spirit, soul, and body, three interpenetrating realms of our being human. It is this anthropology—spirit, soul, and body—that became the core of Bede's teaching and writings. As a matter of fact, once, in a presentation shortly before his death, he said, "The body, mind, and spirit are the main focus of all my thinking presently; we have to integrate these three levels of reality that exist at every moment."[19]

Huxley agrees that this also is actually a return to and a rediscovery of an ancient way of thinking. In *The Perennial Philosophy,* he laments that twentieth-century psychologists have chosen to ignore what the Buddha, St. Augustine, and Pascal were all aware of: "the fact that human nature is tripartite, consisting of a spirit as well as of a mind and body; the fact that we live on the borderline between two worlds, the temporal and the eternal, the physical-vital-human and the divine."[20] Fr. Bede claimed that this view of the human person as body, soul, and spirit was fundamental in the Bible and very clear in St. Paul's writings.[21] The tripartite anthropology was certainly often very clearly taught in the Christian Orthodox tradition until modern times. (You will perhaps have noticed right away that sometimes the word "mind" is used for this middle realm instead of "soul," in Huxley here and, less often, by Fr. Bede as well, although he normally uses the word "soul." I always prefer the word "soul" over "mind," as I will explain below.)

As body we are part of the earth and, just like all of reality, the physical organism of our body is a structure of energies through which *we are part of the physical universe*, connected to every element of creation from the beginning of time. As body, human nature is part of the whole physical universe; it evolves out of the physical universe, from matter and life. Recall the vision of Teilhard here, how the geosphere evolves into the biosphere.[22] In his later years through the language of Tantra, Bede wrote and taught about a very practical spiritual life based partly on embracing our physicality, fully incorporating the body, including one's sexuality. However, although he himself had a great love for nature, which was in fact a large part of his own conversion experience, what Bede did not speak or write about was how an embracing of the body can and should also lead to a greater appreciation for the Earth and all of creation as well. Suffice it to say that this is an area more fully explored in other work, but here let us stress that the idea of being a *part* of the physical universe, not being simply its intervening and impermeable head, is an important neglected emphasis, to which we shall return below.

Our soul then is the whole inner realm, matter coming into consciousness, and then coming into self-consciousness and learning to harness the powers of the mind. Perhaps the rational mind is at the center, but it is surrounded by all the strata of the soul, the psyche—the subconscious, higher states of consciousness, the collective unconscious, and psychic powers and phenomena of all sorts. As soul (again, we can also use the Greek word *psyche*), humanity is the head of the universe. I am being unashamedly anthropocentric here, because I do believe, as the Christian tradition teaches, that the human person has been given a unique role in this economy of evolution, unlike and in many ways more advanced than other creatures, although this again will be attenuated and contextualized in what follows. We are, in a sense, matter coming into consciousness and forming an individual soul. Our psychological organism consists of our appetites, our senses, our feelings and imagination, our reasoning capabilities. I like to stress, as Bede did, that the rational mind forms only one part of this spectrum of consciousness.

This is why I do not care for the popular phrase "body, mind, and soul" (or spirit) and why I always prefer the word "soul" over "mind," because otherwise it seems to abstract the rational mind from the other layers of the soul, especially from the emotive and intuitive realms/functions, as well as from the higher forms of consciousness that surround it and to which it should give way. This psyche (soul) forms our personality and is integrated with the physical organism. In this realm we are also a part of the psychic universe, the collective unconscious and the *anima mundi,* or the soul of the world. The ancients, including St. Thomas Aquinas, thought that plants and animals have some share in this psychic realm, some kind of soul, although of a different quality from ours. So there are theories of plants responding to music, for instance, which suddenly do not seem so far-fetched. This is also similar to Teilhard de Chardin's notion of the noosphere. As a matter of fact, as we saw above, Teilhard takes that idea further in his theory of cosmic embryogenesis, when he insists that whatever manifests at a more advanced degree of evolution has actually been there all along in some way. Applying this to consciousness or soul, we can agree with what Bede says is the oriental view of created reality and say that there is a psychic dimension to all created things.

But then, like matter itself, that soul has the potential to open to something more, which is the *pneuma*, the spirit, the point where the human spirit opens on to the Spirit of God, the universal Spirit.[23] Beyond both body and soul—I like to say, *deeper* than the body and soul—and the source and summit of both body and soul, yet still integrated with them, is the spirit, what St. Paul calls—using the Greek word—the *pneuma*. This spirit in us is the point of our communion with the universal Spirit which rules and permeates the whole universe. Our spirit is the point of human self-transcendence, the point at which the finite and the infinite, the temporal and the eternal, the many and the One meet and touch.

The *realm* of spirit is also beyond all phenomena, beyond all thoughts and words, as the Hindu tradition would say, *a-nama-rupa* (beyond name and form); and *our* spirit is that point where we are one with the Divine Spirit who is beyond all phenomena. Bede pointed out, through his exploration of Universal Wisdom, meditating on the sacred texts of the world's authentic spiritual traditions, that the sense of Ultimate Reality being beyond all name and form is beautifully articulated by the Chinese notion of the Tao, for example, as by the Brahman/atman of Hinduism, the *sunyata* of the Buddha, and the *al Haqq* of Islam, as well as by the abyss of the Godhead of the Christian mystic. And in some way our deepest selves too are beyond all name and form.

The human person first understands himself or herself as a physical entity saturated with soul, and then goes beyond mental consciousness to experience the transpersonal, transmental, or, as Sri Aurobindo calls it, the "supramental" consciousness. And then we discover within ourselves that our ultimate "I" is one with the ground of the universe, God who is Being Itself and the ground of human consciousness. Just as physical reality is pervaded by consciousness, by soul or psyche, so all reality, material and psychic, is further pervaded by the Divine, the Spirit. And so I, too, in some way possess a double nature. I am not only my phenomenal ego, but I am an eternal self, which is my inner person, the spirit, the spark of divinity within my soul. And, more importantly, the end and purpose of life —perhaps better to say that the real *beginning* of a life in the Spirit—is to identify with this eternal self so as to come to unitive knowledge of the Divine and let that unitive knowledge be the source of my strength and action in the world.

This is not the typical Western way to speak of human anthropology. We do not normally distinguish spirit from soul; instead, we normally speak of the human person as either body and soul, or body and spirit, although we do sometimes speak of the "spiritual soul." As a matter of fact, Huxley specifically laments this, that even though St. Paul had drawn the "useful and illuminating distinction between the *psyche* and the *pneuma*," the word *pneuma* "never achieved any degree of popularity," and the "hopelessly ambiguous term, *psyche*" (hence also for most of us the English word "soul") has come to be used "indifferently for either the personal consciousness or the spirit."[24] The English word "soul" usually indicates some nontangible, ethereal part of a person that may even live on after the death of the body. But as we have seen above, what we find in biblical anthropology instead is that words such as *nephesh* in Hebrew and *psyche* in Greek, which are usually translated as "soul," often refer to the physical body itself or at least to some tangible aspects of human existence such as the flesh, the blood, the throat, or the breath. So the English translation "soul" has come to mean something different from what the original words meant. The *Catechism of the Catholic Church*, on the other hand, admits that the soul is sometimes distinguished from the spirit, but insists that even this "does not introduce a duality into the soul." Spirit, according to the *Catechism*, signifies that from creation human beings are ordered to a supernatural end and that one's soul "can be gratuitously raised . . . to communion with God."[25] As beautiful as this is, Fr. Bede, among others, found this anthropology lacking in clarity. He saw the need always to distinguish between the spirit and the soul, between the spiritual and the psychic; and he noted the importance of understanding and accentuating the spiritual realm, which brings the other two realms to their fruition.

Now, the Christian tradition tends to refer to our human condition as a "fallen state," and what I want to propose is that this is what our fallen state is: the state of our spirit, soul, and body being out of right relationship. The norm is psychic consciousness dominated by the rational mind, or else the mind run riot by the appetites of the body. What I suggest further is that the goal (*scopos*) of the spiritual life is to discover, to realize this spirit within us, this deepest aspect of our being, the place of our meeting with the Divine, and find a way to let that be what is the master of our lives, and then to bring the body and soul (with its mind) into right relationship with the inner spirit that is guided by the Spirit of God.

The New Consciousness of a New Humanity

Now let's use these terms to look at Jesus. The birth of Jesus from a Virgin was a sign of the birth of a new humanity, born "not of blood or of the will of the flesh or of [human] will, but of God" (John 1:13). Could we say, born not simply of the body, nor of the soul, but born of spirit, of the Spirit? Jesus' miracles were signs of a new creation, a sign of matter being transformed by being penetrated by consciousness, signs of the mastery of the Spirit over matter, signs of matter being brought into right relationship with Spirit. The stories about Jesus' death and resurrection, his descent into Hell and his ascension, are signs of the passage through death that every person has to undergo in order to realize God, and signs of the penetration of the Spirit into the depths of the unconscious and all the realms of consciousness. But an even more profound truth is that at the resurrection the body and soul of Jesus were transformed by the Spirit; humanity and nature were revealed in an indivisible unity, a unity that was at once physical, psychological, and spiritual; that is, body, soul and spirit. Even Jesus' second coming that we long for can be seen as the final manifestation when all of creation and all of humanity passes out of its present state of being and consciousness into total consciousness of Reality, when all of creation, that is "groaning in labor pains until now . . . while we wait for adoption, the redemption of our bodies" (Rom 8:22-23), will be brought into right relationship with the Spirit who is its source and its summit. This is not only the soul going to heaven; this is the proper end of the spiritual life according to the Christian mystical vision, "a new heaven and a new earth" (Rev 21:1).

And so for the individual, as Abhishiktananda, the French monk who was Bede's predecessor at Shantivanam, wrote, "The outpouring of the Spirit at Pentecost is the symbol, the sign, the sacrament, the 'cosmic origin' of the penetration, the impregnation of all our faculties by the 'mystery of the depth,'" the Spirit.[26]

This following paragraph may be the most important thing that I ever read in Fr. Bede's writings:

> When the Holy Spirit descended on the disciples at Pentecost, the power of the Spirit [that] had transformed the body and soul of Christ at the resurrection was communicated to his disciples. A new consciousness dawned, a consciousness beyond the ordinary rational consciousness, which set the apostles free from the limitations of our present mode of existence and consciousness and opened them to the new world of the resurrection.[27]

This is a fresh approach and new language to express the transformational character of Christianity and Christian mysticism. This is the consciousness that is meant to dawn on us and the transformation that is meant to happen in us through our baptism, and specifically through the sacrament of confirmation, when the Pentecostal Spirit of the risen Jesus allows us to open our eyes and understand the meaning of the resurrection, to see the world once again in right relationship, brought about by Jesus reestablishing the right relationship for flesh and all of creation. And, St. Paul tells us, "if the Spirit of him who raised Jesus from the dead dwells in you, he who raised Christ from the dead will give life to your mortal bodies also" (Rom 8:11), and not just at death, but even now. That same Spirit, if invoked, will bring us into right relationship, spirit, soul and body. "Pentecost is the openness of the mind,"[28] the mind becoming open to this, the deepest reality, the reality of the Spirit who is our source and our summit.

Nothing Gets Left Behind

Why is this new articulation of a depth anthropology important? This is where I find that Ken Wilber's language, which is very popular with a certain segment of contemporary spiritual seekers, fleshes out Fr. Bede's admonition that we need to integrate these three levels of reality that exist, the body, the soul and the spirit, at every moment. This holistic understanding of the human person is a call to an *integral* spiritual life—a word that Wilber inherits from the Integral Yoga of Aurobindo, with whom

Bede was very familiar. This is a spirituality that recognizes that the development of each of these aspects—spirit, soul, and body—is important to the spiritual growth of the whole person. Otherwise so-called spiritual enlightenment could actually make the rest of one's life a disaster! If it is true, as St. Thomas Aquinas taught, that grace builds on, and does not destroy, nature, then no aspect of our being human is not meant to be transformed by the spiritual life.

As Wilber explains it, the human person needs to go through many different areas of development. He calls those areas "lines."[29] They are various intelligences, you might say. One could list dozens; however, the most widely cited are cognitive development, and then the interpersonal intelligences, such as psychosexual emotional development, for instance. Then there is moral and ethical development, and one wonders how much authority someone has about moral and ethical issues if one does not have psychosexual emotional development. There is also bodily or kinesthetic development, verbal and linguistic, logical and mathematical, and the more creative artistic intelligences such as musical, rhythmic, visual, spatial, and finally naturalistic development. Then, of course, there is so-called spiritual development. It is interesting to see spiritual development as only one of those areas, one of those lines of development, that is, only one form of intelligence. And I say "so-called spiritual" not to be cynical, but because from this way of thinking, not everything we call "spiritual" actually is spiritual. Rather, some of what we call spiritual might be religious, but might also be merely psychic phenomena that could be good, neutral, or even evil. More on that later too!

That being said, the main point is this: Someone who has had a profound spiritual experience, such as a religious conversion, might still be at a fairly low level of development in one or several other areas. Wilber points out that this also applies even to a lot of spiritual teachers and religious leaders. This person may have a real gift for the vocabulary and skills of the spiritual life and a knack for the whole ambience of religiosity, but have not developed or have neglected other lines, or those lines might actually be pathological. For example, one might have emphasized personal interior development without ever taking time for inter-personal, sexual, or emotional intelligence. This would certainly provide some explanation for the scourge that has been wracking the Roman Catholic clergy, who may by now be sensing the dire need of a more integral spirituality. But other communions and traditions have had similar problems. (As a matter of fact, Wilber teaches mainly from his experience in Buddhism.)

The problem is that states of consciousness such as spiritual or religious experiences can seem so all inclusive that we could be led to think we are developed in other areas as well, simply because spiritual experience or religious training has imparted a kind of veneer of wisdom that seems to refine everything. In my experience, great damage has been done in this regard. It is for this reason that I say that so-called spiritual enlightenment could actually make the rest of one's life a disaster! If teachers do not have some kind of integrally informed awareness, it will be difficult for them to make decisions in areas in which they are not competent. One could rightly wonder, as the closet continues to reveal skeleton after dancing skeleton, how anyone associated with Roman Catholicism, for example, could dare to expound on healthy sexuality except with a head bowed in absolute humility. Even if our teachings and our anthropology were sound (I am purposefully using the subjunctive mode here), we have certainly not modeled a way to live them healthily! Could it be that the whole body of Catholicism or Catholic religious life is pathologically unintegrated?[30]

The other extreme might be a tendency into a kind of what Catholics used to call "angelism," thinking we have left all those other things behind now that we are "spiritual," a phenomenon that some contemporary spiritual thinkers call "spiritual bypass-ing." But we find out soon enough that nothing gets left behind, and that's the point of this integral spirit, soul, and body teach-ing. We need to develop our *whole persons* at some point, to the glory of God, even (maybe especially) spiritual seekers. Instead of the Spirit making us skip over those seemingly lower lines of development, what if the spiritual life led us to approach those more fundamental aspects of our being with reverence and wis-dom? Wouldn't this be the ultimate in nonduality?

Outside of sexuality, I have sensed a need for growth within Christian spirituality in many other areas as well—such as our understanding of our place in the ecosystem of the planet—often areas where other traditions and even so-called "pagans" have actually continued the incarnational trajectory of Christianity in history without us. If it is true, as the famous aphorism of St. Irenaeus sings, that the glory of God is the human person fully alive, if it is true that Jesus came that "they might have life and have it to the full" (John 10:10), then I am dreaming of a practical integral Christian spirituality, one which reverences and develops the whole person—spirit, soul, and body—into what Wilber calls an "integrally informed" being. What would that look like? Spirit, soul, and body are dimensions that are already a part of us. To be integrally informed means being aware of where we need help—where we are lacking—as well as recognizing what our gifts are.

Bede Griffiths's exploration into this area in both his study and his lived spirituality in the latter part of the twentieth century in India has provided a bridge from traditional Christian spirituality and its lexicon to the sensibility and vocabulary of informed spiritual seekers of the early twenty-first century, hungry for and informed by contemporary incarnations of integral spirituality. Especially under his guidance and rearticulation of ancient truths, Christianity has as much to offer to the discussion as to learn, and as much to learn as to offer.

So many forms of spiritual life work only from the neck up, as if the body didn't exist. We need to find creative ways to include the body in the spiritual journey. . . . The West has had an unbalanced view of the place of the body in the spiritual journey. This lack of balance must be corrected. The body is sacred, and it has to be integrated into the mystical life.[1]

—Wayne Teasdale

6
A New Asceticism

Let's begin this chapter with a reminder of where we started: Sam Keen states that we have to be careful of being seduced by the dualism implicit in the language (which we hear often from Asian traditions) that encourages us to speak of "having a body," as if the possessor and the possessed were different entities. All human knowledge, all human value and aspiration, are stamped with the mark of the body. Keen says that the insight of existential philosophy into the incarnate nature of human existence could be stated like this: Our body is our bridge to and model of the world; therefore, how we are in our body so will we be in the world. This is very important! "As I trust or mistrust the rhythm of my body, so I trust or mistrust my total world. If we lose the self, we lose the other; if we lose the body, we lose the world. Thus the danger of not loving one's body. Love of both neighbor and cosmos rests upon love of self."

Even more important, the sacred rests upon the carnal, and reveals itself through the carnal; as Teilhard and Aurobindo taught, matter will reveal Spirit's face. And Thomas Aquinas agrees, because grace builds on nature. So, as we are in the world, so will we be in that mystery that founds, sustains, and engulfs the known world. Keen says there is a correlation between our attitudes toward our body, our social and material context, and our absolute context.[2]

It is often said of Johann Sebastian Bach that his was a "theology in music." His music itself was a theology. Pope John Paul II wrote a magisterial work called "Theology of the Body," but I am not sure most people understood that he was conveying much the same thing. It was not a theology *about* the body; it was the body *as* theology. The body itself *is* a theology.

Conquering the Flesh

Fr. Bede once suggested, in his typically courteous and understated way, that perhaps the idea of "mortification of the flesh," derived from the Fathers of the Desert and their tendency toward extreme asceticism, "had passed its usefulness." He wrote of the Desert Fathers that "their aim was to *conquer* [emphasis mine] the flesh by watching, fasting, and bodily mortifications. . . . They probably found these disciplines necessary, but it had a very bad effect on the Christian tradition of asceticism. The result is that many people reject asceticism altogether."[3] Bede similarly thought that asceticism such as that found in Thomas à Kempis's classic *Imitation of Christ* is also not a good model for today, because it is so limited and negative.

William Johnston has put it in a similar way, but adds an even stronger claim than Bede's polite understatement. According to Johnston, as Western culture was breaking down and traditional religion was collapsing in the twentieth century, it is hardly surprising that traditional ascetical practices were challenged, criticized, and put to the test. He wrote that the old religious training "contaminated by Stoicism, Neoplatonism, rationalism, and Jansenism" had not merely passed its usefulness; rather, the traditional ascetical practices actually "had strayed far from the authentic spirit of the Gospel." Further, as the study of psychology began to plumb the depths and understand the human psyche more, it became clear that much of the traditional training in houses of formation, novitiates, and seminaries was downright "unhealthy, dehumanizing and destructive."[4]

As Wendell Berry warns, what happens when the body is isolated and set in competition with the spirit—and perhaps we know this as much from existential proof as from hard science—is a counterreaction, often not of reverence and respect but of indulgence and comfort with a disregard for health. This is why the notion of "Follow your bliss," while it has truth to it, is also a slippery slope. How much purification and realignment does it take until we discover what our real bliss is? For many young people bliss is crystal meth and Ecstasy! What all this has led to is a situation where it is difficult for us to establish the proper value of the body in the world; we do not understand that the body, even though fragile and impermanent, is still good.

Jules Monchanin, a brilliant French priest and scholar and another of Fr. Bede's predecessors at Shantivanam, sums up a healthy approach to asceticism, saying, "one must renounce only what has been attained—for one can only go beyond what has been reached—only renounce fullness in view of a greater fullness." And then he quotes the beautiful mantra from the Isha Upanishad:

> *Purnamadah purnamidam*
> *purnat purnamudacchyate*
> *purnasya purnamadaya*
> *purnamevavashishyate*
>
> Fullness beyond, fullness here,
> fullness springs from fullness.
> From fullness take Fullness away,
> fullness still remains.

He goes on to point out that "God is not the other, the competitor jealous of our joys." God is both Totally Other and at the same time Totally Mine. God is "the fullness which sometimes occurs in our fullness, or most often in our emptiness."[5]

However, let's make it clear: Part of what we are up to here is a new approach to asceticism—*new wineskins for new wine*—not a tossing out of asceticism altogether. Some younger people in religious life complain about a certain generation of women and men ahead of them who have tossed out the old without replacing it with the challenge of the new, rid themselves of the unhealthy old ascetical practices and replaced them with a rather vague approach to discipline that has often led to mediocrity, if not downright license. What we are looking for is a new approach to asceticism. Often we are turning to the East for some guidelines but, as I have attempted to show, it is not that Asian asceticism is without its own tendency to dualism. Dualism is rampant in one form or another wherever there is religion, and certainly wherever there is monasticism. It is always the easiest answer: to regard the body as bad and needing to be cast off. However, there is an anthropology at work in a tradition such as that of Yoga that integrates the body into the spiritual life in a way that can be of great service. Jung suggested that a new "Yoga" would have to be developed for the West, and that it actually should and would come out of Christianity.

So it is not that there will be no asceticism, no discipline, but we are trying to find a new healthy one, one that is set about reestablishing right relationship, not isolating the body from the soul and the spirit or the rest of the ecosystem, physical and psychic, in which it finds itself. As Sri Aurobindo wrote, "I have always seen that there has been really a long unobserved preparation before the Grace intervenes, and also, after it has intervened, one has still to put in a good deal of work to keep and develop what one has got."[6] Therefore, according to Aurobindo, some kind of *tapasya* (austerity) or ascetical practice is unavoidable.

Right Relationship

So perhaps asceticism (*tapas*) can and needs to be seen in a fresh light. Fr. Bede taught that through the Yogic approach, for example, "We are trying to learn to appreciate the body and the world, and to integrate them into our Christian lives."[7] Seen through the eyes of Yoga, the discipline of ascesis is understood as control without any strain, complete control in perfect harmony, with an eye toward transformation and right relationship rather than a dualistic notion of punishing the flesh. "Yoga is never a suppression of anything," Bede writes in *The River of Compassion* (and note the hint of Tantra in those words), "neither of the body, nor of the passions, nor of the senses, nor of the mind. It is a bringing of the whole person into harmony, into a perfect order." Therefore, we may even still do the same things, engage in similar practices, but we would do them for different reasons, and that slight change of focus, perhaps with a new vocabulary and a fine-tuning of our praxis, might help us immensely.

This is not far from the thinking of other contemporary Christian teachers. For instance, Anselm Grün, Benedictine monk and author, writes that discipline (asceticism) is not a way that we *suppress* our drives and passions, but a way that we can *transform* and shape them. And he explains that what he calls the three basic drives—eating, sex, and greed—"are *transformed* through fasting, prayer, and almsgiving," the three classic exhortations for Lenten practices, as well as through the evangelical counsels of religious life, poverty, chastity, and obedience. Note here again the resonance with Tantra: Discipline is a way not to suppress the drives, but to shape them, so that the drives can serve us as a *power source*. "We overcome sadness by fleeing dependency on the world, by letting go of what we are clinging to, and by setting ourselves free."[8] As the Amritabindu Upanishad (1–2) teaches:

> Driven by the senses the mind becomes impure;
> but with the senses under control, the mind becomes pure.
> Driven by the senses we become bound;
> but with the senses mastered we become free.

Through discipline, the senses are not suppressed or killed; they are controlled and shaped, trained (might we say "focused"?), and thus become sacraments, hinges of salvation, as Tertullian, second-century Christian writer, teaches that all flesh is for the Christian.

Kata Physin, a Christian Humanism

My favorite example of a healthy, authentically Christian approach to asceticism comes from an ancient writing, "The Life of St. Antony" (*Vita Antonii*), written by St. Athanasius around the year 360. As much as it is a defense of orthodox Christianity against the Arians and a paean to the monastic life, "The Life of St. Antony" is also a lesson in Christian anthropology. Athanasius recounts how, after his initial conversion, Antony of the Desert first moves into an animal shed in the garden of his family home, then withdraws to live in tombs outside of his village, and then at the age of 35 retires into the desert completely. There he spends twenty years living in a deserted fort on the confines of the desert, where bread is brought to him twice a year. After twenty years some friends come and break down the gate and, Athanasius tells us, Antony comes forth, "as from a holy of holies, filled with heavenly secrets and possessed by the Spirit of God." It's worth it here to quote this whole section from "The Life":

> And when they beheld him, they were amazed to see that his body had maintained its former condition, neither fat from lack of exercise, nor emaciated from fasting and combat with demons, but was just as they had known him prior to his withdrawal. The state of his soul was one of purity, for it was not constricted by grief, nor relaxed by pleasure, nor affected by either laughter or dejection. Moreover, when he saw the crowd, he was not annoyed any more than he was elated at being embraced by so many people. He maintained utter equlibrium, like one guided by reason and steadfast in that which accords with nature.[9]

Those last words, "that which accords with nature," are so important. The Greek phrase for this is *kata physin*—according to nature. He is healthy and psychically sound, sound of soul and body.

Saint Athanasius's writing about the ascetism of Antony is an argument against any kind of dualism. Not long after in the Christian monastic tradition (as I recounted in the first chapter) there will be much polemic against the body, influenced by the Neoplatonists. (Porphory says of Plotinus, for example, that he was "a man ashamed of being in his body.") But here Antony's life of ascetism and virtue has led him to physical vigor as well as psychological balance. This is a theme that quietly abides in the Eastern Christian tradition, in spite of the distortions that cropped up and became the norm like weeds among the wheat.

There will be the saying about early monasticism that it is "in the desert a garden," meaning a return to Paradise, the Garden of Eden. And so later in the "Life of Antony" we also see that the relationship with animals has been restored. Through Antony, Athanasius is showing what a deified human being is like, and that he is still *kata physin*, or according to nature. We are somehow not destroyed by our encounter with grace; we are brought to who we are, who we are meant to be. The other word Athanasius uses in Greek is *telios*—that is, perfect. Antony has become perfect. This is a gospel term, a Pauline term, but also a term familiar to Greeks, especially those "initiates" familiar with the secret rites of the Eleusinian mysteries. Antony has become a real initiate into the divine mysteries, and it has not destroyed him; it has made him fully human while deified. Derwas Chitty writes in his classic work, *The Desert a City*, that Antony's perfection is the return to the human person's natural condition. This is the constant teaching of Eastern Christian ascetics, that the aim of the spiritual life, the ascetical life, is not to punish us, not to destroy our bodies, but rather the recovery of Adam's condition before the Fall. That is our true nature, "the whole person in harmony, into a perfect order," as Fr. Bede wrote concerning Yoga. It is our "fallen condition," on the other hand, that is actually *para physin*—that is, unnatural.[10]

In Western theology, the spiritual person is usually thought of as a "natural" person to whom grace has been added. We tend to think that human nature is made up of both the intellectual life and animal life, and that the spiritual life is added on top of that, superimposed on the purely human, thus we often use the term "supernatural." As opposed to kata physin, the word in Greek for "supernatural" would be *hyperphysin*. But I was surprised to find out, as the great Jesuit author George Maloney loved to point out, that in Eastern Christianity, and as far back as the patristic era, the word *hyperphysin*, "supernatural," is rarely if ever used in reference to the human person. It is sometimes used to refer to extraordinary, irregular, or magical occurrences, but not as a human condition. What we in the West might think of in terms of "natural–supernatural," the Eastern authors simply refer to as either human–divine or created–uncreated. But everything in nature or that comes to nature after baptism is kata physin—according to nature. Everything is already within the structure of nature and nothing gets superimposed on it, not on human nature nor on any other aspect of nature. There are only things that are kata physin—according to nature—and para physin—against nature. Everything in us, everything that is given to us in creation, and everything that comes afterwards is kata physin and therefore is good.[11] The term para physin is almost always used in reference to sin. What is natural for us—kata physin—is doing what is truly good: charity, faith, the virtues. Wickedness—evil thoughts, sin, disordered passions—is para physin, against our nature.[12]

Even what the desert fathers called our "passions" are basically good energies gone awry. When Evagrius of Pontus, that great psychologist of the desert, speaks of the *logismoi* and *patheia*, the thoughts and passions, he means the evil thoughts and disordered passions, ways in which our human faculties get trapped in pointless and irrational reactions, ways that are para physin—against our nature. Passions are not just emotions; they are *disordered* reactions, so that passionlessness or *apatheia* is "health of the soul." But it is still not emotionlessness that he is pointing us toward, but "a state of harmony in which all our faculties are doing precisely what they were created to do"—kata physin—"so that they do not disturb our equilibrium or hinder the proper clarity which the mind should have."[13] As Bede says, "The whole person in harmony, in perfect order." Like Antony, "altogether even as being guided by reason, and abiding in a natural state."

So good does not get superimposed on us from the outside; instead, it is evil that comes from the outside, outside of God's creation and outside of our own nature. Evil does not come from our basic nature. It can and does touch our intellect, and it can and does touch our will. But the good news is that it can never touch or destroy or completely corrupt our nature. We can lose grace, we can lose our likeness to God, but the nature given to us can never be destroyed. The image of God, the *imago Dei* that is the very mark of our being, on which all of moral theology is based, can be covered, tarnished, hidden, but it can never be destroyed. It is our very nature.[14] So Evagrius writes, "When we were created at the beginning, seeds of virtue existed in us naturally but no malice at all." That is our natural state. It is the demons that have hounded us and chased us from this state that is naturally ours. Ephrem the Syrian goes further to say that it is not even our nature that is corrupted, but our habits, and the corruption of our habits alters our nature—does not destroy or corrupt it, just alters it. However, deliverance from sin can bring us back to our natural state.

And so our new understanding of asceticism is again actually a return to an ancient understanding of asceticism: returning us to our original nature, our natural condition.

Another more modern example of this understanding comes from St. John Paul II. In 1980, on the six hundredth anniversary of the death of St. Catherine of Siena, he wrote that what we admire in her is the same thing that immediately struck her contemporaries: the extraordinary richness of her humanity, "not dimmed in any way but, on the contrary, increased and perfected by grace, which made of her almost a living image of that true and wholesome Christian humanism." I pause briefly and bow, savoring this beautiful phrase—"true and wholesome Christian humanism"—from one of the great Christian humanists of the twentieth century. John Paul II then goes on to point out that the fundamental law of all this was formulated by none other than St. Thomas Aquinas, Catherine's Dominican confrere and teacher, in the aphorism "Grace builds upon, does not suppress, but presupposes and perfects nature."[15]

The person of complete dimensions is the one who is fulfilled in grace.

A New Language

Father Bede's way of articulating a healthy approach to asceticism was that the body has to sacrifice its autonomy. First of all the body needs to admit its dependence on the soul, that subtle aspect of our being with its rational mind and its power to choose, as well as its emotions and intuitions. But the soul is also a bridge to that deeper realm as well, the realm of spirit.

And so Bede taught further that when the soul "turns," if you will, toward the spirit first—our spirit in communion with the Spirit of God—the soul then becomes the conduit of grace for the whole being. But we will get to those second aspects later.

Here is my own marriage of East and West, the beautiful adage of Tertullian, which the great theologian Cipriano Vagaggini returned to often: *carne cardo salutis es*, "The flesh is the instrument of salvation," and the Sanskrit equivalent of it from Sri Aurobindo: *sariram khalu dharmasadhanam*, "The body is the means of fulfillment of the dharma." Even more, there is the foundational truth upon which Aurobindo and Teilhard de Chardin agree, that "matter shall reveal Spirit's face." The body is not only the instrument; it is also the field of transformation. I think anything we read from any spirituality, Eastern or Western, prophetic or mystical, Christian or Yogic, that tells us we are not our bodies has to be tempered by this truth, the hopeful side of Christianity's incarnational theology, and the rest of the story from Asia.

As I read through what I have of Sri Aurobindo's writings, for example, this is what excites me the most in trying, as has been my aim all along, to articulate a practical integral Christian spirituality (note all three adjectives, "practical," "integral," "Christian"). "In the past," he wrote, "the body has been regarded by spiritual seekers rather as an obstacle." Here there is even what I have been calling a kind of "enlightened dualism." In the past the body has been regarded "as something to be overcome and discarded" rather than as "an instrument of spiritual perfection and a field of the spiritual change." But "if a divine life is possible on earth, then this self-exceeding [i.e., perfection of the body] must also be possible."[16] What we are aiming at is for our outlook and practice to be holistic, in other words, for our physical practices to be at the same time spiritual and psychic ("soulful"), so that even our "vital and physical processes are given a spiritual or psychic turn and raised to a higher motion . . . taking up the activities of human life and sublimating them by the power of the spirit." Aurobindo calls the physical body the "lower perfection" and insists that *it will not disappear*: "it will remain but will be enlarged and transformed by the higher perfection which only the power of the spirit can give." Whatever perfection has already been attained will be "included in a new and greater perfection but with the larger vision and inspiration of spiritual consciousness and with new forms and powers." That sounds to me like the resurrection body, Jesus' glorified body. Recall here, too, Wilber's articulation of this in his "Great Nest of Being" (see chapter 5): each element is judged according to its holistic capacity, so that what is whole at one stage becomes merely part of a larger whole at the next stage. Hence, the notion of interpenetrating or, even better, enveloping levels of reality also within our being human. I do not see any reason why this philosophical approach cannot lend itself to Christianity, indeed become an articulation of transfiguration, resurrection, and ascension, as St. Paul promises, so that our bodies would be transfigured into glorious copies of Jesus' own (Phil 3:21). This passage from Aurobindo could actually be used as a reading for the feast of the transfiguration and easily mistaken for a writing from the patristic era of Christianity:

> The physical consciousness and physical being, the body itself must reach a perfection in all that it is and does which now we can hardly conceive. It may even in the end be suffused with a light and beauty and bliss from the Beyond and the life divine assume a body divine.[17]

Practically Speaking

Establishing right relationship between spirit, soul, and body is essential. The body is a wonderful beautiful thing, but it must be subordinated first to the soul, the psyche, and ultimately to the inner power of the spirit; the body must surrender its autonomy. Then our bodies will come to their full fruition, perhaps ultimately transfigured, walking on water, working healings, rising from the dead. What do we mean by "Yoga"? Yoga is "a means of union, union of the powers of the body in harmony, union of body and soul in harmony, union of body and soul with the inner Spirit." But this can only be attained "when body and soul are 'sacrificed' to the Spirit." According to Fr. Bede, "This is the death the body and soul have to undergo, the sacrifice of their autonomy, their surrender to the inner Spirit."[18]

Our way of meditation is about this as well, of ‿
acknowledging, reverencing, welcoming, and surrendering ‿
incarnate force of the Spirit, the creative energy inside of us that
is a manifestation of Divine Energy, what the Orthodox tradition
would perhaps call the "uncreated energy," and so to set loose
in ourselves, through the training of our senses and the stilling
of our minds, the power of transformation, the power of healing, the power of transfiguration, the power of resurrection, the
power of "the love of God that has been poured into our hearts
by the Spirit living in us" (Rom 5:5).

After citing the invectives against the body that came out of
the early monastic tradition, from the best of the desert monastic
tradition comes this pithy little saying of Evagrius of Pontus also,
from his *Praktikos*: "The monk should always live as if he were
to die on the morrow, but at the same time that he should treat
his body as if he were to live with it for many years to come."[19]
Thus, by keeping death before our eyes we will be able to cut off
every thought that comes from *acedia*—the specifically monastic
vice of "listlessness"—and be more fervent in practices; by treat-
ing our body as if we were to live with it for years to come, we
will preserve it in good health and maintain its continence intact.

Practically speaking, what does this mean? What creative
ways can we find to include the body in the spiritual journey?
What does this new asceticism look like? Let me give just some
of my own broad guiding principles.

There is of course the tradition of self-inflicted corporal punishment in religious life, from the hair shirt called a "cilice" worn
close to the skin, to the practice of flagellation with a whip or a
rod or a stick. Such practices, I believe, are the type of thing that,
as Fr. Bede says, "has passed its usefulness," and if what we have
said above is true, are actually far from the spirit of the Gospel
and an appreciation of the incarnation. Yet it is still essential to
bring our flesh to surrender its autonomy, as Fr. Bede says, and
not let it control us with its passions and tendencies toward
compulsivity and addiction, which may have been the good
intention in those practices. Rather than such extreme practices,
it would be beneficial to take up less punitive disciplines, such
as running, jogging, or even just a brisk walk every day, or a

discipline that trains the senses while stilling the mind, such as one of the martial arts or yoga. To do this consistently might be harder than Flannery O'Connor's character Hazel Motes in *Wise Blood* walking around with glass in his shoe, and much more in keeping with respecting and preserving the dignity of the body as the temple of the Holy Spirit. What if some weight lifting or calisthenics were actually seen as an integral part of my spiritual life and formation? This is what I mean by the new asceticism.

At the same time, from a broader perspective (and, since I have never been an athlete of the caliber of many of my peers, forgive me if I am speaking out of turn) my notion of athletics in the West is that it has quite often not been rooted in a healthy and holistic view of the person. It is quite often steeped in beating the body into submission ("No pain, no gain" and "Pain is only weakness leaving the body"), or, as evidenced by the steroid scandals in professional sports in the early twenty-first century, trying to make the body into something it is not. For example, my friend who is a football coach laments the fact that we might force a young man whose frame is meant to carry 160 pounds to "bulk up" to over 200 pounds. That is not kata physin. Now, recall Sam Keen's phrase: "How we are in our bodies is how we will be in the world." Also, many of our sports are based on militaristic models and engendering a kind of at least temporary hatred for the opponent. (Perhaps the exception to this is track and field where one is competing against oneself?) "How we are in our bodies is how we will be in the world." The case of someone like Phil Jackson and his wonderful little book *Sacred Hoops*, for example, seems rare, and he has turned to Buddhism and Native American spiritualities to flesh out his philosophy. I can only speak from practical experience: in my boarding school in high school the disconnect between the chapel and the soccer field and the gym seemed pretty wide. I don't think it is the fault of the sports themselves, but of the attitude that we bring to them. And yet, as Jung said that a new yoga would emerge in the West out of Christianity, I think that it is out of athletics that a "new yoga" can emerge. I am thinking of the immense popularity of Tai Chi, or of Aikido and Taikwando, for example, and the martial arts in general that unite mind and body, and then at least tentatively point to that deeper thing as well, what we would call the spirit. I must add that I have also been impressed with and educated by many of the athletes I have met in recent years who do have a deep sense of the natural health through diet and self-care. A young friend of mine wrote a marvelous paper for our Sangha, for example, entitled "Sport as *Sadhana*," in which he expounded on how athletics can be reenvisioned as part of our spiritual practice.

As far as diet is concerned, my sound byte for this is that instead of going on what we used to call a "black fast" once in a while, I would rather see someone commit themselves to eating healthily *all the time*! I don't have to point out what this includes; there is plenty of information available to the average consumer about the health benefits or detriments of our common foods. This could be considered an element of the new asceticism. As a matter of fact, at some point what we eat becomes a moral, ethical issue, both personally and communally due to production issues. Anyone who reads a book such as Eric Schlosser's *Fast Food Nation* would first of all realize the economic and social ramifications of our eating habits. But if we start doing analysis of the food itself produced by mass marketing and the insidious practice of just the right chemical cocktail in certain popular fast foods that sets the body up for craving and addiction, we start to get a sense that it is not good to be doing this to our bodies, especially if they are temples of the Holy Spirit! My major problem with many of the popular chain restaurants is not only the practice of driving small local businesses out of business and the incredible waste of resources through the use of single-use disposable items—mountains of paper and plastic—but also the promotion of caffeine, sugar, and fat. This may be the new asceticism and the new fast—mindfulness of our eating habits, fasting not out of hatred for our bodies, but eating carefully out of respect for our bodies and care for the planet. If this is not a Christian value, it ought to be.

We'll spend a whole chapter considering our relationship with the environment, but for now suffice it to recall this simple little formula of Fr. Bede's: "We have a body, a physical organism, which is *part* of the physical organism of nature." What we have learned from modern science is what an intricate web created reality is, and we ourselves are included as part of that web. We can think of it in very practical terms. First of all, we are formed in the wombs of our mothers; everything they eat or ingest in any way becomes part of our very selves. After we are born it is not that very much different, especially as we nurse at the breast. An acquaintance of mine who is a marvelous chiropractic doctor and holistic therapist explained to me once how we used to think of the skin as an impermeable membrane, and so mothers, for instance, slathered their babies with baby lotion that was filled with peanut oil, for example, which inadvertently set up an allergic reaction to peanuts. We are not individual impermeable membranes! Our skin is not like a raincoat! This is one way in which we are vitally connected to the environment around us. How we are in our bodies is how we are in the world, and vice versa! St. Francis is probably the most well known but not the only Christian mystic to refer to the earth as our mother: "Praised by yours through Sister Earth, our Mother / with her leaves and fruit and flowers for cover." Even now we live as if in this womb, the womb of Mother Earth, and the same thing goes: whatever she eats or ingests, we are eating and ingesting. This same doctor reminded me about how much we ingest through our breathing, not only ordinary air pollution from factories and cars with which we have clogged our skies but, he said, the very air we breathe on a day-to-day basis in our homes, schools and places of work. "If you can smell the air you are breathing," he said, "you are taking in whatever it is you are smelling." You will remember the consciousness raising that came about through all the talk of secondhand smoke, for instance; this same principle applies to cleaning solutions, air fresheners, any kind of industrial chemicals around us. This is only dealing with smell; we could spend a whole chapter talking about what kind of chemicals we ingest through eating. We are not impermeable membranes: we are intimately tied to what is around us.

This kind of consciousness is the new asceticism, not life denying, not flesh hating, but care of the precious temple that is the human body and care of Mother in whose wombs we are wrapped.

Re-incarnating

In 1920 Mirra Alfassa, an accomplished French artist, pianist, and writer, permanently joined Sri Aurobindo in Pondicherry. She came to be known simply as "the Mother." Sri Aurobindo entrusted full material and spiritual charge of his ashram to her, and it is under her care and guidance that it grew into a large, multifaceted spiritual community. The Mother, whom we might consider Sri Aurobindo's female counterpart, wrote: "It is only by rising to the summit of consciousness through a progressive ascent . . . that one unites with the Supermind. But as soon as the Union is achieved one knows and one sees that the Supermind exists in the heart of the inconscient as well. When one is in that state, there is neither high nor low but generally it is by redescending through the levels of the being with a supramentalized consciousness that one can accomplish the permanent transformation of physical nature."[20]

This above passage has come to mean a great deal to me. The Mother is referring here to the ascent of *kundalini* in the tradition gleaned from Tantric Yoga, the belief that there is an energy coiled up at the base of the spine—kundalini, the serpent energy—that must rise up through various *chakras*, energy points within the body, until it reaches the uppermost chakra at the crown of the head. (We shall explore this all in greater detail in the chapter on sexuality.) As we have seen in the Tantric tradition, this is understood to be Shakti, the feminine energy, rising to meet Shiva, the masculine principle, who descends from above in the act of grace to meet the willing aspirant. Fr. Bede actually considered this a beautiful image of Pentecost, when the disciples received the tongues of flame on their "crown chakras."

But, the Mother teaches, this is not the end, just as Pentecost was not the end, but indeed the very birth of the church, just as for the human person the descent of the Holy Spirit at the sacrament of confirmation or otherwise does not mean that person's destruction but rather a new creation. It is then, as a new creation, that we descend again, accompanied by grace (another major theme in the writings of Aurobindo), back down into and through the muddy depths of our being, all the way to the furthest reaches of unconsciousness (what Aurobindo and the Mother refer to as the "inconscient"). We do not escape our human condition; instead, we "re-incarnate" (if you will excuse the play on words) with the aid of grace. We do not escape human life on earth at that point; we reinhabit our physical and psychic beings, and let them be filled with grace. It is then that we discover what the Eastern Christian tradition calls our divinization and can reascend, again in partnership with Divine Grace, and divinize all aspects of our being.

What creative ways shall we find to make our bodies full participants in our spiritual life?

Because of Christ's resurrection . . .
there is an upward movement in the
whole of creation, each element raising
itself to something higher.[1]

—Maximus of Turin

7

Sister Earth, Our Mother

When Ken Wilber proposes his Great Nest of Being, he adds another element before the body: matter. It may be that we do not really recover our body without recovering the earth, nature, and creation too. It may be that we do not fully recover our full sense of corporeality without reestablishing right relationship with the earth, with nature, with matter in general.

Right Relationship

When Fr. Bede says that the body has to sacrifice its autonomy, he mainly points to its dependency on the soul (psyche) and then the soul's sacrificing itself to the spirit, but we can safely add here that the body has to sacrifice its physical ecological autonomy as well, to realize its part in the web of the symbiotic ecosystem, to realize that whatever mother (earth) eats, baby (in the womb of the earth) eats, breathes, ingests as well. This perspective in no way denies the primary place the human race holds as a species. Rather, it only reinterprets what St. Paul meant when he said, "the whole creation has been groaning in labor pains until now . . . while we wait for adoption, the redemption of our bodies" (Rom 8:22-23). This, as I have hoped to show, is the significance of the resurrection and the ascension—the incarnation in general: this is the beginning of our bodies being redeemed, and with us all of creation that fell into disrepair at the Fall.

Perhaps the most salient feature of that disrepair is seen in the very myth of the Fall in Chapter 3 of the book of Genesis. Because Adam and Eve have fallen out of right relationship with God, all other relationships fall apart as well. In a sense, we do not necessarily have to see the rest of the story as a punishment, but simply as a consequence. The real punishment is God making known to Adam and Eve what else they have just bought with the knowledge of good and evil, the consequences of the Fall, all the signs of the disordered world. First of all, because they have alienated themselves from the Spirit they are now out of right relationship with their own bodies; they are ashamed of their nakedness. This must be an important point because a chapter earlier we learned that they were naked but that they were not ashamed (Gen 2:25). Then we learn that the blessing of childbirth would be accompanied by pain. This is part of the woman being out of right relationship with her own body but also a general disordering of sexuality: The woman will also desire to possess her man, but he will possess her. (It is an interesting side note that the author of Genesis considered this to be a disorder, that male domination is a result of the Fall rather than a divinely decreed ideal. The Lord had originally intended woman to be man's suitable partner, complement, and peer.) And then there is death itself. Although there are different schools of thought regarding whether or not human beings would have been immortal if not for the Fall, the author of Genesis points out clearly that what was to make them immortal actually reveals them in all their futility, that they will go back to the ground. The ominous words that used to be uttered at the distribution of ashes at the beginning of Lent come right from this story: "You are dust, and to dust you shall return!" And so there is certainly the entry into human consciousness of the awareness of death, and the fear of death, which could be the root of all subsequent sin.

And, of course, the main point for our purposes in this chapter is that as a result of the Fall, Adam and Eve are now out of

the Fall (Gen 1:26-28). We think that to have dominion means to exploit, bend, and shape creation to our will and needs, even to force it to do what it would not do. Like the character in *The Glass Palace*, Amitov Ghosh's marvelous novel about the timber and rubber trades in Malaysia and Burma, who says, "To bend the work of nature to your will; to make the trees of the earth useful to human beings—what could be more admirable, more exciting than this?,"[3] we have not exercised our dominion well. Through our own ignorance, negligence and greed, we have wiped out entire species that will never return. We have forever altered the God-given trajectory of evolution, creation as it was intended to spill forth from God.

It was not always this way, even in Christianity. Tomas Spidlik relates something in the early popular mentality of the Russians that would be helpful for us to recover. He wrote that in Russia there existed a mysterious relationship between the earth and the diseased human conscience. The earth was seen as sacred, the common mother of humanity, which we can injure, profane, and hurt. So the sinner would at times confess to the earth by means of a ritual-like confession, not only asking God for mercy, but asking "the Earth darkened by sin and dishonesty" for forgiveness too, "and, like Alyosha in Dostoevsky's *The Brothers Karamazov*, [the sinner] kissed it and promised to love it for all eternity." Such rituals are probably the survival of archaic pagan beliefs mixed with a form of sophianic Christian religiosity that recognizes an unbreakable bond between the divine world, human perfection, and creation, and insists on "the responsibility of all for all," as Dostoevsky said. "In such a piety," Spidlik explains, "there is no room for any 'private,' merely individual' sin. Every breach carries with it a social and osmic disturbance and 'darkens the earth.'"[4] To give another ample from the West, we turn to Steve Kellmeyer, who writes his book, *Sex and the Sacred City: Reflections on the Theology of Body*, that our stewardship of the earth is more like a type of rriage that takes place. This is where the word "husbandry" s from. "How we are in our bodies is how we will be in the l," and ultimately how we are going to relate to the Mystery nderlies the cosmos as well.

Father Bede says, "We have a body, a physical organism, which is part of the physical organism of nature." What we have learned from modern science is what an intricate web created reality is, and we ourselves are included as part of that web. Many people express this by quoting the first part of the famous, though perhaps apocryphal, words of Chief Seattle (the "bumper sticker version"): *The earth does not belong to us; we belong to the earth.* But what follows on that is even more sublime:

> All things are connected like the blood that unites us all.
> We did not weave the web of life; we are merely a strand in it.
> Whatever we do to the web, we do to ourselves.[5]

Sam Keen, like Francis of Assisi, writes that perhaps the best model to use in thinking about the intimate relationship between the body and the world is the analogy of the relationship between child and mother, self-other-world, baby, mother, and earth are experienced as one thing. "In the beginning is unity, the oneness of the body and the matrix which nurtures and supports it; the embryo and the placenta are inseparable." After nine months in the unitive state within the womb, it is only in the grossest physical sense that the coming out from the womb and the cutting of the umbilical cord separate the baby from the mother. According to most hypotheses about infant consciousness, the newborn baby actually continues to live in a state of undifferentiated consciousness for a time, not categorizing or experiencing, not being able to distinguish between her own lips, the mother's breast, and the swaddling clothes as belonging to three different spheres of reality—that is, self, other, world, or I-Thou-It.[6] How can we recapture the very real sense that this is the relationship we continue to have with Mother Earth, that in some very real way there is a union by communion physically, psychically, and even spiritually between us and creation, and that whatever we do to the web, we do to ourselves?

As I stated at the beginning of this chapter, it may be that we will not fully recover our full sense of corporeality without reestablishing right relationship with the Earth, with nature, with matter in general. The contemporary Sufi teacher Pir Zia Inayat Khan expresses it this way:

Study nature in the horizons and in yourself. Observe the conti-
nuities between your body and the land, and between the land
and its source. The stones, the rivers and birds, and we together
with them, partake of an ancient oneness, a silent communion
that weaves its invisible weft through all things.[7]

We are called to take the world into ourselves because, as the
fourth-century Cappadocian father Gregory of Nyssa taught,
human beings are at the same time *microcosmos* and *microtheos*:
in ourselves we are both a synthesis of the universe as well as
an offspring of God.[8]

Teilhard and Paganism

Having been formed in the First Axial Period, the great world
religions bear the mark of Axial Consciousness in that they tend
to turn toward the spiritual ascent and away from the material.
The challenge for spiritual traditions in this day and age is to
rediscover the material dimensions of existence and the spiritual
significance of the material realm. As we have already seen, the
dominant consciousness of the pre-Axial Period was cosmic, con-
nective, tribal, mythic, and ritualistic. The First Axial Period, with
the birth of the Upanishads, Taoism, Buddhism, the late Hebrew
prophets, and Greek philosophy, brought about a consciousness
of the individual (i.e., "know thyself"). An advance, yes, but this
ascent has slowly but steadily severed the harmony with nature
and tribe, and fostered a radical split between the phenomenal
world and what is considered to be true reality, between matter
and spirit, between heaven and earth. Ken Wilber also says this
is the characteristic difference between the feminine-deity-based
religions of prehistoric times and the male-deity-based religions.
Whereas the former were based in the earth, fertility rites, and
nature mysticism, and saw sin as being cut off from the earth, the
sky, or "father," gods, on the other hand, saw sin as being too attached to the earth and not ascending enough into heaven. What
someone like Ewert Cousins sees (and Wilber agrees) is that the
movement of the Second Axial Period is to recover our connection with the earth without losing the sense of the individual
quest, the First Axial Period Consciousness—thus the transfor-

mation from the tribal identity of pre-Axial Consciousness to individual identity of the the First Axial Consciousness, and now in the Second Axial Period an awakening to global identity or global consciousness, with the whole human race being our "tribe." And one of the dimensions of this global consciousness, according to Cousins, what he calls the "vertical level," is "spirituality rooted in the earth and matter." Whereas the First Axial transformation of consciousness tended to disengage spirituality from matter, the Second Axial Period faces the major challenge of discovering a new spirituality of matter, or more precisely, "a new holistic spirituality that integrates in an organic way the human and the divine."[9]

So there is something of the pre-Axial Consciousness that we actually want to recover. Huston Smith hits the nail right on the head in his section on the primal traditions in his classic manual *The World's Religions*. He first writes about how "world devaluation" figures prominently in the historical religions, starting with Plato's famous invective that the "body is a tomb," to which I always return as the beginning of a slippery slope. But he also adds that for Hinduism (as we have seen, this is admittedly only one way of thinking within the Indian tradition, though the most popular one, it seems) the world is *maya*, only marginally real. In fact, the Buddha likened the world to a burning house from which we had to escape. As opposed to this, in the primal traditions "divisions of such severity never appear"; nor is there anything like the notion of creation *ex nihilo* (from nothing). "Primal people are . . . oriented to a single cosmos, which sustains them like a living womb," Smith writes. Because they assume that nature exists to nurture them, they feel no need to challenge, defy, or refashion nature; nor do they have any wish to escape from it. Creation for the primal peoples is not first of all a place of exile, a veil of tears, or an earthly pilgrimage. Its home has many rooms, many varied marvelous spaces that constitute a single dwelling, though not all of them are visible to the naked or untrained eye. "Primal peoples are concerned with the maintenance of personal, social, and cosmic harmony, and with the attaining of specific goods—rain, harvest, children, health—as people always are." Life after death for the primal peoples tends to be only "a shadowy semi-existence in some vaguely designated place in their single domain," and the overriding goal of salvation that dominates the historical religions—leaving this world for a better world to come—is virtually absent for them.[10] What could a Christian learn from this attitude? How much of Jesus' admonition to pray that God's kingdom come "on earth as it is in heaven" makes us reevaluate the place of nature and see it as the locus of transformation and not only a place from which to escape? And how might that change how we relate to nature?

On the other hand, what many modern "neo-pagan" Gaia-based, or earth-based, movements believe is that there is a fundamental equivalence between everything that exists, and that consciousness and personhood as revealed in the human being are not necessarily an advance or a higher form of life. Unfortunately, this mitigates against legitimate evolution in both consciousness and in the material world. Let's for a second not regard "pagan" as a pejorative word, but think of it simply as "people of the land." The poet Gary Snyder, himself steeped in the Zen tradition, has a great respect for Teilhard de Chardin and what he calls "Teilhard de Chardin Catholics," as a matter of fact, but he still, for instance, criticizes Teilhard for this same thing, what he calls a "hierarchical spirituality which claims a special evolutionary destiny for humanity under the name of higher consciousness." But this is undoubtedly and inescapably the Judeo-Christian-Muslim understanding, as well as that of most of the major spiritual traditions, and even why Hinduism and Buddhism talk about the "precious human birth." This again is part of the greater discussion of holarchy and hierarchy, and the dependence of each strata of growth on every stratum (as we discussed in Chapter 5). Teilhard and his followers actually have an answer to Gary Snyder's complaint.

Intrinsic to Nature

Theologian Brian Schmisek explains our present situation succinctly. "In the past five thousand years," he writes, "humanity has shaped the environment more than we have been shaped by it." And as a consequence, "some anthropologists believe we have altered our environment to such a degree that we have entered a new epoch in the geological time scale: anthropocene."[11]

The new science has helped us recover a sense of our planet as a single multidimensional being. We are imbedded in and dependent upon the biosphere, and failure to adequately understand or appreciate that insight has taken us down some dubious and dangerous paths in our stewardship of this single multidimensional being. All things are connected like the blood that unites us all, so whatever we do to the web of creation, we do to ourselves. That's the holarchy. However, as Carter Phipps explains so well, there is a subtle yet significant difference between understanding humans as being simply *intrinsic to nature* and understanding humans as being *intrinsic to the natural evolutionary process*. Human beings, in other words, are in a unique position in the whole trajectory of evolution, unlike that of other creatures. This does not make us better, but it does make us important in a particular morally obligating sort of way. "Our human intelligence, our unique capacity to think and reflect, is part of nature too, and we dare not underestimate its worth." Human beings are "the progressive edge of evolution as far as we know," Phipps writes (and I very much like that phrase, "as far as we know"!). We are "the creative dynamics of the Earth come alive in human form." As Fr. Bede would say, we are "matter coming into consciousness." I might not have used as strong of words as Phipps does, but he asserts that in the name of combating a false (or exaggerated) anthropocentrism, one that does not understand human beings as intrinsic to nature, some have embraced a "nonsensical egalitarianism" that thereby questions the entire worth of the human experiment.[12] Phipps also shows, through a number of examples in a variety of arenas, just how vital a role hierarchical governance actually is as a spur to evolutionary advance, from the minutest level of cellular organization all the way through the need to "organize, incentivize, and otherwise oversee the many national and transnational entities and processes that now exist on this rapidly complexifying pale blue dot out on the spiral arm of the Milky Way." In fact, hierarchy is "an evolutionary imperative, a developmental challenge for the species itself" and a tremendous moral responsibility.[13] If we do not recognize and own this hierarchy and our tremendous place in it, we will not own the fact that at this point in the history of the universe our very choices are affecting the course of evolution! As a matter of fact, as the visionary mathematician and cosmologist Brian Swimme shocks us into realizing, the force of natural selection has, in this era, in some sense been superseded by human choice! We are, through our decisions and actions based on those decisions, changing the trajectory of evolution, in a way that no other species can.

Teilhard's notions of embryogenesis and creative unions have far-reaching consequences and appeal for everything from science through psychological and cultural development. The greater our depth within, the greater our self-consciousness, the more impact we can and do have on the environment around us. Teilhard too considers the earth as "the Great Mother" and is approaching this topic as much as a paleontologist as a Christian, perhaps even more so. And as a paleontologist he believed that matter was suffused with what he called "psychism" (soul!) and driven by spiritual energy. He taught that the self-reflective consciousness that breaks forth and is made manifest in the human being, that is lauded so much by the spiritual traditions, the precious human birth, was embedded in matter from the beginning, all the way down to the simplest atomic elements that are the building blocks of matter and life, plants and animals. And he believed that that psychism, that consciousness, has grown and been driven forward by the force of spiritual energy inside of it, ultimately the energy of love, which is a desire for union and creative unions. This is what is made manifest in the human person in a way that does not appear to have been made manifest in other primates or mammals or birds or amphibians or fish or bacteria. Teilhard believed that the evolutionary thrust was not just toward more and more complex creatures, but toward this breakthrough into the realm of thought and self-reflexive consciousness, awareness, so much so that evolution broke through the realm of mere life at one point and a new realm was created, what he called the noosphere, the realm of thought, what Fr. Bede refers to as the realm of "soul" that enwraps the material realm. But, remember, this "soul" was already embedded in creation from the beginning, the energy behind its evolution.

Of course Teilhard does want to recover earth. There is his marvelous prayer "Hymn to Matter," in which he writes, directly addressing the person of the First Axial Consciousness: "You thought you could do without [matter] because the power of thought has been kindled in you? You hoped that the more thoroughly you rejected the tangible, the closer you would be to spirit: that you would be more divine if you lived in the world of pure thought, or at least more angelic if you fled the corporeal? Well, you were like to have perished from hunger."[14]

No, instead of fleeing the corporeal, he says, "Steep yourself in the sea of matter, bathe in its fiery waters, for it is the source of your life and your youthfulness." We have no value except for that part of ourselves that passes into the universe; even our noblest theorizing is empty and fragile "as compared with the definitive plentitude of the smallest fact grasped in its total, concrete reality" (I assume here he means the truths of science), the "ridiculous pretentiousness of human claims to order the life of the world," in trying to impose human dogmas, standards, and conventions on the world.[15]

The fine balance we need to find is watching out for what Ken Wilber calls the pre/trans fallacy. Because the post-rational stage of the spiritual life ("trans") in some ways looks like the pre-rational ("pre")—just as an old person ("trans") can in some ways resemble a baby ("pre") and vice versa—we confuse the two. So we do want to immerse ourselves in matter again. But the immersion into matter is not to *worship* matter, and this is the difference between St. Francis's "Canticle of All Creatures"—"All praise be yours, my Lord, *through* Sister Earth our Mother"—and pagan hymns to the earth. Teilhard says that the true summons of the cosmos is a call to share consciously in the great work that goes on within it: "it is not by drifting down the current of things that we shall be united with their one, single, soul, but by fighting our way, *with them*, toward some goal still to come."[16] Once we consciously, intentionally reenter right relationship with matter, we with matter head together toward the reign of God, groaning together, or better yet, creation's groans become our songs of ascent like the pilgrims to Jerusalem. Or perhaps we could use The Mother's image here again, that we might dive down into the muddy depths of unconsciousness, but then we reascend as partners with the Divine. We are set up as the priests of creation, though we must recognize that if we are the head of the body, we are head as servant, a Christ-like priesthood. We might not be fulfilling our duty well, but it is still our duty.

Teilhard asks at one point, rather shockingly, if there has ever, "by definition, been any true mysticism without some element of pantheism? 'And then,' says St. Paul when speaking of the plenitude of the Incarnation, 'God will be all in all: *en pasi panta Theos.*'"[17] As a matter of fact, Teilhard at one point writes about his kind of "Christian pantheism" due to the Incarnation, the "Word made flesh." Although many Christians fight the notion of evolution, Teilhard says that what/who we call "Christ" is the power behind evolution! God brings unity to the world by uniting it organically with himself, by fulfilling creation and purifying it. God accomplishes this by "partially immersing himself in things" (this, of course, again is the basic meaning of the Incarnation), "by becoming 'element,' and then, from this point of vantage in the heart of matter, assuming the control and leadership of what we call evolution." Christ, for Teilhard, is the principle of universal vitality because he sprung up as a human being among human beings, and put himself in the position "to subdue under himself, to purify, to direct and superanimate the general ascent of consciousness into which he inserted himself." And by a perennial act of communion and sublimation, Christ continues to aggregate to himself the total psychism of the earth. "And when Christ has gathered everything together and transformed everything . . . then, as St. Paul tells us, *God shall be all in all.*" This, Teilhard says, is indeed a superior form of pantheism, because it does not have any trace of the poison of either adulteration or annihilation: "the expectation of perfect unity, steeped in which each element will reach its consummation at the same time as the universe."[18] This is an incredible vision of nonduality, in which nothing gets left behind.

We mentioned earlier Jean Corbon's idea of the eternal ascension of Christ, that where the head has gone the rest of the body must go. The rest of the body is not just human beings. The rest of the body is all of creation that is groaning and in agony while we work out our place in this cosmic schema. We mentioned earlier too the image of the burning bush, how it is a symbol for God in the book of Exodus, how then Jesus becomes the burning bush on the mountain of the transfiguration, but how each of us is meant to become in some way a burning bush. "If you want you could be all fire!" Well, Maximus the Confessor fills in the rest of the picture for us. According to Maximus, the Christ event "unites created reality with uncreated reality . . . two are become one. The whole world enters into the whole of God and by becoming all that God is, except in identity of nature, it received in place of itself the whole God."[19]

Thus all of creation becomes the true burning bush.

Two Movements in Creation

As Fr. Bede articulated, there are two movements in creation. One is that creation comes forth from God; the second is that creation returns to God. And when these two movements meet perfectly, that is the Incarnation. These movements are like breathing in and breathing out. We believe that the human being, as represented by Adam, was created as the height of this process of creation, the priest of creation, the creature that was intended to bring creation back to God, because human consciousness is able to reintegrate all the movements of creation and give them voice and will them back to God. But what the myth of the Fall teaches us is the breakdown of the organic unity of creation. So all of creation is lagging in this divided state. And all of our broken-down relationships, including our relationship with the Earth as symbolized by global warming, the depletion of the rain forests, the wiping out of species, and pollution, serve as an icon of the ongoing breakdown of the organic unity of creation.

And yet, it is not for nothing that the classic Catholic doxology had us pray, "world without end, Amen!" God will be all in all in Christ! St. Augustine describes the state of humanity in this world like the human person being scattered over the world, and this is the human nature that Jesus assumes into the Godhead once again at his ascension, and in so doing he reunites all the scattered members, and in some way flesh itself, and all creation, which is *groaning and in agony*, is brought to its glory in the "eternal ascension of Christ" to the right hand of the Father in glory. Fr. Bede says that this is also what every Eucharist symbolizes, a reuniting of the Body of Christ that has been scattered by sin.[20]

Recall William Johnston's four elements of what he calls the "new mysticism," and all of them rooted in the body and in the earth, in Second Axial Consciousness: first of all a *kataphatic* mysticism, a mysticism of light; then a feminine mysticism that emphasizes the earth; then a mystical theology like that of Teilhard de Chardin that sees God in all things—not as a flight from matter but by entering more deeply into matter; and finally a mysticism that is inspired by the movements of social justice and care for the poor. (Note that even that last one is rooted in created reality and the body.) Johnston goes on to say that the gift that we have to receive from Asian cultures is just this: that wise men and women of Asia have always had "a vision of unity." They have experienced what the Hindus would call *advaita*, or nonduality. Asian mysticism also sees the unity of the human person in a different way than Western Europeans typically do. The word "yoga" for instance, means "union," so Yoga is a way of achieving integration in the person through trained senses and stilled minds, but ultimately in union with the Divine. A friend of mine loves to use the acronym SONG to describe the unions meant to be achieved through our spiritual practice: through our yoga, we reestablish right relationship with Self, Others, Nature, and God. It is important to articulate that reestablishing that right relationship with Earth and matter is part of our spiritual *scopos*, or goal, one not often spoken of or thought about. Johnston even says that the Buddhist teachings about emptiness and nothingness are really all "attempts to describe a universe that, as scientists now say, is a unified web of interconnected energies." The "ways" of China and Japan—the way of tea, the way of the bow, the way of Zen, and so on—are likewise meant to lead one to an inner unity, so as to realize that, as the famous Zen saying goes, *shinshin ichinyo*—"mind and body are one." The human person is unified by controlling the energy, even sexual energy, that flows through what are called the meridians and by balancing the *yin* and *yang*, the female and male principles that are within the whole body.

But, most important for our purposes in this chapter, we discover that human energy is linked to cosmic energy. This, in turn, is joined to the Source of All Energy, the Ultimate Reality that Christians call God. Johnston adds too that all this has something in common with the doctrine of Uncreated Energies expounded by mystical theologians of the Orthodox tradition, such as Gregory Palamas's Taboric light that we saw earlier in our discussion about the transfiguration.[21] From this perspective, all energy in life is a manifestation of Divine Energy, what the Hindus would call *shakti,* what the Chinese tradition calls *chi.* Fr. Bede writes that "all energy in human beings is a manifestation of this same Divine Energy, and when we come to consciousness, that Divine Energy becomes conscious in us." The energy that is in plants and animals becomes conscious in the human being. And "we, through the power of the Spirit in us, are able to return to God, to the Word."[22]

What can we learn from the traditions that retain a sense that the energy in us is divine, and that it is an energy shared by all created reality with whom we share the web of life?

We have a mistaken, or at least unchristian, notion of what it means to have dominion over the earth. How is a follower of Jesus meant to have dominion? The clearest example we have is Jesus at the Last Supper. He took off his robe, tied an apron around his waist, and washed his disciples' feet. Followers of Jesus are always servant leaders. And this applies equally to our relationship with, even our so-called "dominion over," the earth. We are heads of the household. Other words that creep into the Western tradition, such as stewardship and husbandry, also give us a clue. Dominion is not about beating creation into submission. It is not about forcing nature to be something that it is not. It is about being a servant leader, a good and loving head of the household, with the commission of care over that which we have been given charge. As Sr. Ilia Delio beautifully writes, we are supposed to be like our Creator, and Jesus has shown us what the Creator is like: "To be like the Creator . . . to be like God, is to become humble in love." Even more "to be an image of God does not separate us from the world but should lead us right into the heart of the matter, literally—the universe, but in a new way, a God-like way, in a way that is transforming."[23]

Strengthening the Covenant between Human Beings and the Environment

The God-given, Christ-driven trajectory of evolution has, in the modern era, in some sense been superseded by human choice. We are, through our decisions and the actions based on those decisions, changing the course of the evolving universe in a way that no other species ever has or can. A recognition of our role in the cosmos awakens us to great moral obligations. How shall we be stewards of the earth? How shall we exercise our dominion, as heads of this household? These decisions and concrete actions are part of our new asceticism as well.

Of all the things that Pope Benedict XVI will be remembered for, such as his stalwart defense of orthodox teaching against relativism, the scandals and mismanagement within the Vatican, and his early retirement, one thing rarely gets noticed: He was the "greenest" of popes. In his World Day of Peace Message of 2009, he altered the famous quote of Paul VI, "If you want peace, work for justice," to "If You Want to Cultivate Peace, Protect the Environment." Environmentalism is often seen as a leftist liberal value, but Benedict placed it right at the heart of our modern ethical challenges. "Can we remain indifferent," he wrote, "before the problems associated with such realities as climate change, desertification, the deterioration and loss of productivity in vast agricultural areas, the pollution of rivers and aquifers, the loss of biodiversity, the increase of natural catastrophes and the deforestation of equatorial and tropical regions?" He too recognizes the common web in which we are but a strand, and how whatever happens to the web happens to us. He asks, "Can we disregard the growing phenomenon of 'environmental refugees,' people who are forced by the degradation of their natural habitat to forsake it—and often their possessions as well—in order to face the dangers and uncertainties of forced displacement?" He also places all this in the context of war, asking astutely, discerning what may actually be at the heart of some of our global conflicts, perhaps presciently prophesying what may lie ahead in terms of global conflict due to environmental issues: "Can we remain impassive in the face of actual and potential conflicts involving access to natural resources? All these are issues with a profound impact on the exercise of human rights, such as the right to life, food, health and development." For all of these reasons, he says, it is imperative that we human beings renew and strengthen "that covenant between human beings and the environment, which should mirror the creative love of God, from whom we come and towards whom we are journeying."[24]

And so our choice of what to drive and how much to drive is a part of the new asceticism. So are our decisions about what we buy and where we buy it. The issue of single-use disposable items, especially of paper products and, even more, of plastics come into play. We need to think about how much garbage we produce and what we do with it. How much energy we need to consume, from where we get it and at what long-term cost, and discerning how much of the world's resources we claim as our entitlement, especially in so-called First World countries, all become concerns of our new ascetical life. We are concerned with issues such as the amount of grain used to feed cattle (as opposed to feeding people), the ethical treatment of caged chickens and the overfishing of our rivers and seas, as well as genetically modified seeds (to name but a few issues); what we eat as well as where and from whom we buy what we eat become a part of our ascetical discipline, bearing in mind the economic consequences and ecological impact of our consumption habits on the intricate web of interconnected life.

I can only briefly touch upon some environmental concerns here, but there are countless people from whom we can learn, people dedicated to "walking softly upon the Earth," repairing the damage done by our neglect, and raising consciousness about how our way of life needs to change in order to be a better, more royal priesthood, exercising dominion in humble love and servanthood over our planet home. We may not always agree with how others (our neo-pagan friends, for instance) articulate the *telos*—the ultimate end—but I think we will find that we can easily agree on the proximate goal of greater care and responsibility for our shared environment, the womb, the web, the nest of Sister Earth our Mother.

Lust and wrath waste the body,
as borax melts gold.
But the gold that can stand the test of fire
is valued highly by the goldsmith.
So it is with the souls.[1]

—"Dakhnī Oṁkār," from the Adi Granth (Sikh Scriptures)

8

Awaken and Surrender!

Now we take a step forward, in some way extending the last chapter on nature, in which we talked about how the energy that is in plants and animals is the energy that becomes conscious in us. But, as Fr. Bede writes, "all energy in human beings is a manifestation of this same Divine Energy, and when we come to consciousness, that Divine Energy becomes conscious in us."[2] I was delighted to discover a book by Jean Bastaire called *Eros Redento* (*Eros Redeemed*), in which he speaks specifically in those terms, again regarding sexuality: "One understands even better up to what point the power of sex is in reality the incarnate force of the Spirit, the creative energy concentrated in its most immediate place of election: that of the transmission of life and the reproduction of the species."[3]

Bede's understanding of this became very real for him in the last years of his life. He wrote a series of letters to his dear friends Russill and Asha in which he writes beautifully about the relationship between *eros* and *agape*. Bede had already for years been in search of, as he put it, "the other half of my soul."[4] Undergoing two strokes indeed opened him up to an overwhelming experience of maternal love; often in his last months when

he spoke of this love his voice would tremble and he seemed to
be on the verge of tears. His relationship with Russill and Asha
(particularly, it must be said, with Russill) at the very end of his
life undoubtedly fleshed out that love, as is evidenced by what
he wrote in these letters. Some years ago I collected a series of
sentences culled from those same letters, and formed them into
one paragraph, which has become for me a sort of manifesto of
sexuality and spirituality. I shall quote the sentences and then
explain what they have come to mean to me.

> What is the meaning of life? The meaning of life is to love and
> there are two ways to love. One is through a dedication of the
> whole of your life to the spirit and the working out of that dedi-
> cation. The other is to love another human being so profoundly
> that that initiates you into the divine love.[5]

First of all what Bede discovered, and what he spoke about
and wrote about openly, was the relationship between love for
another human being and love for God. Not only are the two
related; they are in a sense equivalent paths. Indeed there are two
ways to love, one through a dedication of one's whole life to the
Spirit and the other to love another human being profoundly.

One of the frailties of language is that it can often be too
general. For example, in English we use only one word for the
concept of love. We, however, shall concentrate on the two types
of love that Bede mentions here: eros and agape. Bede says about
them: "Agape without eros simply does not work. It leaves our
human nature starved. Of course, eros without agape is equally
disastrous. It leaves us to the compulsion of human and sexual
love."[6]

Agape is generally thought of as "good love." Dictionaries
sometimes define it as "Christian love." I was taught since my
youth that agape is love as God loves, love that asks for nothing in return. Eros, on the other hand, is generally thought of as
sexual and sensuous love. "Erotic" in common usage usually has
the connotation of being somehow a lesser love, and "dirty" at
that. And yet eros is not just, or even primarily, sexual, at least in
the original Greek conception; it's that and so much more. Eros is
the love that is a longing, the love that draws us out of ourselves

and draws us into others. The Jungian James Hollis describes it this way: "The Greeks thought of Eros as a god, oldest and yet youngest of all the gods, at the beginning of all things and ever-renewing, ever emergent. . . . We have too narrowly confined the work of this god within the bounds of sexuality. Surely he is present there, but we are moved by forces deeper than sex, longer than love, more mysterious than the beloved."[7]

When Bede speaks about "a dedication of the whole of your life to the spirit," I associate that with agape; and when he speaks about loving "another human being so profoundly that that initiates you into the divine love," I associate that with eros. However, what Bede ultimately comes to understand, it seems to me, is that these two ways are actually not two different ways at all, but part of the same process. And so he writes to Russill: "My love for you is not only agape; it is a deep natural urge of love which draws me to you. Often I feel your presence as a tremendous force in my life, making me realize that I cannot experience divine love unless it is united with my human love for you."[8]

Eros and agape are part of the same movement, because agape without eros simply does not work; and, of course, eros without agape is equally disastrous.

Eros and Psyche: Tortured Love

We find resonances with this line of thought in the writing of James Hillman, the great Jungian psychoanalyst, especially in the section on tortured love in his book *The Myth of Analysis*. Rather than eros and agape, he writes about eros and psyche, using the Greek myth of Eros and Psyche by Apuleo, in which the fundamental theme is the torment of the soul (psyche) in its relationship to eros. The myth itself, as well as the various works of art that were inspired by it, especially from the fourth century BCE until the sixth century CE and then again during the Renaissance, tell of Psyche being tortured by love, full of sadness, on her knees, weeping after having been struck by Eros's arrow, depressed and sad at being unable to reunite with him, and destined to fulfill a series of impossible tasks assigned to her by Aphrodite, Eros's mother.

Hillman teaches, based on his own experience in psycho-analysis as well as on studying the archetypes in this myth, that the torture of the soul seems inevitable in every intimate involve-ment. Despite everything we do to avoid or alleviate it, we al-ways seem to end up involved in the very process that generates suffering, almost as if a mythic necessity were compelling us to act out the myth of Eros and Psyche. What the myth tells us, ac-cording to Hillman and Jung before him, is that young girls enter into adult femininity through a type of torture. In Renaissance depictions of this myth, for instance, we see Psyche depicted as a butterfly, with her wings burnt by the flames of Eros. But the soul of a man is also subjected to torment through which he is awakened to the psyche; indeed, Eros is tortured by the same fire as well. While Eros burns others, he also burns alone when he is separated from Psyche, deprived of her gifts of intuition and psychological reflection. But whereas Psyche's torture is depression and nostalgia, Eros's torture is mania.

Hillman says that we experience this separation under the form of a split in ourselves: while Eros burns in mania, Psyche performs her labors without hope or energy, without love, incon-solable, depressed, trying to understand. Before their reuniting becomes possible, Psyche (and our psyche) must pass through the dark night of the soul, the mortification in which she feels the paradoxical agony of a "potential pregnancy in her own depths and yet a sense of guilt and isolating separateness."[9] For Eros, too: his torment transforms the manic energy. Eros will remain in a state of burning unease and agitation (dominated by the mother, but that is a whole other story!) until he realizes that he himself has been struck by his own arrow, that he too has found his companion, his mate, in Psyche—let us say with Bede, "the other half of his soul." In the process he is meant to acquire psy-chic consciousness. And the torment continues until the work of the soul is—the labors of Psyche are—completed, and the psyche is reunited to a transformed eros. It is only at this point that the union takes place, and psyche really becomes Anima, soul.

All this is very similar to the dynamic Bede described. Whereas Hillman speaks of the erotic obsession or erotic mania that occurs in eros when it is separated from psyche, Bede says

simply that eros without agape is disastrous, because it leaves us
to the compulsion of human and sexual love. But agape without
eros is equally disastrous, Bede says; human nature starves.
Hillman explains that Psyche without the wings of Eros cannot
find any kind of proper perspective or raise herself above her
immediate compulsions, which are melancholy and depression.
So Hillman asserts that until our psyche can legitimately unite
itself with the creative energy of eros and bring to a sanctified
birth that which she is carrying in her, we are doomed to live
out our loss of primordial love.

Even though this reading of the human condition presupposes
suffering, this is not blind and tragic suffering, or at least it does
not have to be. This type of suffering, according to Hillman, has
to do with initiation, and with the transformation of the structure
of our consciousness. Jung taught that the ardor of love always
changes fear and compulsion into something higher and freer. The
trials of Eros and Psyche are initiatory; they symbolize the psychological and erotic trials we all have to undergo. All of this gives us
a completely different image, by the way, of neuroses. In this light,
neuroses can become initiation. Consequently, psychoanalysis, at
its best, can become the ritual of our process of psychic and erotic
development, a development that leads to their mysterious union.

Let us also remember that according to the universal archetypes present in this myth, eros is divine energy, because, as
James Hollis reminded us above, Eros himself is a child of the
gods.

Tantric Yoga and the Chakras

In his letters, Fr. Bede continues:

> In meditation we can learn to let our own natural desires, our
> eros, awaken and surrender it to God, that is, let it be taken up
> into agape. It must neither be suppressed nor indulged. It is sur-
> render that is called for.[10]

Bede uses even stronger language than this later when he
says that if the sexual energy is suppressed, even in prayer, it
becomes "neutral or terribly destructive. There is great danger

here which many Christians do not realize," Bede says.[11] Here is where I want to bring in specifically the lessons that can be learned from the psychology of the Yoga tradition, specifically Tantric Yoga, which I am suggesting can help us recast our Christian language and understanding of sexuality. Hillman himself makes reference to Bhakti Yoga, that is, the "Yoga of devotion," in the context of the psychological discipline of developing eros, or the erotic discipline of developing psyche, either of which tend toward "psychic integration and erotic identity." But there is an even more immediate connection with Tantric Yoga and the chakra system. In Bede's *New Creation in Christ*, written very late in his life, he says that Christians should know about this kundalini way of Yoga, and he wrote of it in other places as well.

According to Kundalini Yoga (Tantra), which we explored earlier, the universe is composed of centers of energy known as chakras, literally "wheels." These seven centers of energy in the universe are also within the human person, so that what takes place within the human person—what Tantra sees as the marriage of Shiva (consciousness) with Shakti (energy)—reflects and resonates with what is taking place in the universe outside. Working with the chakras is for the eventual rising of what is known as kundalini, the "serpent energy" coiled in the base of the spine. According to the yogis, all forms of genius and creativity involve some form of awakening this essence. As Bede writes:

> This idea is particularly worked out in Kundalini Yoga, where the understanding is that Kundalini is the serpent power. The serpent was always the symbol of this earth power. That power is supposed to be coiled up like a serpent at the base of the spine and is understood to be the source of all psychic energy. That energy, kundalini, rises up through seven chakras, or energy centers, from the base of the spine to the crown of the head. As the kundalini . . . rises up through the body, the whole being is gradually transformed, from the physical, through the psychological, until finally spiritual evolution is attained.[12]

You will see here again Bede's tripartite anthropology at work: "from the physical, through the psychological, until finally spiritual evolution is attained."

The chakra system begins with the *muladhara chakra*, the muddy area at the base of the spine where the kundalini energy is said to be coiled. This is the place of creation and eros, or primal passion. The awakening of the muladhara chakra is very important; all the passions are stored there, as is all guilt, every complex and agony. The yogis believe that when kundalini is ascending from the muladhara to the next chakra, *svadhisthana*, the practitioner experiences a crucial period in which all repressed emotions, especially those of a primal nature, express themselves. In this period all kinds of infatuations can ensue, but it should be pointed out that this is in a sense presexual, more primordial than sexual.

The *svadhisthana chakra* is located in the region of the genitals. This is the place of sexuality, but also of good taste and aesthetics, where seeds within seeds of generativity are stored. One swami wrote that when kundalini is residing in the svadhistana chakra, we enter a purgative stage, well known in the Christian ascetical tradition, what John of the Cross calls the dark night of the senses: "When the explosion takes place and svadhistana begins to erupt, the aspirant is often confused and disturbed by the activation of all this subconscious material . . . which is often attributed to a disturbed mental condition."[13]

Perhaps here we have Hillman's neuroses, which can actually be embraced as rites of initiation, the constellation of eros in psyche. Unfortunately, according to Swami Satyananda Saraswati, if one fluctuates even slightly, kundalini will return to muladhara and the real awakening will be more difficult.[14] Bede says "the energy must not stop there . . . if the energy is stopped at any of these centers it becomes destructive."[15]

The next chakra is the *manipura*, in the abdomen. Its symbolic element is fire. The manipura is where rising passion begins to be transformed by the heat. This is the center of honesty, independence, and autonomy. According to the Buddhist tradition, actual spiritual awakening takes place here, and from here the awakening is ongoing, so if one has made it this far there is practically no danger of devolution. Only then comes *anahata chakra*, at the solar plexus, sometimes thought of as the heart chakra, where passion starts to become nonphysical compassion.

This is also the place of devotion and self-service, where need is transformed into love and courage. This is the stage where one attains the freedom to escape from a preordained fate and determine one's own destiny, and where love overcomes ego. Perhaps this is where Eros finally frees himself from the grip of his mother, Aphrodite, where love overcomes fear and compulsion. Most importantly, and this is what I am aiming at, this is where eros transforms into agape!

From there we reach the *vishudha chakra* in the throat region, where passion is transformed into dispassion and tranquility. And then on to the *ajna chakra* at the brow, called "the third eye of wisdom," where passion becomes *vairagha*—the wisdom of nonattachment—before reaching *sahaswara*, the chakra at the crown of the head, where the restrictions of time, space, and mortality are transcended. But we are most of us not ready for that. My main point lies back in the anahata chakra.

According to Kundalini Yoga, the teaching of the chakras suggests that we cannot even experience authentic agape until it has been brought to fruition by the rising of eros, until eros constellates in psyche, until the primordial energy has been brought up from muladhara where it has been stored. Even further, I want to suggest that we cannot adequately transform our eros into agape until we first not only acknowledge it but reverence it as a sort of divine madness planted in us. So Bede says, "I cannot experience divine love unless it is united with my human love for you."[16] One yogi told me that he thought the problem with Christians, and monastics in general, is that we try to start with the heart chakra, that is with agape, and forego acknowledging and reverencing the eros, which he says would be a very difficult enterprise.[17] We find out along the way that *agape* without our full humanity behind it often is codependence masquerading as altruism instead.

What is to be noted, not unlike what we said of Eros in the thought of James Hillman, is that this energy within us, according to the Hindu tradition, as in Greek thought, is itself divine. For the Hindu it is really the goddess Shakti herself. It is also important to keep in mind the idea of transformation and surrender, not suppression; it is important to keep in mind that we need not only to accept but also to reverence eros, reverence the creative madness within us. Whether we are speaking of actual loci in the body or not does not matter to me; what I love about this chakra system is the notion of awakening, reverencing the divine madness of eros within us and, as Bede adds, neither indulging it nor suppressing it, but surrendering it, allowing it to be burnt and transformed into another kind of love.

The Path of the Renunciate

How then are we to understand the way of renunciation, and the path of the renunciate, of which Bede was a prime example himself? There is a rather shocking poem from the Zen tradition:

> A sex loving monk, you object!
> Hot blooded and passionate, totally aroused.
> Remember, though, that lust can consume all passion,
> Transmuting base metal into pure gold.[18]

Bede understood the development of Tantra as rising in opposition to the *sannyasa* path, the monastic path of total renunciation. In the earlier Upanishadic tradition, a tradition rising right out of the First Axial Consciousness of the fifth/sixth centuries BCE, the aim had been always to go beyond the physical and beyond the psychological to the Supreme Reality, which in practice entailed a strong tendency toward the asceticism that up to that point had prevailed in Hinduism as a whole, and ought to sound familiar to traditional Catholic teaching on ascetic practice. "Leaving behind the body, the soul, the mind and all its activities, the aim [of the Upanishadic teachers] was to unite oneself with the supreme Brahman, the supreme atman."[19] Bede then marvelously traces how historically the Tantric texts, which first begin to appear in the third century CE, rise up out of the indigenous Dravidian Shaivism of southern India. (As we saw earlier, this is corroborated by many other authors.) The important thing about that is that in southern India devotion to God as mother is very strong, so the tendency instead is to assert the values of nature and of the body, of the senses and of sexuality. Many things that tended to be suppressed in the very masculine

Brahmanical Aryan Vishnu tradition came to be reverenced by Tantra. A key doctrine of the Tantras is "that by which we fall is that by which we rise." In other words, as we may fall through the attraction of the senses, through sex, passion and desire, so we have to rise through them, using them as the means of going beyond. "As the Kundalini . . . rises up through the body, the whole being is gradually transformed, from the physical, through the psychological, until finally spiritual evolution is attained."[20] Again, note our anthropology at work: from body through soul to spirit.

But is the opposition of Tantric path to the sannyasa path of renunciation a false dilemma? At first glance it seems as if the path of total renunciation is opposed to the way of total embrace. But perhaps we could also find a synthesis of the masculine way of renunciation and the feminine way of embrace that is still in keeping with traditional Indian thought, in which Tantrism is not seen as opposed to the sannyasa way, in which the way of eros is not opposed to the way of agape.

The traditional Brahmanic pattern is of four stages (*asramas*) of life: one passes first through the stage of *bramacharya* when one is young, a student learning literally "the ways of Brahman." Then one becomes a householder, *grihasta*, at which point one is expected to have a good career and make money to care for one's parents and offspring. At some point one can become a *vana-prasta*, a forest dweller, retiring to a more contemplative life even with one's spouse. And then, according to classical tradition, one reaches the age to enter the last stage of life, *sannyasa*. These rules, codified in the second century by the semi-historical Hindu law-giver Manu, apply to males, mind you, so at this point the man, after having fulfilled all the obligations of faith and family, could leave his home, renounce all signs of his caste and forms of outer worship, and become a wanderer, a renunciant. Even though even in present-day India most of the monks actually begin as younger men who "take sannyasi" without ever having gone through the other asramas except for brahmacharya, what I am suggesting is that in this classical pattern we can understand that healthy renunciation might only come after some integration has already taken place. When the kundalini energy in the natural flow of life has been reverenced and allowed to work its transformation in and on the human person, then it can be surrendered. Perhaps one is only ready for the great renunciation after the kundalini has been reverenced and allowed to rise up and begin the work of transforming the whole being, starting with the physical, working through the psychological, until finally spiritual evolution is attained. This makes a lot of sense, and stands in contrast not to the path of renunciation itself but perhaps in contrast to the monastic practice—Buddhist and Hindu as well as Christian—of young people "taking sannyasa," attempting a lifelong commitment to celibate chastity without ever having gone through the necessary stages of reverencing their eros, of allowing this divine creative sexual psychic energy to do its work of transformation, particularly the work of eros being transformed into agape.

I am amused and somewhat consoled to discover that the tendency toward dualism is not limited to Christians but is shared by monastics in general, as evidenced by this, one of my favorite Buddhist stories, from China. There was an old woman who had supported a hermit for years, giving him a hut and feeding him while he spent his life in meditation. One day she decided to test him to see what kind of progress he had made, so she sent a beautiful young woman to his hut. The girl sat on his lap, threw her arms around him and pressed her body close up to his, and then asked the old man, "What are you feeling right now?" And the old man answered, "I am like a withered tree that grows on a cold rock in winter. Nowhere is there any warmth." Well, the young girl went and reported this to the old woman, and when the old woman who had been supporting this hermit for years heard this reply she immediately grew furious, went to the hermit's hut and kicked him out, and burned his hut down saying, "And to think I supported that guy for twenty years! What a waste!" So, agape without eros leaves our human nature starved. It is like a withered tree that grows on a cold rock in winter. Nowhere is there any warmth. What a waste!

According to Fr. Bede, the Tantric understanding is particularly important today because many in the West consciously or not have already discovered this way, what he calls the way of the Mother, or have at least intuited something similar to its rightness. Furthermore, when understood correctly, it may especially have lessons to teach Western Christians reeling in the wake of a sexual crisis among its professional celibates. Because agape without eros starves, and eros without agape is madness.[21]

Christian Asceticism: Transformation in the Holy Spirit

In *New Creation in Christ*, Fr. Bede writes this summary, which I think may be one of the most important summaries of the fruits of his own spiritual life.

> So shakti rises and eventually reaches the sahasrara chakra, the thousand petalled lotus at the top of the head. This is where we open up to the whole universe and the transcendent mystery beyond. . . . I like to see it flowing from above, with the Holy Spirit descending through all the faculties, right down through the whole body and then rising up again and returning to God.[22]

I hope the reader will have noticed in the above quotation the Pentecostal imagery—*the love of God poured into our hearts by the Spirit living in us* (Rom 5:5)—and a resonance with the teaching of the Mother about the redescent after the flooding down of Divine power: *from out of the believer's heart shall flow streams of life-giving water* (John 7:38)! And Hillman agrees too, specifically citing Kundalini Yoga, saying that it "insists upon the circulation downward, continually returning to the anal-genital root of muladhara; it is not left behind. Beauty would unite both in yet a further mystery."[23]

Now I'll tie this in with Christianity. Hopefully it will be clear why I might propose a kind of "Christian Tantra."

In the best of the Christian tradition, eros is not to be avoided. As a matter of fact, early Christian writers speak about our eros for God, and God's eros for us. Dionysius the Areopagite from *The Divine Names* writes: "In God, eros is outgoing, ecstatic. Because of it lovers no longer belong to themselves but to those whom they love."[24]

Similarly, Maximus the Confessor writes, in *On the Divine Names*, that God is the producer and generator of tenderness and eros and that God is the moving force in those who look to God and who possess the capacity for desire, according to their own nature. And to further corroborate our theme, St. John Climacus taught that for those who love God with the strength of eros, eros is transformed into agape. The most direct connection is made by Origen, who says that although "eros is usually experienced in terms in relation to a human lover, it is in reality a heavenly force."[25] Even more to the point, Origen makes the bold move of equating the agape, with which the Greek Bible identifies God, and the eros of the Greek tradition. As Bernard McGinn explains it, the Christian belief in a transcendent God who "chooses to go out of himself" in creation (however we might understand that) for Origen is something akin to the yearning desire of eros, and so Origen wrote in his *Commentary on the Song of Songs*, "I do not think one could be blamed if one called God eros, just as John called him agape. . . . You must take whatever scripture says about agape as if it had been said in reference to eros, taking no notice of difference in terms; for the same meaning is conveyed by both."[26]

In modern times Ronald Rolheiser has a beautiful treatment of eros, using Goethe's phrase the "holy longing" in his book of the same name. Rolheiser says eros is "an unquenchable fire, a restlessness, a longing, a disquiet, a hunger, a loneliness, a gnawing nostalgia, a wildness that cannot be tamed, a congenital all-embracing ache that lies at the center of human experience and is the ultimate force that drives everything else."[27]

For Rolheiser, our contemporary search to define Christian spirituality needs to be rooted in eros. He writes that, for the Christian, spirituality is not an uprooting of desire; it's about what we *do* with desire. Our spirituality "takes root in the eros inside of us and it is all about how we shape and discipline that eros." He gives the example of John of the Cross, whose "love's urgent longings" were none other than the eros that is the starting point of the spiritual life. And according to Rolheiser, spirituality is how we handle that eros.[28] Eros, carrying with it desire, disquiet, nostalgia, lust, appetite, and hope, "is soul and soul gives energy." He writes that Christians should agree with the Greeks (and the Hindus) who say that we are fired into life with a madness that is the root of all love, hate, creativity, joy, and sadness, and we should add that God has put this eros inside of us, so that we might share in God's work of creation, and ultimately contemplate that which we have helped create and burst with a joy and "swell in a delight that breaks the prison of [our] selfishness." And for this reason, according to Rolheiser, sexuality lies at the center of the spiritual life: "A healthy sexuality is the single-most powerful vehicle there is to lead us to selflessness and joy, just as unhealthy sexuality helps constellate selfishness and unhappiness as does nothing else."[29]

Reflecting on the sexual scandals in the Roman church that surfaced in the early years of the twenty-first century, one does not have to reach far to guess that they are quite possibly a result of the destructive and dangerous character of blocked sexual energy. "Eros driven underground becomes rage, and great violence ensues," writes James Hollis,[30] and Richard Rohr agrees with this, also citing Fr. Bede in his book *Adam's Return*, and adding that if religion does not integrate and validate the sensual, pleasure-loving, erotic aspect of spirituality—he is specifically referring to male spirituality here—eros can take devious and destructive directions. Rohr says, "If you do not bless it and bow to it, it turns on you and controls you. . . . If you bless it, it also shows its limited value and longs for something higher."[31]

Thus sexuality too, with all of Christian asceticism, needs to be seen in a fresh light. Once again it is apt to bring in that advice of Benedictine Anselm Grün, who changes the language just a bit by saying that our discipline is not a way that we suppress our drives and passions; it is a way that we can transform and shape them "so that they can serve us as a power source."[32] The senses are not suppressed or killed; rather, they are focused and shaped, and thus become sacraments, hinges of salvation, as Tertullian teaches that all flesh is for the Christian.

St. Pope John Paul II made bold new moves forward with his "Theology of the Body," which was as much a language event as a theology. Whereas so much of the teaching about sexuality was pejorative if barely permissive in past generations, John Paul II writes about it as a great gift, and the body itself as a theology. Religious people (especially, but not only Christians) are much more accustomed to an emphasis on the spiritual realm, and tend to become uncomfortable with too much specific emphasis on the body. The noted conservative scholar Christopher West points out in his reflections on John Paul's teaching that the human body itself is in some sense sacramental, in the broadest more ancient sense of the word "sacrament": it is a sign that makes visible the invisible mystery of God. The body is the primordial and preeminent sign of the ultimate spiritual reality.[33] And so John Paul II wrote that the erotic urge is actually an aspiration for goodness, truth, and beauty, what philosophy calls the transcendentals. So we can study the body as a theology, as a sacrament, as a sign of the ultimate spiritual reality, the divine mystery. Without that recognition, West says, we will constantly be swinging back and forth between such polarities as angel-ism, prudery, rigorism, and repression on the one hand, all the way to indulgence, permissivism, and indecency on the other. The solution is never to swing from one end of the pendulum to the other,[34] but to find the integration in right relationship, to find the unity of body and soul, of spirituality and sexuality.

The real surprise came from Pope Benedict, whose first encyclical, *Deus Caritas Est*, dealt with the relationship between eros and agape (to the disappointment of many of his friends who wanted a little more discipline and a little less "love and Mozart," as I heard one conservative commentator complain). In *Deus Caritas Est* he says that human beings are truly themselves only when body and soul are intimately united, and our erotic tension can only be "truly overcome when this unification is achieved." If we try to be pure spirit and to reject the flesh, then spirit and body both lose their dignity. On the other hand, if we deny the spirit and consider matter, the body, as the only reality, we likewise lose our greatness. With a wry touch of humor the pope recounts how the epicure Gassendi used to offer the philosopher Rene Descartes the greeting, "O Soul!," to which Descartes would reply, "O Flesh!" Only when both dimensions are truly united do we attain our full stature. "Only thus is love—*eros*—able to mature and attain its authentic grandeur."[35]

While noting that Christianity has often been rightly criticized for having been opposed to the body, Benedict also warns that the contemporary way of exalting the body is deceptive:

If eros is reduced merely to "sex" the body becomes an object. That is a debasement of the human body because it is no longer "integrated into our overall existential freedom; no longer . . . a vital expression of our whole being," but instead "relegated to the purely biological sphere." At that point, the *apparent* exaltation of the body can quickly turn into a hatred of bodiliness. Authentic Christian incarnational theology always considers the human person "a unity in duality, a reality in which spirit and matter compenetrate, and in which each is brought to a new nobility." True eros tends to rise "in ecstasy," it becomes more sublime, it rises to agape, it rises towards the Divine, it can lead us beyond ourselves. It is for this very reason that it calls for a path of ascent, and that ascent sometimes calls for renunciation for the sake of purification, healing, and discipline "if it is to provide not just fleeting pleasure, but a certain foretaste of the pinnacle of our existence, of that beatitude for which our whole being yearns."[36]

All of this, as Fr. Bede noted, comes terribly close to what Tantric Yoga would suggest as well (aside from the decadent forms of it that have worked their prurient way into the Western consumer culture). As strange as it may sound, I wonder what lessons we Christians could learn from the best of the Tantric tradition, especially the various elements that worked their way into Hatha Yoga, the chakra system that teaches us to reverence the various energies of our being and sublimate them by allowing them to rise to more and more sublime expressions, or the exercises of *pranayama* (breathing exercises) that are practical tools for training the senses and stilling the mind to prepare ourselves for encounter with God. One of the best practical guides I ever read about celibacy, for individuals and for couples, originally titled *Passions of Innocence*, was written by a scholar adept in the field of Kundalini Yoga. The book ends up making a very good case for observances for which conservative Catholics take a good deal of ribbing in popular culture, such as periods of celibacy and procreative intentionality.[37] I dream of this approach and even the yogic techniques that aid Tantric celibacy, or something similar, being introduced into our seminaries and houses of formation.

Meditation

Let's end this chapter with a note on meditation, which is so vital in the spiritual, ascetical life. As we consider it here, "meditation" means more the Asian sense of meditation as a psychosomatic practice, involving training the senses as well as stilling the mind, common in both the Hindu and Buddhist as well as Taoist traditions. For Fr. Bede, meditation is a primary necessary step in learning to deal with and shape our eros. He uses a wonderful expression when he says that in meditation we learn "to let our own natural desires, our eros, awaken and surrender it to God, that is, let it be taken up into agape."[38] While the awakening can be very exciting, the surrender can be very difficult. But it does seem worth the effort in order to be fully alive and offer our whole being both to God and in service of the world. It is specifically in and through meditation that we learn to turn our mind to the inner light of the Spirit, which is able to direct the mind and bring it into right relationship with the senses. As the Buddhist scholar Andrew Olendzki says about his own tradition, the reason meditation is such a crucial tool is that there is a wisdom that is really only accessible to a settled and focused mind.[39] It is in meditation that we still the mind and train the senses, so that we may learn to surrender what we have awakened, the surrender that is necessary to be guided by our spirit, and by the Holy Spirit. It is in meditation that we may learn to surrender to God who, as Maximus the Confessor reminds us, is the moving force, the producer and generator of tenderness and eros, and come to possess the capacity for outgoing and ecstatic creative desire.

Awaken and surrender!

As the Holy One fills the entire world, so the soul fills the entire body. As the Holy One sees but is not seen, so the soul sees but is not seen. As the Holy One sustains the entire world, all of it, so the soul sustains the body. As the Holy One is pure, so the soul is pure. As the Holy One dwells in the chambers that are innermost, so the soul dwells in chambers that are innermost.

—Talmud, Berakot 10a[1]

9

Map of the Inscape, the Soul

The word "soul" is how we normally translate the Greek word *psyche*.[2] You will, of course, notice the root of "psychology" and "psychiatry" in this Greek word as well. At their best, psychiatrists and psychologists are "doctors of the soul."[3] In this context, we are using the word "soul" in a very broad sense, to mean the whole range of the psyche, from the senses and emotions through the intellectual and rational capacities to the higher forms of consciousness, super consciousness, and psychic gifts, even cosmic consciousness. The mind— the rational mind—as we normally understand it, is not separate from the soul in this understanding, but is instead an element, one stratum of the soul. We, in the West especially, have a tendency to abstract our rational intellect from all of the other aspects of the psyche (shall we again blame poor old Descartes?), and this is a real problem, rationality removed from intuition or from the mythic sense, or even from emotions and dreams. Cold, dry intellectualism gets us into all kinds of trouble.

On the other hand, while we are speaking of the soul in a much more ample way, we are also distinguishing it from the spirit. In this understanding, the spirit, *our* spirit, is beyond all phenomena, beyond all thoughts, forms and images, beyond descriptions and understanding, especially beyond all the psycho-mental phenomena with which we normally identify ourselves. But more on that later.

At the same time I want to stress that we must keep in mind psychosomatic unity, the inseparability of body and soul. We are simply turning the human condition around like a precious gem looking at its various facets. In the ongoing debate about the use of psychotropic drugs to treat various psychological and mental disorders, this is exactly what comes to the fore. On the one hand there was a recognition of how much the chemistry of our physicality affects our psychological states. On the other hand, it might be argued that we have grown overly reliant on chemical solutions that may serve as a palliative rather than a cure, and indeed bring about a certain dullness that short-circuits a slower, deeper, more natural process. I have been convinced of the thinking that lands somewhere in between, neither reducing everything to a chemical solution nor shying away from using it to reestablish proper chemical balance in the body. But the underlying recognition, as the author Russell Shorto put it and Fr. Bede would surely agree, is that we have to see ourselves as spiritual beings who have the capacity to transcend ordinary ways of knowing. And this "spiritual side of the human being is tied, in unfathomed ways, to the physical side and to the emotional." And if that is so, then the work of psychology and psychiatry has the ability to go deeper than those professions at their best have traditionally believed and are ordinarily conceived.[4]

In Western culture we generally have the notion that the soul is something contained in and by the body. This too probably comes more from Greek philosophy and the idea that the soul needs to escape the body. As the philosopher-poet John O'Donohue wrote in *Anam Cara*, most Christians grow up believing that the soul is "confined to some special, small refined region within the body. It is often imaged as white." (I remember clearly in my own experience, in preparing for first penance in second grade, being told that when I sinned my soul was stained with a black mark, which had to be cleaned in confession every Saturday.) According to this construct, when a person dies, "the soul departs and the empty body collapses." But O'Donohue says that this "version of the soul seems false" according to the more ancient way of thinking.[5] Christianity does not actually believe that the soul is something contained within the body, much less "trapped" within the body. The body is something contained within the soul, interpenetrated by soul. The ancient formula for this is *anima forma corporis*—the soul is the form of the body. The soul is that which gives form to the body and holds it together, and the two are and always will be in some way an indissoluble unity. This is why the human body is treated with such high regard, because it is not just flesh and meat to be used and discarded at will. Rather, the body is interpenetrated by a soul, and that organic unity is further interpenetrated by the Spirit that vivifies and gives life. So instead of thinking of the soul as something we have, we can think of the soul as something we *are* and, perhaps even more, something in which we are contained. The soul is a realm in which we share, the realm of the psyche.

Keep in mind here our earlier discussion of Teilhard's notion of the noosphere. After the geosphere, there was the biosphere; and the biosphere then gives rise to this noosphere, the realm of consciousness, the realm of the psyche or "psychism." This is the realm of abstraction, logic, invention, art, emotions, and love. Teilhard writes that the "*within, consciousness* and then spontaneity" are three expressions for this same phenomenon. In *Phenomenon of Man* Teilhard writes, "The term 'consciousness' is taken in its widest sense to indicate every kind of psychism, from the most rudimentary forms of interior perception imaginable to the human phenomenon of reflective thought."[6]

A Map of the Inscape

We have especially learned in this day and age from depth psychology about what an incredible "inscape" the world of the psyche is, and that the rational mind is only a fraction of it. As Aurobindo taught, there are many planes of consciousness between the Soul and the Nature.[7] Part of our work in contemplative prayer, in meditation, is grappling with our psyches, taking them seriously, and then being able to surpass them, to arrive at the deepest aspects of our souls. The desert fathers and mothers were masters of spiritual psychology, as are many of our Buddhist and Hindu counterparts. There are many different and wonderful maps of the inscape of the soul, but Bede Griffiths often used a schema from the Katha Upanishad, and so that is what we shall use as a framework for our discussion and to take a journey into the levels of our psyches. The Katha Upanishad teaches that

> Beyond the senses there are the objects.
> Beyond the objects there is the mind—*manas*.
> Beyond the mind there is the intellect—*buddhi*.
> Beyond the intellect there is the Great Self—*mahat*.
> Beyond the great self is the Unmanifest—*avyakta*.
> Beyond the Unmanifest is the Great Person—*Purusha*.[8]

The senses and the objects of the senses account for the material world and our bodies. I want to add in here, besides the senses, the emotions, which serve as a sort of bridge between the physical and psychological. Emotions are half chemical and half spectral. As a popular expression goes, we don't have emotions; they have us! Emotions can drive us, they can be our enemies or our slave masters; or, as with so many other elements of our human condition, they can be our friends, our servants. Even more, at their best they can serve as a bridge to the interior world. This is why developing what in modern times has come to be called "emotional intelligence," especially popularized by the work of psychologist and author Daniel Goleman, is vitally important in the path of self-knowledge and interiority.

Let's keep in mind that we are in a sense mapping out a hierarchy, but that that hierarchy is also a holarchy, and that the lower stages of the mind or soul should not be left behind as we explore its more advanced or refined capabilities. So as we explore the next layer of mind, let us not leave the sensual and emotive behind, but let these be absorbed and refined by the rational mind.

Manas/Ratio

Beyond the senses and emotions is the mind itself, the rational mind, what Thomas Aquinas called *ratio*. The Katha Upanishad uses the Sanskrit word *manas*, a word we have already encountered. Manas is the root of many words, such as "mantra," which is sometimes translated as a "tool for the mind." The rational mind, the manas, works through the senses; Swami Prabhvananda calls it "the recording faculty which receives impressions gathered by the senses from the outside world."[9] This is the capacity of the mind for discursive thought and logic, the ability for abstract thinking and defining, categorizing, and drawing conclusions. When anything is observed, the senses register the impressions, but it is the mind that interprets the data. It is this capacity of the mind that evolves more fully in the First Axial Period, the rational mind piercing through the mythic mind that was much more rooted in the senses and emotions. This is where many of us remain, at least in our conscious awareness, at the level of rational thought, quite often in fact caught up in a tangle, a rush hour of conflicting thoughts. But just as it is important to allow the senses and emotions to have their voice in the rational mind's conclusions—in other words not to make decisions based solely on cold hard facts—it is also imperative to go farther yet, to another layer of the psyche, beyond, deeper than the rational mind.

Buddhi/Intellectus

Beyond the *manas*, beyond this first level of mind, is what the Katha Upanishad calls the *buddhi*. Now we are entering into some fascinating territory. I have never found a satisfying English translation for this word. It is usually translated as the "intellect"; as a matter of fact, Fr. Bede says it is akin to what Thomas Aquinas calls the *intellectus*. But it is a special kind of knowledge that may be more mysterious than what we normally think of as "intellectual."

The word *buddhi* comes from the Sanskrit verb root *budh*, which means "to enlighten." Whereas the manas is akin to what we in the West would call *ratio* or rational knowledge, the power of discursive and logical thought, we might say that the buddhi like the intellectus is the capacity for simple intuition. Whereas the rational mind breaks things into separate parts, the buddhi can grasp the whole in a flash. The buddhi/intellectus is our capacity for nonconceptual knowledge. This is not discursive reasoning that moves from effect to cause; it is a type of knowing that is not sequential, but direct and immediate. In a word, it is contemplative knowledge, and just as in the Christian conception of prayer contemplation is a grace, so the knowledge of the buddhi is given, not earned; it is more inspired than induced. It is not within our own power, and so it can never become a possession, as distinct knowledge can. The knower is passive and receptive. One might say it is more feminine knowledge as opposed to the masculine rational mind.

The thinkers of the Middle Ages considered the intellectus to be a higher form of knowledge and deeper than rationality, closer to the knowledge of God and the angels. Fr. Bede thought of this level of knowing as the pure intelligence that opens us to the source of reality. While the manas/rational mind works through the senses and is the logical, scientific mind, the buddhi goes beyond the senses and beyond the ordinary functioning of the mind. Furthermore, the buddhi is open to transcendence. Our openness to transcendence is vitally important for us to understand. We are not leaving the rational mind behind, but we are bringing it into the broader sky of consciousness. Perhaps this is akin to what Jungian psychology calls the "transcendent function," because part of the transcendent function, according to Jungian psychology, is the capacity of the psyche to unite conscious and unconscious contents, giving rise to a whole new way of thinking that assimilates material that was formerly unconscious into consciousness. Jungians make the bold claim that this is the "psychological equivalent of the birth of Christ (the incarnation of God)," a " 'special development of the human soul,' the incarnation, the realization of the divine being in human life."[10]

For this reason we can also think of the buddhi as the intuitive mind. Though Fr. Bede, especially in his book *Marriage of East and West*, points out that intuition is meant to function at every level of consciousness, this is the level of the mind that in a sense pulls all the lower forms of knowledge up to greater heights and capacities. The Carmelite author Ruth Burrows makes an analogy between the mystical knowledge that we are talking about in this experience of transcendence and what happens in us when we experience beauty in art or music, for instance. She says that it is "knowledge without form," that is inexpressible, even to ourselves! We cannot hold it; it holds us. It is also "shy" and elusive knowledge; if we try to examine it or clutch at it, it flees like the deer. We may seek to communicate something of our intuition, like an artist attempts with images and words, but we can never fully succeed. Our works of art, as beautiful as they may be, are still limited attempts, which in their turn at their best are still pointing away from themselves to that which transcends them. Sr. Ruth writes,

> There are innumerable occasions when this shy visitant knocks: contemplation of the vastness of the universe as well as its infinitesimal constituents—mathematics, a flower, an insect, a human person, the encounters of love, death, disaster, to name a few. Such visitations we may call high points.[11]

However, there is an even more fundamental, constant experience than this shy visitant, an experience that we usually do not perceive: the experience of our very existence, our sharing in Being itself, who is God. It is from this that all distinct thoughts flow; without this they could not be. Ilia Delio writes about this shy visitor as well, but she refers to it as "contuition": "the awareness of the presence of God attained in the consciousness of a being. . . . Contuition, like contemplation, is a penetrating gaze that gets to the truth of reality."[12] This is *satchitananda*, the bliss of being aware of Being!

The Ego

Here we are still in the realm of the ego, what the Indian tradition calls the *ahamkara*—the "I maker." Why this transcendent function of the Jungians is so important is, as James Hollis writes, because the ego, the center of our consciousness, is like "a thin wafer floating on an immense ocean." We all know this, intuitively and by experience, for example, in our dreams while we sleep or when we are stormed by uncontrollable powerful emotions or obsessions. Certainly at some point on the meditative path we learn that we need to confront everything that courses within. Hollis says that we might think that what we do not know will not hurt us. But, Hollis says, "This is worth repeating: what we do not know, controls us."[13]

We are also here at that borderland between psychosis and mysticism. I want to rush in to say that I do not think that psychosis and mysticism are the same thing, even though they may resemble each other in the way that a baby resembles an old man. However, this may be because psychosis and mysticism may actually have the same starting point. In his book *Saints and Madmen,* Russell Shorto uses the same image as James Hollis when he writes that the mind taken "as a whole—including the unconscious, the place of dreams and phantasms and the source of awe," is like an ocean, of which the ego remains mostly ignorant. We think that psychotics are "out of their minds," but they are actually way, way *deep* in their minds, and that is the problem! They are in touch with this ocean, indeed they are swimming in it, maybe drowning in it. It is we supposedly sane ones who are out of our minds, or at least not in touch with or never access the rest of our minds. What psychotics may have in common with mystics is that they are not content with the ordinary ways of knowing what the ego offers, and so may be on "a profound, dangerous, mystical voyage whose purpose is to find new deeper ways to communicate."[14] I believe the great Jungian James Hillman would agree that often neurosis and psychosis are invitations and attempts to find deeper meaning. It is the mystics who are able to fathom these depths without being destroyed.

We should not think of the ego as a bad thing, or something that needs to be crushed or destroyed, no matter what kind of hyberbolic language we hear used in speaking of these things. As a human being develops from child to adult, he or she has to develop a sense of self, has to become conscious of difference from mother and father, brothers and sisters. The ego is a function of the soul, what gives one the happy ability to relate to others, to be in communion, to love, and to relate. It's a natural thing for a young child to be very self-centered, thinking of self in the process of becoming somebody. Ken Wilbur often used the wonderful practical teaching that there is a normal growth from selfishness to care to universal care (usually for females) or from selfishness to rights to universal rights (usually for males). It's okay to be egoistical as a newborn! As the contemporary Sufi teacher Kabir Helminski describes it, the ego is formed "through trying to hold a place for ourselves in a world that has many contrary forces. As we grow into life, we face challenges and demands. We attempt to establish a position from which or through which to act."[15]

As I once heard a Zen teacher describe it, the ego should be like a screen door, easily swinging in and out, keeping out the flies but letting in the breeze and the scent of the morning flowers. Unfortunately, perhaps after a series of hard knocks or years of abuse and neglect, our ego can become supersized, hardened like someone who is muscle bound, several times his or her normal size pumped up on steroids, or imbedded in layers of fat from gorging on comfort foods to ameliorate the pain of life. What my ego needs is the same thing my body needs—some exercise and a good diet, to bring it down to size, lean and mean. Of course, and this is essential and the most difficult part, in order for the ego to be able to do this, it needs a safe and healthy environment.[16]

Kabir Heminski writes beautifully in his book *Living Presence* about the positive qualities of the ego. He says that the ego is "a fundamentally positive energy with many positive qualities: aspiration, diligence, responsibility, self-respect, discipline, integrity." These positive qualities belong to and come from the Divine Source and are then reflected in us, and as we develop the positive aspect of ego, we find that the ego can be supported by spiritual intelligence and wisdom, and then act as an instrument of this greater intelligence rather than as a proponent of its own self-interest. What is needed is "to establish a subtle balance—the ego in co-creatorship with the Spirit." I love this essentially optimistic approach: What is positive in us is much greater than what is negative because whatever exists is essentially good. (Spoken like a true Thomist!) "If there were not some good in it, it would not exist at all." Sometimes, however, these positive qualities are appropriated by the unhealthy ego's self-importance or insecurity, and can stand between us and Reality. This tyrannical ego is what Thomas Merton, writer and mystic, refers to as the "false self," and, according to Helminski, the false self "can ruin anything it touches. The tyrannical ego, which mercilessly drives us, needs to be brought down to its proper size and become a useful servant, messenger, friend. We need the power of an integrated ego, but we need it as our servant, not as our master."[17]

Our psychic being tends to constellate around that ego, whether we are conscious of it and its workings or not. If we advance that far in our inner journey, our journey of self-knowledge, it would still be a problem if we stop at the ego, that sense of self which is still limited. Fr. Bede taught that if we remain centered on the ego we condemn ourselves to a limited experience and, worse, we cut ourselves off from the Supreme, the Beyond, the Transcendent, all that which is beyond the small sense of self. He thought that we are all more or less imprisoned in the ego and that that was exactly the effect of original sin:

> Original sin is the fall from the transcendent into the ego. Instead of being open to the divine and being led by the Spirit, you fall into your psyche, your ego. Then you become a self-centered being and you find yourself in opposition with the other egos all around you and the whole conflict and confusion comes about.[18]

The *Mahat*

> Your soul reaches out farther than your body, and it simultaneously suffuses your body and your mind. Your soul has more refined antennae than your mind or ego.
>
> John O'Donohue[19]

So what is beyond the ego? Now we get to that which produces the ego according to the Upanishads: the *mahat*, an area, a level of mind of which we do not speak often in the Christian tradition. *Mahat* is the "cosmic ego sense, the first dawning of differentiated consciousness." Bede always described it as the Great Self, the cosmic order or cosmic consciousness. The Sanskrit scholar Juan Mascaró translates the *mahat* as "the spirit in the human person" and Swami Prabhavananda says it "may perhaps be compared to the Spirit moving on the face of the waters which is mentioned in the book of Genesis."[20] It is from the mahat that the buddhi, the discriminating faculty, and the manas, the rational, recording faculty, evolve.[21]

It is a dangerous enterprise to try to locate the human "spirit" that Bede refers to, and which will be the subject of the next chapter. I have come to think of it more as a capacity, a function or an openness, than a "thing" to be pointed out or some "place" in us. However, it seems to me that it is at the level of the mahat as it is described here, that we discover or, perhaps better, begin to *experience* our own pneuma, our spirit, what St. Francis de Sales called "the fine point of the soul," the point which Karl Rahner mentions as the point of self-transcendence, and we find ourselves open to the transcendent, the infinite, and ultimately to the Divine, indeed "the point of contact between the human and the divine."[22]

Fr. Bede teaches further that at this depth of our being we are also in communion with one another. "In our bodies and our souls we are all different and divided, but at this point of the spirit we are in communion with God and with one another."[23] Indeed, we are in communion with all creation, as a matter of fact we are matter coming into consciousness. This too seems to me to be another explanation of this deep realm of the soul, the mahat, cosmic consciousness, when we discover that we are in communion with one other and all creation.

This has great resonance with the thought of Rupert Sheldrake, a British biologist who lived with Fr. Bede at Shantivanam for a year and a half while he wrote his first book, *A New Science of Life*.[24] Sheldrake's morphogenetic theory starts out as a biological one, positing that there are invisible fields, like gravitational or magnetic fields, fields of pattern, order and structure that organize, shape, and form both living and inanimate matter. These morphogenetic fields impose patterns on activity that would otherwise be random or indeterminate. However, these fields are not static; they evolve, handed on by past members of species through "morphic resonance." What is most interesting for our purposes is that Sheldrake believes these morphic fields also underlie our mental activity and our perceptions. A social group can have a morphic field, for instance, that can connect group members "even when they are many miles apart, and provide channels of communication through which organisms can stay in touch at a distance."[25]

This also applies to memory; Sheldrake says it is a mistake to think of memory as existing in space, as if stored somehow in the brain. For him memory is a relationship in time and is a "direct relationship between past experiences and present ones."[26] In this way the brain is more like a television receiver (albeit an old noncomputerized one) that does not store images and programs but tunes into and transmits them. In this he is actually close also to the thought of philosophers Henri Bergson, Bertrand Russell, and Ludwig Wittgenstein, who all challenged the notion that memory resides in the brain. If Sheldrake is correct, then the "whole of the past is potentially present everywhere," another example of Jung's collective unconscious, that "does not develop individually but is inherited."[27] It consists of preexistent forms, the archetypes, and it forms a sort of second psychic system of a collective, universal and impersonal—or is it transpersonal? or hyperpersonal?—nature, which Jung thought was identical in all individuals. And we can access this level of the spectrum of consciousness, tune into this realm of the mind, as it were.[28]

Not only is this similar to what the Katha Upanishad says about the mahat. There is also the concept of the "akashic record," which comes from Indian thought and made its way into occult and theosophical usage. *Akasha* in Samkhya and Advaita Vedanta is basically space or ether, regarded as one of the five basic elements; in Buddhism and Jainism too, it is thought of as a kind of permanent, omnipresent, immaterial substance. But it is also understood as the inner mind or consciousness of an individual, which can access this collective record because it is "a common substratum shared by all human minds."[29] Ideas that once might have sounded far-fetched suddenly have a certain validity and plausibility. Again, perhaps science is giving new language to phenomena that mystics have intuited or experienced for ages.

The *Nous*

We are in very subtle territory now, a subject for which we do not have much vocabulary in the Christian West, but which is being uncovered by Western science. And here is where the spiritual psychology of Asian traditions can help us map out the inscape and invite us to explore hidden depths of our own selves. There is, however, one key concept in the Greek Christian vocabulary that is a bridge for us as we move further into our discussion of the "spirit" in the context of the spectrum of consciousness and the inscape of the mind, and its relationship to the Spirit of God, and that is the *nous*, which Fr. Bede associates with the *mahat*.[30]

The term nous occurs in Plato and Socrates but goes back to the fifth century BCE Greek philosopher Anaxagoras, who described the nous as the transcendent cosmic order. (Heraclitus before him had referred to the transcendent cosmic order instead as the *logos*, the rational principle that governs the cosmos, but is equally manifest in the human power of reason.) For Plato nous is the high point of the soul, that which differentiates the animate from the inanimate. The nous is also that which can sort out and pass judgments on sensual perceptions.[31] Plato also gives us the first real use of a tripartite anthropology—*nous, psyche, soma*, or reason, soul, and body—in this passage from the *Timaeus*: "when the god [or *demiurge*] framed the universe, he fashioned reason [*nous*] within the soul and the soul within the body."[32] Some think that Plato is referring to two different souls here, one mortal and liable to passion and fear and the other immortal and above all temptation. But others hearken an explanation similar to Bede's ancient worldview of the three interpenetrating realms, the nous within the psyche, and psyche within the *soma* (body), with the cosmos too reflecting the supreme goodness of its creator, who for the Greeks is the demiurge. So not only every human being, but the very cosmos itself, is a living creature endowed with soul and intelligence. After Plato the nous/logos was always associated with both human reason *and* universal intelligence: "the transcendent source of all archetypes, as well as the providential principle of cosmic order."[33] Through those archetypes (or the Ideas) this universal intelligence permeates the created world, operating both in the natural world and the human mind. The tension of this double meaning—both in the cosmos and in the individual human being—is instructive to us as we explore Bede's idea of the "spirit" in the human being.

It's interesting to note how these two terms, logos and nous, separated from each other as they made their way into the Christian lexicon. The logos of course is the principle of intelligence that governs the universe, the fullness of which Christians also believe was made flesh in Jesus, the scandal of what theologian Hans Urs von Balthasar calls "concrete universality." As for the nous, I think here we have a concept quite close to what Fr. Bede and many other, especially Eastern Christian, thinkers call the spirit in the human person, especially given this dual resonance of the universal particularized, or at least operative, in the individual. This is the universal intelligence that both governs and is made manifest in the individual. We are each a nous.

As the Jesuit scholar William Harmless describes it in his magisterial book *Desert Christians*, the nous in the Greek Christian tradition is very similar to what we said about the level of consciousness that the Katha Upanishad, as we saw above, calls the buddhi. (The Indian tradition of course goes on to describe layers of consciousness between the buddhi and the Purusha in a way that I have seen no Christian mystic do.) The nous is our intuitive side, the level of consciousness that "enables us to know and recognize the truth of things instantly, whether a friend's face or a mathematical proof."[34] For Evagrius of Pontus, the great fourth-century psychotherapist and calligrapher of the desert, who was probably the first to write down the great *apophthegmata,* or wisdom sayings, of the desert fathers, the way the mind knows God is not a matter of logic or thinking; it is a direct intuition, and it is the function of the nous to receive inspiration by intuition. And so Evagrius wrote, "For knowledge of God, one needs not a debater's soul, but a *seer's soul.*"[35] In the Eastern theological tradition, the nous is the highest dimension of the human person, the mind of the seer, what India calls the *rishi.* It is also the "image of God within us," it is "that which is most like its creator. And since it is the most Godlike part of us, it is the faculty most capable of knowing God."[36]

The Unmanifest

The Katha Upanishad continues, "Beyond the great self—the *mahat*—is the Unmanifest—*avyakta.*" Before anything comes into manifestation to be known by the mind, it is first Unmanifest, in seed. This is where Fr. Bede turns to modern science that has stumbled upon mystical vocabulary, and he quotes the theoretical physicist David Bohm (1917–1992), who calls this the "implicate order." The great physicist Fritjof Capra uses similar language in his book *The Tao of Physics*, in which he describes how science through quantum physics has discovered an underlying reality in which everything is indeed interconnected. In Indian philosophy this is called the *mulaprakriti*, root nature or cosmic nature from which all creation comes forth. More importantly, in the spectrum of consciousness, this is the deepest level of our own psyches.

It is interesting to note that Mascarò translates this level as "the spirit in the world." Again to understand this in Western terms, we can turn to Jungian psychology, where we find some resonances. We have a tendency to think of our psyche as merely subjective, somehow only about me and my experience of the world. But Jungian psychology has discovered that the archetypes are outside of us as well as inside of us, and the psyche "is really something that extends outside of us, outside of time, outside of space. . . . Our psyche can function as though space did not exist. The psyche can thus be independent of space, of time and of causality."[37] Perhaps this is the function of the avyakta, a deeper level of the inscape of our soul. Jungian Lawrence Jaffe adds further that this is what makes us feel one with the universe. In fact, according to Jaffe, the psyche—perhaps Teilhard would say "a form of psychism"—permeates the cosmos. "Through the psyche we are enabled to feel a kinship with animals, plants, even the wind and the stars—not just because we imagine it so, but because we are in fact of one substance with them."[38]

We are "one substance with them," both organically in that we are a part of a tremendous web of interrelationships in this womb of Mother Earth, and also one substance with all things at a psychic level, as both Eastern mysticism and Western psychology will suggest. This is the avyakta, "the sphere of consciousness in which the human mind opens upon the universal mind." Bede speculated that this corresponds to the realm of "ideas" in Plato.[39] He also thought that this is equivalent to the *alaya-vijnana*, or "store consciousness," of the Yogacara school of thought that grew out of Mahayana Buddhism. Let's explore that a little bit.

In the Buddhist *Lankavatara Sutra* we read, "Out of mind spring innumerable things."[40] This word "mind" is how we often translate the Sanskrit word *chit* (as we saw in Chapter 2), but it's not really an adequate translation. According to the Yogacara school, this chit (or *citta* in Pali) is made up of eight different kinds of discriminating consciousness (*vijnana*): one for each of the five senses; one that is a kind of sixth sense that unifies the five senses; followed by the manas, the rational mind, which we have discussed above; and finally this alaya-vijnana, the store consciousness. The store-consciousness is supra-individual, because it is prior to any kind of differentiation. The whole world of forms arises out of this store consciousness spontaneously, playfully, the Hindu tradition might say, through the *lila*, the play of the Divine. As the forms flow out from this store-consciousness, they pass into the manas, the rational mind, and only at that level do differentiations appear and then pass into the senses. According to the late scholar of spirituality Alan Watts, what he calls "Buddhist Yoga"—using the word "yoga" in the broadest sense, as a practical meditative practice—consists in reversing this process, stilling the discriminative, abstracting activity of the rational mind, and letting all the categories and all the projections "fall back into potentiality so that the world may be seen in its unclassified 'suchness.'"[41] In other words, meditation at one point is an experience of having conscious contact with this deep layer of consciousness, the avyakta, the level of consciousness that underlies the differentiation and abstraction of multiplicity.

Remember too what we said about Teilhard's notion of the Omega, that it is the point where the universal and the personal, having grown in the same direction, culminate simultaneously in each other. But far from being impersonal, Teilhard thought, the Omega point is actually hyperpersonal, the convergence of our collective consciousnesses upon a center toward which all have been tending. The Omega point, the ultimate concentration of the conscious universe, reassembles in itself *all consciousnesses* as well as all *the conscious*.[42]

Then, beyond the *avyakta*, beyond everything according to the Katha Upanishad, is the Purusha, the Great Person who for us, of course, is God.[43] "Beyond that there is nothing."[44]

Buddha Nature

It is significant that we bring up Buddhism here, because we have now bumped smack dab into our diverging understandings about the *telos*, the ultimate end. This is in a sense where we part ways, at least at first glance, in our language. The Hindu tradition says beyond the unmanifest is the Purusha, the Great Person, the term now used as another way of naming God, besides Brahman and Atman. But the Buddha says specifically, *"an-atman"* (or *anatta* in Pali)—there is no Self of God or of the individual. Beyond the unmanifest there is *sunyata*, the emptiness that is the very nature of reality.

One can get the impression that for the Buddhist "it's all about the mind," and one would not be far from the truth. I remember suggesting this to a Korean Buddhist monk once, who responded to me with a big laugh and a smile and said, "Yes! It's all about the mind! Little mind and big mind!" In the *Lankavatara Sutra* we read, "I say there is nothing but Mind" and "Out of mind spring innumerable things."[45] Here is how the Tibetan teacher Sogyal Rinpoche describes the mind in *The Tibetan Book of Living and Dying*: "The still revolutionary insight of Buddhism is that life and death are in the mind and nowhere else. Mind is revealed as the universal basis of experience—the creator of happiness and the creator of suffering, the creator of what we call life and what we call death."[46]

This is the specifically Tibetan way of describing the mind, but there is the same basic teaching throughout all the schools of Buddhism, with perhaps different vocabulary. There is the ordinary mind, which the Tibetan tradition calls *sem*, the mind which "thinks, plots, desires, manipulates," flares up in anger, creates and indulges in negative emotions and thoughts, and "has to go on asserting, validating, and confirming its 'existence' by fragmenting, conceptualizing, and solidifying experience."[47]

Ah, but beyond this sem there is what the Tibetan tradition calls *rigpa*, the very nature of mind, the innermost essence of mind, "which is absolutely and always untouched by change or death." This rigpa, the very nature of the mind, is hidden within the sem, the ordinary mind; it is "enveloped and obscured by the mental scurry of our thoughts and emotions."[48] It is the "jewel in the heart of the lotus" that the famous Tibetan mantra sings of—*Om mani padme hum*. Awakening consists of this:

> Just as clouds can be shifted by a strong gust of wind to reveal the shining sun and wide-open sky, so, under special circumstances, some inspiration may uncover for us glimpses of this nature of mind. These glimpses have many depths and degrees, but each of them will bring some light of understanding, meaning, and freedom. This is because the nature of mind is the very root itself of understanding. In Tibetan we call it *Rigpa*, a primordial, pure, pristine awareness that is at once intelligent, cognizant, radiant, and always awake.[49]

This rigpa is not exclusive to the mind though. It is the nature of everything; it is what Buddhism calls "Buddha nature." And so to have this awakening and realize the nature of mind is to realize the nature of all things.

Now for the Christian, our vocabulary is different about this. What is beyond the unmanifest in our understanding is closer to the Hindu understanding: the high point of the soul (or *psyche*), where our spirit is in union with the Holy Spirit as our ground (as the Rhineland mystics would say), our source and our summit, is the Purusha, a person, even though beyond any concept of "person" we might be able to conjure up. But interestingly enough, when Fr. Bede wrote about this, in an article on the Tibetan meditation practice of *dzogchen*, he said that we go beyond our body, and beyond our psyches and "arrive at our pneuma, our spirit, which is the atman in Sanskrit." He then went on to say something that I found at first shocking: "It is in every human being. It is what is called the Buddha nature."[50] So he equates our "spirit" with Buddha nature! I often wondered how Buddhists would react to a statement such as that, until I read Sogyal Rinpoche, who pretty much agrees:

> Saints and mystics throughout history have adorned their realizations with different names and given them different faces and

interpretations, but what they are all fundamentally experiencing is the essential nature of the mind. Christians call it "God"; Hindus call it "the Self," "Shiva," "Brahman," and "Vishnu"; Sufi mystics call it "the Hidden Essence"; and Buddhists call it "Buddha nature."[51]

All this to say that, whatever words we use to describe it, whatever we call it, "there is a movement in the human being taking us always beyond the physical and the psychological to the spiritual, which is beyond word and beyond form, beyond all images and beyond all concepts."[52] And this is the art of meditation: to go beyond our body and beyond our psyche to this underlying and overarching reality, this highest point of the soul, our spirit where we are in communion with the Spirit of God which has been poured into our hearts.

I find that the words of the fourth-century desert monk Evagrius of Pontus sit very comfortably next to Sogyal Rinpoche's description of the rigpa. Evagrius uses the image from Exodus 24, when Moses with Aaron, Nadab and Abihu, and seventy of the elders of Israel went up the mountain and "saw the God of Israel." Scripture tells us that "under his feet there was something like a pavement of sapphire stone, like the very heavens for clearness" (Exod 24:9-10). This sapphire stone is for Evagrius a symbol of the tranquil mind.

> When the mind—having stripped off the old person—has been reclothed in the new one who comes from grace, then it will see its state, at the time of prayer, similar to sapphire or the color of the sky. This is what Scripture describes as the "place of God," what ancients saw on Mount Sinai.[53]

So keeping in mind the Christian conception, logic, and requirements of prayer and grace, we believe that this "place" in our own consciousness at the depth of our psyche, the fine point of our soul, is the place of encounter with God when, as the anonymous fourteenth-century author of *The Cloud of Unknowing* describes it in his other known work, *The Book of Privy Counsel*, we offer our "blind, naked being to the glorious being of . . . God."[54]

Cultivating the Realm of the Soul

What is the point of this exploration, this map of the in-scape? I do not expect that most of us need to spend a great deal of time exploring the fine points of the various descriptions of these levels of consciousness in comparative studies, as is the fascination of some of us in the field. My point here is merely to excite a sense of the depth of our minds, our consciousness, our souls, and to point out that in the Christian tradition too, we believe that at the height and depth of our soul there is union with God that is somehow already extant—and already achieved by Jesus and in the sacramental life of the Church, so Christians believe—and needs to be realized, and can be realized by this inward journey, an inward journey on which others from other spiritual traditions are embarked, though having different poetry to describe the points of entry, landmarks and destinations.[55]

The human soul is multilayered, and the rational mind, what is referred to here as the *manas*, is only one part of it. There is also the intuitive mind (the *buddhi*), very important in the spiritual traditions of Asia, where some say the real awakening takes place. And then there are all these other layers of consciousness as well. For ourselves, and for our children, for the people we teach and serve, it seems to me very important that we speak to these other layers of the soul.

A few years ago a high school principal and English literature teacher and I were having a discussion about liberal arts education and the notion of developing a philosophical and theological matrix upon which to build. Part of the project even for religion classes, it seems to me, besides ethical training or familiarizing young people in ritual, is immersing them in the stories, the myths of Judeo-Christianity, as well as perhaps even the mythology of Greco-Roman civilization before and surrounding it. I could imagine spending a semester just having students read the Bible as literature (as Fr. Bede did before converting to Christianity) so that they have the symbolic and mythological vocabulary, the archetypal vocabulary upon which to build the foundation for a spiritual life, that is always going to call one to the more subtle areas of consciousness. I was teaching a group of high school students once in a world religions class about the bridge between Hinduism and Buddhism, and I was keenly aware that many of the young people did not have a sense of history or any knowledge of their own philosophy on which to hang this new information, or a sense of why it would be relevant in a world that is ever more focused on expediency. And our souls are starving! But Jungians warn us that even if we were to rid ourselves of all the religious symbols in the world they would rise up again, because they arise from a subtle level of shared consciousness, the collective unconsciousness, the storehouse of the archetypes. If there is a vacuum of "soul vocabulary" it will be filled, and so rock stars and Hollywood actors get raised to mythic priestly status, Harry Potter and Nemo take the place of Jesus, drum circles replace liturgy, not to mention the fact that thousands of our friends leave Christianity for Asian spiritualities because our own have grown bankrupt of depth and imagination. I am not suggesting that any of these things are bad in and of themselves; instead they are signs that people are hungering for a sense of both the transcendent and the communal. Alongside of this then is a cultivation of the arts, which often gets lost in the expediency of business and IT: literature, poetry, painting, sculpting, drama, and music. These things are not just a preservation of culture and civilization: these things *cultivate soul*, and encourage the depth of the inner journey. Ewert Cousins wrote that this ought to be one of the major retrievals of tradition in the Second Axial Period, that the West would rediscover the kind of thinking that was characteristic of the consciousness of the primal peoples, the rich realm of spiritual symbols that is a part of our spiritual heritage, and the "reappropriation of our symbolic imagination."[56]

Let's end with this beautiful quote of Origen that sums up our asceticism when it comes to the soul:

> We are not asked to tear out or annihilate the natural activities of the soul but to purify them. That means we have to rid it of the defilements and impurities with which our negligence has covered it, so that it may be restored to its natural youthful brightness with the native vigour that belongs to it.[57]

In what imaginative ways—through the cultivation of our psycho-sexual-emotional growth, through the arts and literature, through exploring the spiritual literature of our own tradition and that of the other great world religions, through our immersion in the ritual and liturgical life and the practice of meditation—can we cultivate our souls and make this inner journey and allow our psyches to be vehicles for the inner light of the Spirit to shine through the whole of our being?

The Self is not known through discourse,
splitting of hairs, learning however great.
The Self comes to those whom the Self loves
and takes their bodies as his own.
Blunderers, charlatans, weaklings cannot attain the Self.
The Self is found by the pure, daring, cautious.
They who have found the Self seek no more;
the riddle is solved; desire is gone and they are at peace.
Having approached from everywhere that which is everywhere,
whole they pass into the Whole.
When ascetics have mastered theory and practice,
they forge the body, remember Spirit, attain immortality.
As rivers lose name and shape in the sea,
the wise lose name and shape in God, glittering beyond all distance.
They who have found the Spirit, are Spirit.

—Mundaka Upanishad (III.2.2-8)

10

Spirit: The Fine Point of the Soul

While we are dissecting these elements of our being, let's also recall the goal: to integrate the three levels of reality that exist—the body, soul, and spirit—at every moment. But in order to integrate them we need to give primacy to the spirit, and to the Spirit.

It could be said that we each begin life in a kind of unitive state, as we said about the baby in the mother's womb. And perhaps we could say that the evolution and growth of each individual person also mirrors the evolution and development of humanity as a whole. The Judeo-Christian foundational myth of the Fall points us toward just such a reality. Before the Fall, Adam and Eve are walking through the garden in the cool of the evening breeze with God, able not to sin, as the ancients taught, still caught up in a unitive experience with God, between themselves, and with the earth as well, a sort of union by communion, unity in diversity. Then came the Fall, with its consequences: The blessing of childbirth would be accompanied by pain; and the woman will desire to possess her man but he will possess her. There is enmity with the earth: Adam must now fight with the earth for it to bring forth crops by the sweat of his brow. Last of all, Adam and Eve are said to be somehow out of union with their own bodies, and so they needed to cover their nakedness. This must be a significant point because we heard twice in the story that they were both naked, and not ashamed; whereas after the Fall Adam says, "I was afraid, because I was naked; and I hid myself" (Gen 2:25; 3:10). And death enters the picture too, the entry into human consciousness of the awareness of mortality, and the fear of death, which could be the root of all subsequent sin. This is the fall out of unity. And all creation suffers for this and is in agony even now while we await the redemption of our bodies.

All this comes about as the result of the primary relationship being ruptured, the relationship with God, who is Spirit. And it can only be made anew by the reestablishing of right relationship with Spirit. But that Spirit is not just the Holy Spirit who hovers over the water; this is also the breath blown into the center of the lump of clay that animates and makes of it a *living being.* It is not just the Holy Spirit who rests on the heads of the apostles like flames; it is also the Spirit who is the love of God that has been poured into our hearts and shall flow from out of the believer's heart like a stream of life-giving water. So while we are reestablishing right relationship with God, we are also reestablishing right relationship with that deepest part of ourselves, our real self, hidden with Christ in God, the point of our being where we are already somehow in union with God, where that breath, that stream of life-giving water, that love of God, is its source. This point of our self-transcendence, this place within us that is our point of encounter with God, is what we refer to as our spirit.

Fr. Bede taught that this is the movement for each human being: from the original unitive experience of the mother's womb, we fall, if you will, into differentiated consciousness. The memory of the original unity will spur us on to the new unitive experience ahead of us, the Omega point, a journey in which our intellect and will play a decisive role.

Spirit, Soul, and Body

To recap, just as all created reality has a spiritual, psychological, and material dimension, so each human being can be spoken of as spirit, soul, and body. As already mentioned, this is not the typical Western way to speak of Christian anthropology. We do not normally distinguish spirit from soul, but we speak of the human person as either body and soul or body and spirit, though we do sometimes speak of the "spiritual soul." For example, the *Catechism of the Catholic Church* teaches that, "Sometimes the soul is distinguished from the spirit." The *Catechism* is quick to point out, however, that this "does not introduce a duality into the soul." "Spirit" merely signifies that from creation human beings are "ordered to a supernatural end," and that one's soul can be "gratuitously raised . . . to communion with God."[1] The word "gratuitously" is important here; this is part of the Christian conception of prayer, its logic and requirements, that this is not a self-powered exaltation, but a work of grace, God's initiative. This is fundamental in a Christian understanding of any spiritual work. Note also the use of the word "supernatural," which, while obviously having its place, is a word that was rarely used in the patristic era.

At any rate, Fr. Bede, among others, found this articulation of our spiritual anthropology lacking. On the one hand, he saw the need to distinguish between the spirit and the soul, to clarify that often phenomenon that we label as "spiritual" are actually psychic. On the other hand, he saw the need to understand and accentuate the importance of the spiritual realm, which brings the other two realms to their fruition. He believed that "we have to integrate these three levels of reality that exist at every moment."[2] Fr. Bede said that this tripartite anthropology of body, soul, and spirit was the main focus of all his thinking late in life.

That being said, there are actually two tensions involved when dealing with this term "spirit." The first is distinguishing the spirit from the soul. And the second is distinguishing, in

Christian terms, a human being's spirit from the Holy Spirit, the Spirit of God.

The Atman in Indian Thought

There is a similar tension in Sanskrit and the notion of the atman. Some words can have several different meanings in different contexts; and some words can have several different meanings and hold all those resonances together at the same time. The Sanskrit word *atman* is one such example. At one end of the spectrum, its root meaning is "breath" or "wind," "moving or pervading air." (It is fascinating that the word for "spirit" in so many different languages derives from this same root meaning, such as *ruah, spiritus,* and *pneuma,* all of which mean wind or breath, in Hebrew, Latin, and Greek, respectively.) At the other end of the spectrum, atman is a name for the Divine or Ultimate Reality. But then atman has a whole host of nuances in between. In the Upanishads atman is the ultimate essence of the universe as well as the vital breath of human beings, the spark of the Divine, immanent in everything that is, the unborn and undying reality behind reality. According to Samkhya and classical Yoga, the atman is identical with consciousness, we might say, "the ground of consciousness," which has no attributes, and is self-luminous and omnipresent. The Nyaya and Vaisheseka philosophies, two other Indian darshanas at which we have not looked thus far, think of atman as the substratum of cognition, but say that it is of two kinds, supreme and individual. And finally, the most fascinating understanding of atman and the one that we, along with Fr. Bede and his predecessor Abhishiktananda, wrestled with the most is that of our friends of Advaita Vedanta. They too teach that atman is the substratum of both individual and universal reality, but they insist that atman, ours and the universal, is identical with Brahman, hence *advaita*—"not two." To an advaitin the transcendent self of things is also the transcendent self of human beings.

My favorite way to understand this is to think of Brahman as the "ground of being," a term not uncommon to Christian mystics, and atman as "ground of consciousness," a concept not totally unfamiliar to Christian mystics but rarely spoken of in this way. Hence, Advaita would teach that the ground of being and the ground of consciousness are not two different realities. In other words, if I were to make that journey down through the layers of my own consciousness, beyond the senses and the rational mind, deeper than the intellect, the ego, and the store consciousness, and experience the very ground of consciousness, I would simultaneously discover that this ground of consciousness is also the source of all being, which/who we understand God to be, in accord with St. Thomas Aquinas. And so the Upanishads teach *ayam atma Brahman* (Brahman is atman) and *aham Brahm'asmi* ("I am Brahman"); the transcendent Self in the individual human being is the same as the transcendent Self of the Universe. Or, simply, the famous mantra, *so'ham* ("I am He").

In Sanskrit, distinguishing between what we are calling the soul and the spirit is sometimes done with the prefix *jiva*. The *jivatman* is the individual self. Bede and the Sanskrit scholar Sharma agree that this is equivalent to our notion of "soul." Fr. Bede employs the sense used by late Vedic and Sanskrit literature, referring to the jivatman or soul as the "lower self," or the self with a small "s." Here "soul" includes the senses, the mind, the ego, and the intellect, and the deeper layers of consciousness, all those separate components in Hindu psychology—in Sanskrit the indriyas, manas, ahamkara, and buddhi, of which we have already spoken. The intellect (buddhi) is of special importance because it is at the point of the intellect, which is our capability for self-transcendence, where we can go beyond ourselves. To us human beings belongs the psychological world that stands between the spiritual world of heaven and the material world of earth by virtue of our soul and its intellect. It is important to remember, however, that the rational and conscious mind is only one aspect of the jivatman; the soul is a complex organic structure in which many other levels of the mind exist—the subconscious, unconscious, preconscious, and higher forms of consciousness. Together they embrace the whole world of consciousness; there is a whole "spectrum of consciousness."[3]

But, to this way of thinking, beyond the lower self or soul (jivatman) of each human being, there is the higher self, the atman, which is actually the true Self, "the Self of our striving." The term *Paramatman* is also used, which means the Great Self, the Absolute, equivalent to God or Brahman.[4]

Of course, this way of thinking also entails a jivatman transmigrating from one body to another until the individual soul increases enough in knowledge to be freed from the cycle of birth and death (*karma*) by overcoming ignorance (*avidya*).[5] So, the Svetasvatara Upanishad teaches:

> On this ever-revolving wheel of being
> the individual self goes round and round
> through life after life,
> believing itself to be a separate creature,
> until it sees its identity with the Lord of Love
> and attains immortality in the indivisible whole.
>
> He is the eternal Reality, sing the Scriptures,
> and the ground of existence.
> Those who perceive him in every creature
> merge in him and are released from the wheel
> of birth and death.[6]

Liberation (*moksha*) is only achieved, and this ignorance overcome, by realizing one's true nature, precisely by realizing one's identity with the Paramatman. And so the Kena Upanishad teaches,

> Brahman is really known when it is known
> as the Self of each state of consciousness;
> thereby one gains immortality.[7]
> Power is acquired through the Self (*atmana*),
> Immortality is attained through wisdom.
> If one has realized Brahman here, then there is truth;
> those who do not realize it here, then there is great destruction.
> The wise ones, having realized Brahman in all beings,
> become immortal.[8]

Here is how the renowned historian of religion Mircea Eleade (1907–1986) explained it: "For Samkhya and Yoga the problem is clearly defined. Since suffering has its origin in ignorance of 'Spirit'—that is, in confusing 'Spirit' with psychomental states—emancipation can be obtained only if the confusion is abolished."

We human beings have a tendency to believe that our psycho-mental life—activity of the senses, feelings, thoughts, and voli-tions—is identical with Spirit, with the Self. We thus confuse two wholly autonomous realities. But we need to realize that "between psychic states and Spirit there is a difference of an on-tological order," Eleade writes. According to Eleade, liberation or *moksha* occurs when one has understood this truth, and when the Spirit regains its original freedom.[9] The ascetical life and all of our spiritual practices are about reestablishing this mastery, this primacy, this freedom of the Spirit.

St. Paul and the Bhagavad Gita

There is a fascinating section in the Bhagavad Gita that Fr. Bede used to explain his understanding of the dynamic between soul and spirit, in chapter 6, verses 5 to 7. Note how many uses of the word *atman* come into play.

> 5. *uddhared<u>atmanatma</u>nam <u>natman</u>amavasadayet*
> *<u>atma</u>iva hy<u>atmo</u> badhur<u>atma</u>iva ripur<u>atmanah</u>*
> "One should lift oneself by one's own effort and not degrade oneself.
> One's self is friend-self and one's self is enemy-self."
> 6a. *bandhur<u>atmatman</u>astasya yenamaiv<u>atmana</u> jitah*
> "One's self is friend-self when lower-self has been conquered."
> 7a. *jit<u>atma</u>nah prastantasya param<u>atma</u> samahitah*
> Supreme Self is rooted in the consciousness of the tranquil self."

Fr. Bede interprets this as follows: "With the help of your higher self, lift up your lower self; with the help of your spirit, lift up your soul. For your soul can be your enemy or your soul can be your friend."[10] When our lower self or soul is not controlled by our higher self or spirit, we are *an-atman*, literally "no-self." (It is interesting that this same word *an-atman* is used by the Buddha to describe one of the characteristics of existence; he teaches that there actually is no self! And note the use of *param-atma* in verse 7.)

How much of this can we convert to Christian terms? Well, Bede sees the same tension going on in Pauline language. A classic example of this in the Christian tradition is St. Paul's First Letter to the Corinthians (see 2:14-15). If we pay attention to the original Greek words instead of the way they are usually translated, Paul's words have a whole new sense in this regard: "Those who are unspiritual (*psykikos*) do not receive the gifts of God's Spirit, for they are foolishness to them, and they are unable to understand them because they are spiritually discerned. Those who are spiritual (*pneumatikos*) discern all things, and they are themselves subject to no one else's scrutiny." And then later we hear in 1 Corinthians 3:1: "And so, brothers and sisters, I could not speak to you as spiritual (*pneumatikos*) people, but rather as people of the flesh (*sarkikos*), as infants in Christ."

So you see, it is just as bad to be a "person of the soul" (*anthropos psykikos*) as it is to be a "person of the flesh" (*anthropos sarkikos*). There is something beyond both: to be a "person of the spirit," anthropos pneumatikos, because the spirit brings both the body and the soul to their fruition. Note how similar this is to the anthropology of the Bhagavad Gita above. According to Bede, if we were using Pauline vocabulary to express the translation of the verses from the Gita above we might say, "With the help of your pneuma, lift up your psyche. A person's psyche is a friend when by the pneuma one has conquered the psyche; but when one is not lord of one's psyche then this becomes one's enemy."

In some way our soul can be our enemy! It stands between the atman (the spirit and the Spirit) and the world of senses, passions, and activity. It is the soul with its intellect that makes the choice either to turn toward the world and the body, or to turn toward the Spirit within and live by the Spirit's law. It can be the means to go beyond to the realm of the Spirit, or it can in some way also be an obstacle. It is this function of the soul to choose between the world of sense and activity and the world of the Spirit that Fr. Bede uses to make the connection to biblical, specifically Pauline, thought: according to St. Paul, to live by the flesh is to live solely by one's mind and natural feelings, whereas to live by the Spirit is to live by the Holy Spirit who dwells within, at the point of *our* spirit. The former Paul calls anthropos psykikos (i.e., a person of the soul); the latter anthropos pneumatikos (i.e., the person of the spirit). And it is the function of the soul to choose to turn to the world first, or to give the Spirit primacy by focusing on our own spirit, our openness to the Divine.

Recall Gregory Palamas's notion of the Taboric light, how he taught that those who receive this spiritual light, first of all, can perceive that which is beyond all intellect, but also may participate in the divine energies and become themselves a kind of light. Evagrius, in his famous writing called the *Praktikos,* tells us that the proof of what he calls *apatheia* (the contemplative state of tranquility) is had "when the spirit begins to see its own light."[11] What is this light and where does it come from? Is this God's light illuminating the mind, as the sun illuminates the moon, a direct vision of God? Or is this the purified light of the mind itself, in its luminous primordial nature? Both Evagrius and the fourth-century "seer" John of Lycopolis, to whom Evagrius and his friend Ammonius journey seeking the answer to this dilemma, are cagey and ambiguous about it. Abba John says: "It is not in the power of human beings to explain it. Besides, the mind cannot be illuminated during prayer without the grace of God." And sometimes Evagrius says that the light seen during the time of prayer is the "light of the holy Trinity"; other times, as in the passage from *Praktikos* above, he says that the mind "sees its *own* light."[12] The passage we already cited above can now be seen in this context: "When the mind—having stripped off the old person—has been reclothed in the new one who comes from grace, then it will see its state, at the time of prayer, similar to sapphire or the color of the sky. This is what Scripture describes as the 'place of God,' what ancients saw on Mount Sinai."[13]

And where is the dwelling place of God but in the human soul?

An Open Window

The great writers of the Christian mystical tradition seem to dance respectfully around, like an Indian classical musician introducing a raga, hesitant to name this place, function, element, aspect in us that Fr. Bede calls the "spirit." Is it the nous? Is it the "image of God" stamped on the soul? For Origen, the "image of

God" in the soul is actually an image of the logos, primal reason, primal spirit, primal life, and the inner human being only truly lives and grows when we are in a dynamic personal relationship with that logos. Hans Urs von Balthasar, in writing about Origen, describes the place of encounter with a very attractive phrase: the "fundament of the soul." This fundament, he says—and this too is a gorgeous image for this aspect of human being that we are attempting to bring into consciousness—is "like an open window through which enter the illuminating rays of the Logos who is also present in each spirit as personal conscience." Ah, that's it! There is a part of us that is like an open window through which the illuminating rays of God's own Spirit enters us and floods our whole being, body and soul, with light. As to the question of whether the Logos and human spirit are different, like Evagrius and perhaps every smart mystic, Origen deftly avoids it, by using scriptural images of nearness instead.[14]

Fr. Bede explains that in the normal understanding of the Advaitic school, the school of nonduality, the individual self is identified with the Supreme Self. And so one can say, "I am Brahman" and "Thou art that." "It is an identity with the Absolute. That is a genuine and profound mystical experience without a doubt. By contrast, in the Christian understanding the human spirit is *never identified* with the Spirit of God."[15] Alduos Huxley's explanation helps too. According to Huxley, the Hindu categorically affirms that "thou art That"—that the indwelling atman is the same as Brahman. But for Orthodox Christianity there is not an identity between the spark and God. Union of the human spirit with God takes place—union so complete that the word "deification" is applied to it. Yet it is not a union of identical substances. According to Christian theology, the saint is "deified" not because atman is Brahman, but because God has assimilated the purified human spirit into the divine substance by an act of grace.[16]

Whereas much of the Hindu tradition understands that union with God is by identity ("I am Brahman"), the Christian insight and experience is that the Godhead is a communion of persons. Fr. Bede focuses on the language of love and points specifically to the Trinity as the example of this. Hence, for Christians, we look forward not to "union by identity" but "union by communion":

> . . . in love we go out of ourselves, we offer ourselves to another, each gives [oneself] to the other but you don't lose yourself in the other, you find yourself. That is the mystery of communion in God and with God—the Father and the Son become a total unity and are yet distinct, and that is true of [human beings] and God as well. We are one, and yet we are distinct. There is never a total loss of self. In consciousness there is pure identity, but in love there's never pure identity because love involves two, and yet the two become one. That's the great mystery. It's a paradox.[17]

Hence, Bede says that the Indian metaphor of the self disappearing in the Self of God as a droplet disappears into the ocean is not adequate for the Christian. You could say that the drop merges in the ocean, but you could also say that the ocean is present in the drop. According to the Christian articulation of this great mystery, "in the ultimate state the individual is totally there, totally realized, but also in total communion with all the rest."[18] What is unique in Jesus is that Jesus' jivatman does not disappear at death nor does it dissolve into the Godhead. Rather, the individual being of Jesus is fully realized; his body and soul are permeated by the Spirit and totally transfigured in the transcendent One. Bede says that this is where the Christian tradition has more in common with the Tantra of Kashmir Shaivism and some understandings of Mahayana Buddhism than it does with other articulations of Advaita, such as Shankara's, because they (the former) leave room for interrelationship within the Absolute.[19]

Now, this is all beyond our comprehension, but make no mistake about it: this is unapologetically an articulation of the Christian mystery at its most refined.

Distinguishing Soul from Spirit

What is the difference between the soul and the spirit in this way of speaking of them? First of all, to review, what is the soul? It is a realm, really, a spectrum of consciousness that pervades material reality and the body. Fr. Bede was very insistent that not only do we need to understand the physical in relation to the psychic, but we also need to take the psychic realm seriously, neither fearing it nor dismissing it, and then furthermore to distinguish the psychic from the spiritual, because most people confuse the psychic with the spiritual. For instance, in this understanding most of what we think of as "spiritual gifts" or "spiritual experiences" are actually psychic gifts and psychic experiences. This is a common usage (I would say a misusage) just as much for Christians as for non-Christians. There are psychic gifts (what we might consider paranormal gifts) that any person can have, not necessarily a good or virtuous person. This whole realm of the psyche is not only not necessarily spiritual; it is not even necessarily good. This is the major danger of psychedelic drugs, for instance, that may allow entry into the world of the psyche, but once "there" in the realm of the psyche there are good powers, there are neutral powers, and there are also destructive powers. And even if these powers do come to a virtuous person, even the great yogis tell their disciples to go beyond these *siddhis* or "powers" if they want to reach the knowledge of the Self or atman. Here's how Bede speaks of it: "They all recognize that this psychic experience is dangerous. . . . If you have miraculous powers people will flock to you and think that you are a very holy man, and your ego grows and grows until you are lost in your ego. It's very dangerous. Any kind of psychic power, any psychic experience, bliss or so on, it's okay as far as you accept it, but don't cling to it! You must let it go, because we must go beyond the psyche, the whole soul world to the transcendent."[20]

Prabhavananda, commenting on the Yoga Sutras of Patanjali, says that a "community of degenerated yogis, using psychic powers for business and political ends, would be even more unpleasant to live in than our atom-wielding world." So he advises his student to "stop hankering after the psychic powers and turn back to the true path toward spiritual growth," and he reminds his students of Patanjali's warning in the Yoga Sutras: "They [the *siddhis*] are powers in the worldly state, but they are obstacles to Samadhi."[21]

We must go beyond our psyches! This is also what St. John of the Cross counsels his directees, to ignore visions and locutions, and press to the height of Mount Carmel, because these phenomenon "can be a serious obstacle to souls in their journey toward divine union because by paying attention to them souls are drawn far from the abyss of faith."[22]

Then what is this spirit, that which is beyond our psyches? What is *our* spirit?

The Fine Point of the Soul

The human spirit is, to use St. Francis de Sales's phrase, the "fine point of the soul," the place of our encounter with the Spirit of God, where we experience God's presence. When we enter into the depths of our soul, or rather the depths of our own spirit, we discover the depths of God, the Lord dwelling within us. The human spirit is a dynamic point, the point where the human being is open to God, who Saint John of the Cross tells us is "the center of the soul."[23] This is the point of human self-transcendence, and if we respond to grace we open to the divine, like an open window through which enter the illuminating rays of the Logos who is also present in each spirit as personal conscience. Fr. Bede also seems to equate this human spirit with the thought of Karl Rahner, whom he said he "admired more than anyone else," specifically in regard to Rahner's notion of the "supernatural existential." He notes how Rahner taught that in every human being there is the capacity for self-transcendence. "Beyond our body" (note again the same language), "beyond the normal faculties of the soul, we are open to the transcendent reality. That capacity is in us at all times, and it can grow and become total, so it is possible for the human being to give oneself totally to God."[24] In describing the human spirit, Fr. Bede again even goes so far as to link up Rahner's supernatural existential, atman, the pneuma, and Buddha Nature, which we explored in the last chapter.[25] One of my favorite writers about meditation in the Christian tradition, who Fr. Bede also thought was one of the finest voices in our day, John Main, describes it this simply: "we have a divine origin, a divine source . . . the incandescent energy of our own spirit emanates from the Spirit of God."[26]

It is important to point out that in this understanding the spirit, *our* spirit, like God's own self, is beyond all phenomena, beyond all thoughts, forms and images, beyond descriptions and understanding, especially beyond all the "psychomental phenomena" with which we normally identify ourselves. That is to also say that God is beyond all of this. Both our Hebrew and Muslim brothers and sisters are in touch with a very real truth when they refuse any kind of image of God to be portrayed, just as the fourth-century Alexandrian and Cappadocian Christians, influenced no doubt by the desert monks and theologians, considered it akin to idolatry to anthropomorphize God—that is, to think of God being like a human being only in greater proportions—even in prayer. Any image we could come up with is surely limited and could never grasp the fullness of who God is. And there is also a part of *us* that is beyond all of this, that is the observer of the mind-soul, and that is our meeting place with God, the point toward which we are aiming in our meditation, beyond all phenomena, beyond all thoughts, words and images, the place of what the desert tradition calls pure prayer. The Orthodox theologian Paul Evdokimov has a very attractive phrase for this: our "apophatic theology corresponds to an apophatic anthropology."[27]

Articulating this truth is especially the gift of India, and the Asian traditions in general, including, maybe especially, the Chinese Taoist tradition, which we have barely touched on here. As Abhishiktananda wrote at the beginning of *The Further Shore*, his seminal work on the sannyasa tradition, India's spiritual tradition has made us aware of our own deepest center, "beyond what in other cultures is termed 'mind', 'soul', or even 'spirit' . . . beyond all its actual or even possible manifestations, beyond every sign which claimed to represent it, beyond all formulations, names and concepts or myths." Simultaneously they discovered that their own true self was "likewise beyond everything that signifies it, whether it be body or mind, sense-perception or thought, or that which is normally called consciousness."[28]

This is the subtle point that is the key to everything: Our most real self is our spirit which is—or *when* it is—in union with the Spirit of God, and when body and soul—our psychic being with its rational mind and all the levels of consciousness—are submitted to that deepest part of our being, then body and soul become flooded with the light and power of the Spirit of God.

Maximus the Confessor wrote that the gift of deification is "a grace of the Holy Spirit, a grace by which God alone shines through the intermediary of the soul and body of those who are truly worthy of this."[29] Our spirit is what we are calling that point where the Spirit of God meets us.

On the other hand, when the soul withdraws from its own spirit and the Spirit, it creates an illusory self, or what Thomas Merton calls the false self. What we imagine to be our real self is usually only our outer self, our personality. We may identify with our ego or we may identify with our persona, which is even more limited and illusory than the ego. But neither the ego nor the persona is our real self. In fact, the ego and the persona can and often do mask or hide the true self. ("Persona" literally means "mask.") Bede says that "To get through those outer superficial layers of personality and to discover our true person is only possible if we are seeking God. Otherwise we have no real self." Or, as the Bhagavad Gita teaches, we are an-atman. If we try to be a self without Spirit, "we are living an illusion."[30]

The Spirit Permeates

Now let's go back to one of the central ideas that we glean from Teilhard, that the Spirit, just as we can say of God in general, is not just an interventionist, breaking in from above or outside; rather, the Spirit permeates reality, or at least is meant to and, we can even say, wants to!

The twentieth-century French theologian of the *nouvelle theologie*, Jean Mouroux, sums up this concept beautifully, while conjuring up images from both Thomas Aquinas and Teilhard. We are embodied spirits, he writes—this is fundamental to our anthropology—and the telos, you might say, of life is for the spirit to spiritualize the whole person, body and soul.[31] It's that simple. As Aurobindo and Teilhard would say, "matter will reveal Spirit's face."

But Mouroux says the problem is that our embodiment is far from perfect; our body is only partially permeated by our spirit. We spoke at the beginning of this chapter of the unitive experience, both our personal one and the one we believe that the first human beings enjoyed. The imperfect embodiment in us is actually due to a certain lack of *being itself*, the being which, according to our foundational myth, God gave by grace to the first human beings, but which was lost at some point in evolution after what Christians call the Fall, and we do not get that fullness of being back even after our redemption. This is the state into which we are born: The human spirit alone does not have the power of spiritualizing its body; the spirit cannot become fully embodied. Recall what Fr. Bede said about death, that for most of us the process of transformation remains incomplete, and at death the matter of our flesh is not "fully assimilated by the Spirit," and is returned to the earth. Remember too how Fr. Bede says that the body has to sacrifice its autonomy, as does the soul, to the spirit and the Spirit. Mouroux uses similar vocabulary when he writes that the body's "far-reaching and tenacious" autonomy is the great peril and the great anxiety of the embodied spirit.[32] While we are in this present mode of existence, we await "in anxiety, in distress and in tears," what St. Paul calls in the letter to the Romans "the redemption of our bodies" (Rom 8:23).

There is another way, too, in which the spiritualization of the person is incomplete that has more to do with the soul, the mind, and the emotions. There is an "unruliness of the emotions" that threatens and enslaves us; and "there is division and temptation within the very spirit itself. The forces of egoism and pride are always active, always menace the fragile likeness to God." This unruliness and these forces are always threatening our fundamental orientation and compromising our free response to Eternal Love. This is the wrestle between the old person and the new. Here again, the root of the conflict, Mouroux says, is a lack of being, and being is associated with the Holy Spirit who is meant to *permeate our being through our spirit*! And that's exactly the problem: Our spirit "is not sufficiently penetrated by God"; our spirit is "not united to Christ to the whole extent of its capacity"; our spirit is "not yet entirely saturated by grace." And so neither our souls nor our bodies are permeated by our spirit or the Spirit. Prior to all personal sin and even after our redemption, we still harbor these virulent seeds of conflict because our beings have not yet been permeated by the Holy Spirit.

And so we suffer from a double lack, "a twofold deficiency, issuing in difficulties of every kind": We suffer from a lack of spirit to cope with our body, and we suffer from a lack of spirit in our soul to attain to God. Our personal history, our spiritual itinerary, begins with this recognition: We can be more and more captive to our emotions, egoism and pride, and empty of Spirit, or we can be "more and more freed and enriched with the true life."[33] But we are people of hope. We await the fullness of life; we await the full consummation of our being; we await the "coming of our Lord Jesus Christ who will transfigure our lowly bodies into glorious copies of his own" (Phil 3:21). We await the fulfillment when we shall attain to absolute communion with Christ, when Christ shall be all in us as he is "all in all" (1 Cor 15:28). Mouroux strikes a Teilhardian note when he writes about the Omega point as the union of individual perfected selves brought into communion: when perfect unity shall be realized in the bosom of perfect distinction, one sole image in a profusion of images. And each of these images, each of these members, each of these children, will be fully achieved in their being by their full relation to the Father and to the Spirit in the Son. "Because then they will all be one in Christ, and Christ in them, and the Father and the Spirit in Christ."[34]

Here again we have the distinctive Christian vision of the telos, the end. Remember Bede said that though a Hindu might say that the self disappears into the great Self like a drop into the ocean, this is not quite adequate for the Christian, because we believe that we will be "not absorbed but consummated," in and by the very act that unites us and makes us a body. And here a verb needed to be coined in English that is a wonderful play on words. Mouroux says we will be *"Consummed in one."* Not "consumed" with one "m" as in food we consume; but "consummed" with two "m's, which could only mean we will be brought to our supreme completion, our ultimate consummation.[35]

The Spirit Is Energy

The soul becomes God by sharing in divine grace, after it has halted all activity of the spirit and of the senses as well as all the natural energies of the body, for the body becomes divine at the same time . . . then God alone appears in the soul and in the body.

—Maximus the Confessor

One other modifier for spirit (and Spirit) that needs to be mentioned, perhaps the most important for our purposes: the divine Spirit is energy, and at the point of our spirit we receive the Spirit's divine energy. Note how often in the Gospel of Luke, for instance, the spirit is associated with power and dynamism: "With the spirit and power of Elijah he will go before him," "The Holy Spirit will come upon you, and the power of the Most High will overshadow you," and "I baptize you with water; but one who is more powerful than I is also coming. . . . He will baptize you with the Holy Spirit and with fire" (Luke 1:17, 35; 3:16). Back to my favorite bookends: God's love has been poured into our hearts through the Holy Spirit that has been given us, Paul tells us in the letter to the Romans, and that love of God is meant to flow from out of the believer's heart like rivers of living water, Jesus tells us in the Gospel of John (Rom 5:5; John 7:38). The Spirit of God is not a static thing and the Spirit working in us is not a static thing.

Here again I like the thought of our fourteenth-century hesychast Gregory Palamas, and the distinction he and his contemporaries made between God's essence and God's uncreated energies. Recall our earlier discussions about kundalini and shakti, not to mention the chi of Chinese medicine and perhaps even the divine madness of eros of the Greeks, which I associated with Teilhard's certain type of love behind evolution. William Johnston thought that Asian psychology and physiology might play an important role in the mystical theology of the future, and that this Orthodox doctrine of the uncreated energies could serve as an invaluable bridge between Christianity and the religions of the East.[36]

We cannot know God's essence, nor are we consubstantial, one substance, with God in the same way that the great councils of the church say Jesus was (the famous *homo ousias*). But we can know God's energies, which Gregory and his friends call the *uncreated energies* of God, which are at work in us. They are "supernatural" in the sense that they come from beyond the body and its senses, and are not natural to the body and its senses; nor are they merely mental and intellectual powers of the mind or the soul. This power comes from beyond all that, as Fr. Bede would say, beyond our bodies, beyond our souls. But at the same time, by virtue of our spirit, we can participate in this uncreated energy of God. It can flow through us. As a matter of fact, this is our right by baptism! Gregory and his circle truly believed that our intelligence and our senses, our souls and our bodies, could be, should be, transformed by grace. And it is this transformative experience that would allow us to participate in the supreme end for which we were created: union with God. Gregory writes that our sensual and intellectual abilities constitute two different ways of knowing, the ways we usually operate. "But those who possess *not only* powers of sensation and intellection, but have also attained spiritual and supernatural grace, are not limited beings in their knowledge, but know also spiritually, above sense and intelligence"—beyond body and soul—"that God is Spirit, for in their entirety they become God, and know God in God."[37]

Our created faculties, the abilities of our body and our soul with its whole spectrum of consciousness, are not enough for us to see God. For that we need God's own peculiar power, God's life and God's energy, in other words, grace. The Orthodox theologian John Meyendorff says that this is what Jesus did in his person: he united human energy with divine energy, enabling human beings to be in union with God.[38] In Jesus, because of the Christ event, a new portion of grace was poured out on the human race.

This is also what it means to be deified, to become God by participation, and this is our version of union by identity! Gregory Palamas spoke about identity with God in a way that was shocking, especially to those who were suspicious of—if not outright hostile to—his teaching. "All that which flows from the Spirit towards those who are baptized in him according to the Gospel of grace and who have become spiritual . . . still remains attached to its source; it comes from there and it dwells in there in its present and in its past existence."[39] Although we cannot know or see the essence of God and are not of one substance with God, Gregory emphasizes the inseparability of the essence and energies of God, because divine grace, the divine life granted to us, is not distinct from God. Meyendorff explains it this way: "In Christ and in the baptized, there is one sole indivisible Spirit and, in him, all distinction between created and uncreated is inadmissable."[40] When we participate in the energy of God through grace, the life of God becomes our life. Maximus the Confessor says that God and the saints have one and the same energy! And not only do we rejoice in the presence of God, but that presence is manifested to others through us. So deification is not only an individual gift of sanctity; it is also a way to manifest God to the world. Gregory taught that the saints not only participate in God; they also *communicate* God: "They not only live, but also bring to life." He also associates this with the divine light that we saw in the burning bush, in Jesus on the mount of the transfiguration: the divine light is "a gift of deification . . . a grace of the Holy Spirit, a grace by which God alone shines through the intermediary of the soul and body of those who are truly worthy of this." Meyendorff comments that the true likeness to God consists in making God appear through oneself.[41]

Another important point about Gregory's teaching, especially for our integral view, is Gregory's stress on the surpassing dignity of the human body, and not just that of the rational soul. William Johnston noted that this was a great breakthrough for someone who was so deeply influenced by Neoplatonism, and the "body as a tomb for the soul."[42] Even though this divine energy comes from a supernatural source—a source beyond body and soul—neither the body nor the soul are left behind. Not only the soul but also the body shows forth the glory and beauty of God; both body and soul are transformed by this divinization. As a matter of fact, the transformative divine light continues to be manifest in the bodies of saints even after death, hence the veneration of relics and tombs of the saints.

Could it be that other traditions, such as those of the Greeks and Hindus who have intuited something about a divine power with which we are fired into life, a divine "madness" that is the root of all love and creativity, have a Christian equivalent? Can we come to recognize that God has put this energy inside of us, so that we might share in the work of creation, so that we might become participants in the divine nature?

An Invitation to Divinization

Gregory of Nyssa said, "Our spiritual dimension, which is precisely that wherein we are the image of our Creator, is beyond our ability to explain. . . . By this mystery within us we bear the imprint of the incomprehensible godhead."[43] In commenting on this, Olivier Clement says that this is "the opening through which God comes to dwell in humanity, and through which humanity itself can ascend to God,"[44] an aspect of our being which is more important than our biology, our sociology, or our psychology. There is in us a spiritual depth that we rarely reach or realize. From our creation we human beings are ordered to a spiritual end. There is something within the human person that permits an encounter with the Spirit of God, a part of human being that can enter into dialogue with God's own Spirit, a permanent substantial invitation to a spiritualization that will permit the created to partake of the Creator's uncreated life. It is specifically this that distinguishes humanity from all other orders of creation. Our spirit possesses a knowledge that is deeper than our ordinary and even higher ways of knowing—the knowledge of intuition, where the knower and known are one, where love and knowledge come together and are not two, a knowledge that is relationship. There is in us a self-conscious inwardness, which is the product of the Divine Spirit as the principle of life, a created participation in the Holy Spirit, where the Holy Spirit is present to the human person. It is that to which our minds—indeed, our whole soul—must turn in order to be illumined by the Spirit of God, to be informed by deeper unitive knowledge. There is a mysterious part of the human being that has been stamped with God's image, steeped in the love of God. It is the means of communion with the transcendent that allows us to go so far as to say that we are God's offspring. There is a capacity within us that can receive and conform to the Spirit of God. It is the hidden person of the heart, one's innermost person, closely connected to the biblical notion of the heart, but the deepest heart, through which we can come to know God and enter into communion with God. It is the truest and highest aspect of oneself, deeper than our bodies or our souls, our capacity for God, the capacity to receive that can be filled by God and transformed into God, the gift of pure grace.

Perhaps most importantly, it is by virtue of this spirit that we are invited to divinization. At the high point of the spiritual journey, the Christian mystic describes the telos—that is, the end—in words similar to other traditions but shocking to many ordinary Christians. My favorite is St. Basil the Great's treatise *On the Holy Spirit.*

> As clear, transparent substances become very bright when sunlight falls on them and shine with a new radiance, so also the souls in whom the Spirit dwells, and who enlightened by the Spirit, become spiritual themselves and a source of grace for others.
>
> . . .
>
> Through the Spirit we acquire a likeness to God; indeed, we attain what is beyond our most sublime aspirations—we become God.[44]

The only real practical application of this notion of spirit is that it is to this that we are aiming when we speak about Christian meditation and contemplative prayer: to be in conscious contact with our own spirit and so with the Spirit of God, which, as Bede says, leads us to communion with God, and communion with one another, and hopefully through that also to recover the deepest most sublime understanding of our Christian faith.

For us the whole world has been purified
by the coming of Christ. . . . the whole
world has become holy, holier than the
innermost shrine of the temple.[1]

—St. John Chrysostom

Conclusion:
The End Is Not the End

Toward a Practical Integral Christian Spirituality

This book, like my first one, *Prayer in the Cave of the Heart*, is really the product of presentations that I gave mainly over a ten-year period. When I was asked to come and lead a retreat or give a talk somewhere, I usually didn't have to think about what title to give it or what the topic was going to be. Nine times out of ten it was "Spirit, Soul, and Body: The Universal Call to Contemplation." I garnered both of these themes from Fr. Bede Griffiths. *Prayer in the Cave of the Heart* dealt with the call to contemplation, and this book has now treated the spirit, soul, and body anthropology. Another way of expressing what my scope has been is captured in the subtitle: "Toward a Practical Integral Christian Spirituality."

From the beginning of my life as a monk I have been fascinated with praxis, the actual nuts and bolts of how to live the spiritual life, the monastic life being essentially an ascetical life;[2] and I have been equally entranced by the motivation, the philosophical matrix, if you will, that undergirds and inspires that praxis. Often, after all the theorizing on the "why" of the praxis, I would end a retreat or a conference by drawing on a white board, chalk board, or drawing paper a simple diagram of a large circle divided into four quadrants. And I labeled three of those quadrants body, soul, and spirit, but was always hesitant about what to name the last one. For the body quadrant I would ask the same question that I have asked in these pages—"What creative ways shall we find to make our bodies full participants in our spiritual life?"—and then make some suggestions based on my own personal practice. And so for the soul: "In what imaginative ways can we cultivate our souls and make this inner journey and allow our psyches to be vehicles for the inner light of the Spirit to shine through the whole of our being?"; and for the spirit: "What practical spiritual tools do we need to learn in order to cultivate this deep interiority?" But that last quadrant? I played with different words. At times I called it "incarnation" or "participation" or "charity" or simply "work" or "labor." Gradually I settled on "immersion," meaning both immersion in our own being and immersion in our world.

Sometimes there is a tendency to think that we need to pull off into isolation for a long period of time to achieve our own enlightenment before we can help others in the world. There is some truth to that, especially if one feels called to be a leader, a teacher, a minister, or a spiritual director in any way. But at the same time our immersion in the world and our involvement in the messiness of relationship itself is a "yoga," a praxis, a spiritual exercise.

Along with this re-embrace of our own being comes a re-embrace of the world and all its activities as well, another theme common to both Sri Aurobindo and Teilhard de Chardin. In this last movement I am also addressing the specifically monastic asceticism of withdrawal into silence and solitude. I believe and hope that there will always be a place and a need for the purely contemplative life. When so much of the Body—the Body of Christ, the body that is the human race—is busy and active, moving at a frantic pace, bombarded with constant input and stimuli, immersed in a culture of consumerism and materialism and a shallow yet insidiously seductive and ubiquitous entertainment industry, some part of the Body needs to counterbalance that on lonely mountaintops and in desert huts, dark cloisters and arid retreats. But at the same time even this monastic withdrawal needs to be relativized and put in its proper place. We often forget that the famous Scripture passage from the third chapter of John used to prove the unicity and necessity of Jesus starts out with the tender words "God so *loved* the world" (John 3:16). Sri Aurobindo admonished his followers not to get caught in the trap of a total withdrawal from activity. While in the past it was ordinarily thought and taught that a yogi (or a monk!) "should draw away from action as much as possible and especially that too much action is a hindrance because it draws off the energies outward," this is only true to a certain extent. He taught that neither the abstention from all physical action nor aversion to either mental or corporeal action was desirable.

I think again here of Carter Phipps's worry about the world-denying tendencies of spiritual traditions. The seeker of the integral state should be free from *attachment* to action, as is the prevalent theme of the Bhagavad Gita, but also equally free from attachment to inaction! Especially in Aurobindo's reflections on the Bhagavad Gita, similar to Bede's own thought on it, the great sage is always urging that one should arrive at a state where "the life and body perform as mere instruments of the will of the Purusha." Then there will be an ease and a grace about our presence and action in the world, and we "come to work as forces of nature without the fret and toil and reaction" that are characteristic of our lives before we have mastered the physical or, in Bede's words, surrendered the autonomy of our physical beings to deeper realities—the soul and the spirit. In other words, at some point "action and inaction become immaterial"; at some point neither action nor inaction can interfere with the freedom of the soul nor draw it away from its urge towards the Divine or its poise in the Divine.[3]

Father Bede was particularly attracted to this theme, and referred often to it as the *sahaja samadhi*, the "natural contemplation" as taught in the Bhagavad Gita. In an article about Hindu-Christian monasticism he wrote that the great message of the Bhagavad Gita was that "one can find God not only through the way of the ascetic, in silence and solitude," but also through one's daily duties, "if one offers to the Lord all that one does,"[4] in the same way Jesus never seemed to be bothered by being called out of his solitary moments of communion with his *Abba*, but rather "had compassion on them for they were harassed and helpless, like sheep without a shepherd" (Matt 9:36). The end is not the end. Our ascetical life is always meant to resolve itself in a life of immersion in the world in some way, a life of co-creation, bringing forth "a new heaven and a new earth" (Rev 21:1).

Aldous Huxley calls for the same thing in his chapter entitled "Contemplation, Action, and Social Utility" in *The Perennial Philosophy*. He concedes that monks, be they Buddhist solitaries or the desert monks of Christianity (the "hermits of Tibet and the Thebaid"), have certainly been single-minded, one-pointed (what Yoga would call *ekagrata*), but it has often been a one-pointedness of "exclusion and mutilation." He suggests that if they had truly been docile to the Spirit of God, they might have come to understand that the one-pointedness of exclusion is only a preparation for the one-pointedness of inclusion—"the realization of God in the fullness of cosmic being as well as in the interior of the individual soul. They would at last have turned back into the world riding on their tamed and regenerate individuality," like the Taoist sages, or the hero in the legendary ox-herding pictures of the Buddhist tradition; or they would have been like Jesus as he is presented in the Gospels, eating and drinking with publicans and sinners (or the Buddhist equivalents, "wine-bibbers and butchers"). Huxley writes that for those who are fully enlightened and totally liberated "*samsara* and *nirvana*, time and eternity, the phenomenal and the Real, are essentially one." Our whole life ought to be an "unsleeping and one-pointed contemplation of the Godhead in and through the things, lives, minds and events of the world of becoming." There ought to be no mutilation of the soul, no atrophying of any of the soul's powers or capacities. Rather there should be an "enhancement and intensification of consciousness, and at the same time an extension and transfiguration."[5] Huxley then goes on to quote none other than that bastion of Catholic orthodoxy, Thomas Aquinas, who taught that action should be something added to the life of prayer, not something taken away from it. And Huxley follows that with a beautiful quote attributed to Meister Eckhart: "What we take in by contemplation, we pour out in love."[6]

The end is not the end! *Streams of living waters shall flow from out of the believer's heart* (John 7:38).

And finally Teilhard sums this all up beautifully and poetically in an essay entitled "Christology and Evolution." Formerly, he writes, to adore meant preferring God to things, by referring them back to God and sacrificing them for God. But now to adore means "pledging oneself body and soul to the creative act, by associating oneself with it so long as to bring the world to its fulfillment by effort and research." In the past we understood loving our neighbors mainly as binding up their wounds and not defrauding them. But he writes that we have a broader understanding of charity now. Without leaving out compassionate action, loving our neighbor means that we give our life over for common advance. If being pure or chaste used to mean "standing aside and preserving oneself free from stain," in the future hopefully we will understand that chastity calls above all (and here he sounds like a perfect Tantrika!) "for a sublimation of the powers of flesh and all passion." Whereas being detached formerly meant not concerning oneself with things and only taking from them the least possible, much in keeping with the spirit of the Bhagavad Gita, he says, "being detached now means step-by-step moving beyond all truth and beauty by power of the very love that one bears for them." And my favorite one of all: "Being resigned formerly could signify passive acceptance of present conditions of the universe. Being resigned now will be no longer allowed, save to the warrior fainting away in the arms of the angel."[7]

The Four Oratories

I was fortunate to be involved with two Salesian schools for a time, both in ministry and by friendship. The Salesians are a religious congregation of sisters, brothers, and priests named for St. Francis de Sales, a saint whose definition of the spirit as "the fine point of the human soul" Fr. Bede loved to quote (from St. Francis's seminal work on spirituality, *An Introduction to the Devout Life*, which, incidentally, was written for lay people). But the religious congregation that bears Francis de Sales's name was actually started by an Italian saint named John Bosco, who dedicated his life to ministering to poor and homeless boys. I grew to love Don Bosco and his unique approach to education, especially his teaching about "the four oratories," the four places of prayer, *cortile, casa, scuola, chiesa*—playground, home, school, and church, which winds up being a pretty good example of exactly what I am after with my four quadrants. Don Bosco taught that not just the church, but also the playground, the home, and the classroom should all be considered oratories, places of prayer. Everyone (even, or especially, monks!) can take a lesson from this beautiful teaching. So let me use it as a summary of our work in the previous pages.

Cortile really means a "courtyard." In the Piedmontese region especially, I'm told, where John Bosco was from, houses are built with a kind of an open-air quadrangle court in the middle. But the word usually comes to be translated as "playground." The playground as oratory—I like that a lot! I gave a talk once at Notre Dame University on this same topic, "integral spirituality" from a Christian perspective, but I wanted to give it the subtitle (especially since it was at Notre Dame) "Why is it so far from the gym to the church?" As I mentioned earlier, what I have experienced of what competitive sports has become in the West—the behavior, the language, the attitude, the whole ecosystem—is usually quite different from the kind of environment one hopes to cultivate in a spiritual setting, let alone an oratory. One of the reasons I have been so fascinated with the Asian traditions, whether it be the martial arts or Yoga or the various Buddhist physical disciplines, is that there usually tends to be a certain attitude of a spiritual presence, or at least a mindful concentration on the unity of the body and mind involved. What would it be like if all our physical activities, even taking a walk, calisthenics, lifting weights, running, were seen as part of our spiritual practice? The bigger issue of course is what would it be like if we really understood that caring for our physical being is also an important part of the spiritual life?

I like also that the *cortile* is outside, because we need to recover more and more our relationship to nature, the out-of-doors, and understand how symbiotically we are tied to it, and how much our own evolution and survival is tied to that of greater nature. And this too is an integral part of our spirituality, if for no other reason than that we are stewards, servants of creation.

Between *cortile* and *casa*, there is also the issue of work. When I was a young monk I had a tendency to think that my work was something I had to get done so that I could get back to my cell and pray. But at some point my postulant master reminded me that I was supposed to be praying constantly; that's the goal of the monastic life. This is what we learn from the best of the monastic tradition, or from someone like Brother Laurence of the Resurrection finding God amid the pots and pans as he wrote about in his classic work, *The Practice of the Presence of God*. Not only ought we pray while we work; our work is also meant to be a prayer, and even the laundry room, the kitchen, the garage are all oratories. That's why in his Rule for Monks Saint Benedict says that we should *regard all the utensils and goods of the monastery as sacred vessels of the altar* (RB 31:10). I think here of one of our elder monks, Brother Emmanuel, sprinkling holy water on the tractor.

The *casa*, the home, means to me our emotional and interpersonal development. This applies to monks and other religious too. There is a communal aspect of our life and a relational aspect to being human. Our former prior general Don Benedetto Calati, of happy memory, used to say, "Before a man can be a monk, he must be a man!" There's a phenomenon spoken of often in contemporary spiritual circles called "spiritual bypassing." What spiritual bypassing means is that because we are outwardly "spiritual," we might have the tendency to think we can skip all that messy work of psychological and emotional (i.e., human) development, and just be like angels floating above it all. It doesn't work that way! We're not made that way. What if we were to understand that our interpersonal skills and our emotional and psychosexual growth, are all a part of our spiritual life, just as important as saying our prayers? I think this is why even the marriage bed in the Christian tradition is supposed to be viewed as a holy place. We only grow through, with, and in relationship—even hermit monks! That's how God made us.

Of course Don Bosco's *scuola*, school, is a symbol of the intellectual life. I love the title of Jean le Clerc's famous book, *The Love of Learning and the Desire for God*. It is one of those book titles that contains the whole message of the book, and this summarizes the monastic tradition at its best. Learning not just for the sake of learning, not for the sake of a degree that will get you a better job, not just to show how smart you are, and certainly not as an escape from the real world, but learning as a valid path to knowledge of God. Yoga calls this *jnana marga*—that is, the path of knowledge. The *whole* person needs to be developed. We do not leave our intellect behind either, but we reverence it as a part of the ecosystem.

And then finally *chiesa*, the church, what we think of as the proper place of prayer. All that has gone before is what we bring to worship; everything from the *cortile* and the *casa* and the *scuola* is what gets collected and offered up in our prayer; everything from the playground, home, and school is what is symbolized in the bread and wine that we offer at the altar; and everything of our physical, emotional, and intellectual beings is what gets accepted and changed into the Body of Christ, *the fullness of the one who fills all in all* (Eph 1:23).

I think of Don Bosco's *cortile*, playground, mainly as the realm of the body, and with it work and the material world. The *casa* and *scuola*, home and school, are the realm of the soul, both psychological emotional growth and intellectual training, developing the full spectrum of consciousness. And finally *chiesa*, the church, obviously, is the symbol of spiritual development. But note that they must all be held as oratories: all of this is "spiritual work"; none of this is done removed from immersion in relationship, the world and society.

Our World Has Eternal Value

Let's have one last word in summary from Fr. Bede. It may seem (and at times it even seems to me) that all this mumbo-jumbo, splitting hairs in differences between arcane philosophies, is just so much sophistry and a waste of time. But we all live with a certain philosophy and anthropology, a worldview that undergirds our lives, our thoughts, our actions. The worldview that we presented and examined here, based on Fr. Bede's experience and wisdom, has a very practical meaning, which is *that our world has eternal value!*

> It means also that our life in this world
> day by day, and hour by hour,
> has eternal value.
> And it means that history itself,
> the evolution of humanity and of the world,
> is all part of this divine drama.
> The whole universe is to be taken up into the divine
> along with the whole of humanity in all the stages of its history.
> All is part of this movement of the divine
> in matter, in life, in humanity,
> and we are all being drawn into that,
> such that our ultimate state is a total fullness of being
> as we experience the whole.[8]

Let's hope that one day we can see the whole world as purified by the coming of Christ, the whole world as holy, holier than the innermost shrine of the temple, the whole world as our oratory. The end is not the end. We are participants, co-creators.

Notes

Chapter 1   The Problem of Dualism

1. Marco Vannini, *L'Esperienza dello Spirito* (Palermo: Edizioni Augustinus, 1991), 41.

2. Jacques Dupuis, *Gesù Cristo incontro alle religioni* (Assisi: Cittadella Editrice, 1989), 154–55.

3. All recorded in Tomas Spidlik, *The Spirituality of the Christian East* (Kalamazoo, MI: Cistercian Publications, 1986), 109–10. See endnotes for specific references.

4. Sam Keen, *To a Dancing God: Notes of A Spiritual Traveler* (San Francisco: HarperCollins, 1970), 142. Gnosticism consistently saw an alien God—the *Demiurge*—as the creator of the body, the *plois*, and the cosmos. Thus all were to be equally suspected and rejected in quest of salvation.

5. Louis-Marie Chauvet, *The Sacraments: The Word of God at the Mercy of the Body* (Collegeville, MN: Liturgical Press, 2001), 6.

6. *The Dhammapada* 11:2-3, trans. Ananda Maitreya (Berkeley: Parallax Press, 1995).

7. Bernie Clark, *Yinsights: The Philosophy of Yin Yoga* (Self-published in Canada, 2007), 150–51.

8. Sri Aurobindo, *The Supramental Manifestation upon Earth* (Pondicherry: Sri Aurobindo Ashram, 1952, 2006), 10–11.

9. Sam Keen, *To a Dancing God*, 148. Emphasis not in original.

10. Ibid., 150.

11. Ibid., 155.

12. Cipriano Vaggagini, *The Flesh, Instrument of Salvation: A Theology of the Human Body* (Staten Island: Alba House, 1969), 16.

13. Ken Wilber, *No Boundary: Eastern and Western Approaches to Personal Growth* (Boston: Shambala, 2000), 6–7.

14. Ibid.

15. Wendell Berry, "The Body and the Earth," in *Recollected Essays, 1965-1980* (Berkeley: North Point Press, 1981), 279.

16. Ibid., 278–80.

Chapter 2   Axial Consciousness and the Darshanas

1. Sri Aurobindo, *The Synthesis of Yoga* (Pondicherry: Sri Aurobindo Ashram, 1957), 521.

2. Some, such as Karen Armstrong, set the beginning of this period much earlier. See her magisterial work, *The Great Transformation* (New York: Anchor Books, 2007).

3. Theologian Ewert Cousins (1927–2009) wrote that primal pre-Axial Consciousness did not contain that distinct idea of individuality that was necessary to produce a religious type such as a monk, someone who would adopt such a radical stand on the margins of society, not only in stripping oneself of material goods, but especially in opting for celibacy and chastity, which means withdrawing from family and community. Ewert H. Cousins, *Christ of the 21st Century* (New York: Continuum, 1998), 133.

4. Aldous Huxley, Introduction to *Bhagavad Gita: The Song of God*, trans. Swami Prabhavananda and Christopher Isherwood (Hollywood, CA: Vedanta Press, 1987), 7. See also Huxley's own *The Perennial Philosophy*. We'll need to ask ourselves at some point what it means to be a "manifestation of" something.

5. The six orthodox *darshanas* in generally accepted chronological order are Samkhya, Yoga, Purvamimamsa, Vedanta, Vaisheshika, and Nyaya.

6. There is also some speculation that Samkhya and Yoga, at least pre-classical Yoga, grew simultaneously.

7. Bernie Clark, *Yinsights: The Philosophy of Yin Yoga* (Self-published in Canada, 2007), 156–57; John Grimes, *A Concise Dictionary of Indian Philosophy* (Varanasi: Indica Books, 2009), 415.

8. Perhaps it is more accurate to say they are attributed to Patanjali, who is associated with two different figures, one a grammarian and the other a compiler. His name means "small snake" and "palm," the snake being the symbol of the cosmic serpent *Sesa*, who was in the hand of the grammarian.

9. The term *advaita* itself is also used by other Indian schools of thought that teach nonduality while still allowing for some distinctions within their system. For instance, as we have seen, Samkhya is forced

into a kind of duality between *purusha* and *prakriti*. But the Advaita of Shankara is pure nonduality.

10. *Pancadasi of Sri Vidyaranya Swami*, 2:66. English translations and notes by Swami Swathânanda (Madras: Sri Ramakrishna Math, 1967).

11. Shankara quotes the Atharva Veda, "The universe is Brahman," saying that the delusion is when we see it as having a separate existence apart from its ground. *Shankara's Crest Jewel of Discrimination*, translated by Swami Prabhavânanda and Christopher Isherwood (Hollywood, CA: Vedanta Press, 1947), 70.

12. As we shall see below, Sri Aurobindo thought that Shankara overstressed the notion of *maya*, whereas he himself preferred to fix on the idea of *lila*, the cosmic, divine play.

13. *Atta* is the Pail form of the Sanskrit *atman*.

14. John Peacocke, "Investigating the Buddha's World," *Tricycle* (Fall 2008), 47.

15. Peacocke, 47. He writes further that in the formation of certain Mahayana ideas he sees the irresistible tendency to "essentialize" phenomena, for example, when Buddhism arrives in China and in Tibet:

> In some cases I see them almost smuggling the *atman* in through the back door somehow. For example, if you talk about Cittamatra philosophy, then you're talking about the *alaya vijnana*, or "store of consciousness." In some interpretations this sounds very much like a self. When you talk about, say, *rigpa* [the Tibetan name for the inner mind], the notion of pristine awareness—awareness without an object, the only true knower—it sounds very much like Advaita, which defines Brahman as pure consciousness and the only knower.

16. Bede Griffiths, *New Vision of Reality* (Springfield, IL: Templegate, 1989), 159.

17. Ibid.

18. Bede Griffiths, *Return to the Center* (Springfield, IL: Templegate, 1976), 136–37.

19. Carter Phipps, *Evolutionaries: Unlocking the Spiritual and Cultural Potential of Science's Greatest Idea* (New York: Harper Perennial, 2012), 271–72.

20. One theory based on Aryan religious texts and human remains in an area called Mohenjo-Daro suggests that the Aryans entered the area violently, killing its inhabitants and burning the cities. Another theory supported by more recent evidence suggests that the Harrappan civilization was in decline before the Aryans arrived and the indigenous inhabitants of the Indus Valley already dispersed before the nomadic

Aryans entered the area, and the Aryans were simply able to take the region over. Also, even though only part of their language has been deciphered today, leaving numerous questions about this civilization unanswered, some still assume that the Harappan people "were literate and used the Dravidian language," modern day Tamil. (David Koeller, http://www.thenagain.info/webchron/india/harappa.html, ©2003.)

21. June Singer, *Androgyny* (New York: Anchor, 1976), 184.

22. Some argue the central ideas of Tantra were "largely lost or discarded in the Bhagavad Gita and in raja yoga as described by Patanjali." See Mark Stephens, *Teaching Yoga* (Berkeley: North Atlantic Books, 2010), 15. No matter in which tradition Tantra began, Hinduism or Buddhism, it is easy to see Hinduism as the original matrix of the Tantric elements in Buddhism also. Kogen Mizumo, *I concetti fondamentali del Buddhismo* (Assisi: Cittadella Editrice, 1990), 41.

23. Stephens, 13.

24. Carter Phipps also identifies two traditions that still offer hope in overcoming the antiworld bias: Judaism, with its emphasis on healing the world, and Kashmir Shavisim.

25. "Creation as Explained in the Tantra," in *Studies on the Tantras* (Kolkata: Rama Art Press, 1989), 120, 124.

26. Singer, 184.

27. This masculine-feminine polarity does not involve any duality in God, however, because there is, in fact, no difference or distinction between Shiva and Shakti. It is one and the same reality called by the name Shiva when the power of Self-reflection lies absorbed or is inactive or passive, and called by the name Shakti when that same power is active, and it is *chitshakti*—"consciousness-power"—when viewed or experienced as one. The entire outer world of objects is *within* this consciousness.

28. This feminine principle "does not supplant the male aspect but rather asserts symbolically the complementarity of the two, even on a spiritual level." Thomas Matus, *Yoga and the Jesus Prayer Tradition* (Bangalore: Asian Trading Corporation, 1992), 21–22.

29. Stephens, 14–15.

30. Singer, 186.

31. Matus, 22.

32. Kalidas Bhattacharyya, "The Advaita Concept of Subjectivity—A Modern Understanding," in *Philosophy: East and West* (Bombay: Blackie & Son [India] Limited, 1976), 11. He contrasts this with the Advaitin perspective, saying that the "Advaitin has no preference for this alternative."

33. Stephens, 13.

34. Including, we must add, some experiences outside the limits of conventional morality (Matus, 22).

35. Singer, 186.

36. Clark, 175.

37. Many of the *pranayama* practices (mostly breathing exercises), as well as the teachings about the *chakras* and the subtle body, and the chanting of mantras and some use of *yantra*, trace their direct lineage to Tantra. Hatha Yoga understands the body as the instrument of transformation by focusing its practices on "building a healthy body, one that would be perfect for the higher practices of meditation and samadhi," and serves as a "ladder to Raja Yoga," the royal yoga which contains the higher limbs of *dharana, dhyana, samadhi*—concentration, meditation and absorption (Clark, 182).

Chapter 3   Aurobindo, Teilhard, and the Second Axial Consciousness

1. Pierre Teilhard de Chardin, *The Phenomenon of Man* (New York: HarperCollins, 1959), 259.

2. "*prajna prasrta punîni* ['Wisdom that went forth from the beginning']. Omnipotent Wisdom created the World": "The Object of Our Yoga" in *The Penguin Sri Aurobindo Reader*, ed. Makarand Paranjape (New Delhi: Penguin, 1999), 165.

3. "Integral Yoga and Its Sadhana," in *Reader*, 165.

4. "The Yoga and Its Objects," in *Reader*, 9.

5. Aurobindo uses the word "inconscient."

6. From the Introduction by Makarand Paranjape, and the essay "Integral Yoga and Its Sadhana," *Reader*, xxvi, 176.

7. This threefold realm of mind-life-matter is pretty much identical to Teilhard's notion of the noosphere, biosphere, and geosphere, as we shall see below.

8. Paranjape, and the essay "Integral Yoga and Its Sadhana," in *Reader*, xxvi, 176.

9. "Letters on Yoga," in *Reader*, 212.

10. Ibid., 213.

11. Teilhard, *Phenomenon*, 78. Usually Teilhard refers to this simply as "cosmogenesis" and or "embryogenesis," but early on he uses this fuller term.

12. Ibid., 135.

13. Ibid., 78.

14. Ibid., 169.

15. Ibid., 180–81.

16. Ibid., 57, plus footnote.

17. Ibid., 78.

18. Joseph V. Kopp, *Teilhard de Chardin: A New Synthesis of Evolution* (Mahwah, NJ: Paulist, 1964), 30.

19. Ibid.

20. Kopp, 31. Later we will see this same idea of a spectrum of consciousness applied to our own individual consciousnesses, as Fr. Bede loved to point out à la the Katha Upanishad and Ken Wilber.

21. Ibid., 32.

22. Ilia Delio, *Christ in Evolution* (Maryknoll, NY: Orbis, 2008), 174.

23. Beatrice Bruteau, *Evolution Toward Divinity* (Wheaton: Theosophical Publishing House, 1974), 81. This had significant importance for Fr. Bede. At the end of his chapter on "God and the World" in *New Vision of Reality,* in which he addresses these divergent world views about the relation of the One to the many, he writes in very Teilhardian language: "We all form a unity which yet embraces all diversity . . . we are fulfilled in that Absolute in our own individual being, and in the whole cosmic order and the fullness of Reality" (175).

24. It seems as if this term is attributed to Teilhard much more than he uses it himself, which is rare. But he does use it, for example, in the essay "Human Energy": "Cannot a further and final metamorphosis have been in progress since the birth of love in Christianity: the coming to consciousness of an 'Omega' in the heart of the Noosphere—the circles' motion towards their common centre: *the appearance of the 'Theosphere'*?" Pierre Teilhard de Chardin, *Human Energy* (New York: Harvest, 1969), 160. (See also *Let Me Explain* [London: William Collins Sons, 1974], 69.)

25. Teilhard, *Phenomenon,* 291.

26. Ilia Delio, *The Unbearable Wholeness of Being* (Maryknoll, NY: Orbis, 2013), 69.

27. *Human Energy,* 145–46.

28. *Human Energy,* 33.

29. Delio, *The Unbearable Wholeness of Being,* 47, 49. Cf. Teilhard de Chardin, *Human Energy,* 73.

30. Sri Aurobindo, *The Synthesis of Yoga* (Pondicherry: Sri Aurobindo Ashram, 1957), 137. Aurobindo also adds frequent appeals to grace: "Every evolutionary leap is accomplished by the wedding of an aspiration from below and the descent of grace from above."

31. Ursula King, *Towards a New Mysticism: Teilhard de Chardin & Eastern Religions* (New York: Seabury, 1981), 29–30.

32. Perhaps in line with Ken Wilber's wonderful teaching about how both humanity and the individual human person are meant to evolve in the normal course of growth from selfishness to care/rights to universal care/rights.

33. Jacob Needleman, *An Unknown World: Notes on the Meaning of the Earth* (New York: Jeremy P. Tarcher, 2012), 37.

34. Ibid., 40.

35. William Johnston, *Arise My Love: Mysticism for a New Era* (Maryknoll: Orbis Books, 2000), 162–63.

36. Cousins, 133.

37. Bruno Barnhart, *The Future of Wisdom: Toward a Rebirth of Sapiential Christianity,* (New York: Continuum, 2007), 150.

Chapter 4   Incarnational Theology

1. On the Refutation of All Heresies, Cap. 10, 33-34; *Liturgy of the Hours,* vol. 1 (New York: Catholic Book Publishing, 1976), 460.

2. Ursula King, *Towards a New Mysticism: Teilhard de Chardin & Eastern Religions* (New York: Seabury, 1981), 34.

3. Note that I am using the word "myth" here in its broadest sense possible, not as something that is not true but that such truth is being proclaimed in terms that are not necessarily scientific or historical.

4. Hans Urs von Balthasar, *Origen, Spirit and Fire: An Anthology of His Writings* (Washington, DC: Catholic University of America Press, 1984), 57.

5. Jerome Murphy-O'Connor, *Jesus and Paul: Parallel Lives* (Collegeville, MN: Liturgical Press, 2007), 78.

6. So, even the New Testament, specifically Pauline, notion of the flesh warring against the spirit is not body against soul, but body/soul as contrasted with spirit.

7. José Pagola, *Jesus: An Historical Approximation* (Miami: Convivium Press, 2011), 392.

8. Bede Griffiths, *New Vision of Reality* (Springfield, IL: Templegate, 1989), 167, 169. The theory of the three bodies comes from the Yogic/Vedantic idea that reality is wrapped in a series of *koshas,* or sheaths. The gross body is made up of the food sheath and the gross portion of vital-air sheath—in other words, gross matter. The subtle body is formed of the subtle portion of vital-air sheath combined with mental and intellectual sheaths, and is constituted of passions, desires, emotions, feelings and thoughts. The causal body—*karana-sarira*—refers to

the bliss sheath, the highest or innermost subtle body that veils the true soul. We'll see later how this corresponds with Bede Griffiths's notion of spirit, soul, and body.

9. See, for instance, Matt 9:29; 15:28; Mark 2:5; Luke 7:9.

10. Pagola, 166–67.

11. And we are not even touching at this point on the social implications of the gospel, which also make Jesus and his teaching very earth linked, more or less accented by various Christians (from liberation theologians to conservative Republicans), but unavoidable nonetheless.

12. This theory was attacked by a man named Barlaam, who thought that this was polytheistic because it seemed to postulate two eternal substances, a visible (the divine energies) and an invisible one (the divine being or *ousia*). "In answer to this the Byzantine councils of the fourteenth century adopted the Palamite distinction between the divine essence and energies." John Meyendorff, *Gregory Palamas and Orthodox Spirituality* (New York: St. Vladimir's Seminary Press, 1974), 92.

13. *Apology, Coisl. 99, fol. 13r-v.* Quoted in John Meyendorff, *A Study of Gregory Palamas* (New York: St. Vladimir's Seminary Press, 1964), 175.

14. *On participation in God, Coisl. 99, fol. 26.* Quoted in Meyendorff, *A Study,* 175.

15. Jean Corbon, *The Wellspring of Worship* (Mahwah, NJ: Paulist Press, 1988), 35.

16. N. T. Wright, "Mind, Spirit, Soul and Body: All for one and One for All. Reflections on Paul's Anthropology in his Complex Contexts," Society of Christian Philosophers: Regional Meeting, Fordham University, March 2011, 2–3.

17. Wright, "Mind, Spirit, Soul and Body" 2–3.

18. *The One Light: Bede Griffiths' Principal Writings,* ed. Bruno Barnhart (Springfield, IL: Templegate, 2001), 277–78.

19. Ibid.

20. Gerald Vann, "The Water and the Fire," quoted in *Word in Season: Readings for the Liturgy of the Hours,* ed. John E. Rotelle (Villanova, PA: Augustinian Press, 1995) 4:142.

21. Griffiths, *New Vision of Reality,* 168.

22. Ibid.

23. As so often happens in Western Christianity, perhaps also in the Judeo-Christian tradition in general, the texts that speak about the interior way are brief, hidden, and go by so quickly that we often miss them. Take, for instance, the second story of Creation in the book of Genesis, chapter 2, in which the creation story is recounted relatively quickly so as to get to the point, a point which could also be a vital

lesson about the Holy Spirit for Pentecost: that breath blown into the mud becomes a living soul.

24. . . . to borrow a word from the theologian James Allison.

25. This event is known as "the cleansing of the temple," but I have come to think of it as the cleansing, the purification, the redemption of the human body.

26. There is one other place where these images of "Spirit like water poured into our hearts" come together in the liturgical tradition, on the Third Sunday of Lent (Cycle A). These are readings specifically chosen to prepare candidates for baptism at Easter: the first reading is Exodus 17:3-7, about Moses striking a rock at Horeb so that water flowed from it for the people to drink; the second reading is Romans 5 again (vv. 1-2, 5-8), the marvelous image of Pentecost, "the love of God has been poured into our hearts through the Holy Spirit living in us," which sets us up for the other moment in John's Gospel when Jesus uses the running water for the indwelling Spirit, when he tells the Samaritan woman at the well, "the water that I will give will become in them a spring of water gushing up to eternal life" (John 4:14).

27. King, *Towards a New Mysticism*, 34.

Chapter 5   Bede Griffiths's New Vision of Reality

1. Bede Griffiths, *The Marriage of East and West* (Springfield, IL: Templegate, 1982), 51.

2. Cousins, *Christ of the 21st Century* (New York: Continuum, 1998), 9.

3. Bruno Barnhart, *The One Light: Bede Griffiths' Principal Writings* (Springfield, IL: Templegate, 2001), 397.

4. For years I assumed that Bede himself had discovered this perennial philosophy through the Vedanta after his move to India, but later research showed me that he had come to this understanding as early as 1941, as evidenced by mention of it in his letters to friends, long before his full immersion in the Hindu world, though having already been introduced to Huxley. He then saw it latent everywhere, not least in his own Christian faith at its best.

5. Aldous Huxley, introduction to *Bhagavad-Gita: The Song of God*, trans. Swami Prabhavananda and Christopher Isherwood (Hollywood, CA: Vedanta Press, 1987), 6–7.

6. *Bhagavad Gita: The Song of God*, trans. Swami Prabhavananda and Christopher Isherwood (Whitefish, MT: Kessinger, 2004), 7.

7. Griffiths, *The Marriage of East and West*, 51.

8. Ibid.

9. The five *koshas* are the *Annamaya-kosha*—the material covering of food, the physical body and the material world, nonliving matter and energy; the *Pranamaya-kosha*—the vital covering manifest as breath; the *Manomaya-kosha*—the mental covering, the rational mind; the *Vijnana-maya-kosha*—intelligence covering, the higher form of mind, what we often refer to as the subtle realm; and the *Ananda-maya-kosha*—the bliss covering, the causal realm, the formless, beyond.

10. The five *skandhas* are *rupa*—material composition, *vedana*—sensing (including the sixth sense of mental perception), *samjna*—perception, *samskara*—mental formations, and *vijnana*—consciousness.

11. Ken Wilber, *The Eye of the Spirit: An Integral Vision for a World Gone Slightly Mad* (Boston: Shambala, 1998), 40–42. See also "Completing the Great Chain," from *One Taste* quoted in *The Essential Ken Wilber: An Introductory Reader* (Boston: Shambala, 1998), 108.

12. Griffiths, *The Marriage of East and West*, 51.

13. Bede Griffiths, *New Vision of Reality* (Springfield, IL: Templegate, 1989), 58.

14. Bede Griffiths, *Return to the Center* (Springfield, IL: Templegate, 1976), 96.

15. Ibid.

16. Griffiths, *New Vision of Reality*, 59.

17. Ibid., 57.

18. Ibid., 11.

19. Bede Griffiths, "Integration of Mind, Body, and Spirit," An Occasional Paper of the Fetzer Institute (Kalamazoo, MI: Fetzer Institute, 1994), 1.

20. Aldous Huxley, *The Perennial Philosophy* (New York: Harper, 1945), 115.

21. Griffiths, *New Vision of Reality*, 97.

22. See especially chapter one, "The Advent of Life," in Pierre Teilhard de Chardin, *The Phenomenon of Man* (New York: HarperCollins, 1959).

23. Griffiths, *New Vision of Reality*, 97.

24. Huxley, *Perennial Philosophy*, 165–66. Huxley raises an interesting point that devotional writers in the Western church chose to speak of the *anima*, the feminine noun that for Romans meant the lower, animal soul, instead of *animus*, the masculine noun that was normally used for the rational soul, because "the human soul is normally regarded as feminine in expositions of the Perennial Philosophy."

25. *Catechism of the Catholic Church* (United States Conference of Catholic Bishops: 1994), no. 367, 93–94.

26. Abhishiktananda, *Ascent to the Depth of the Heart* (Delhi: ISPCK, 1986), 216.

27. Griffiths, *The Marriage of East and West*, 36.

28. Abhishiktananda, *Ascent*, 274.

29. Wilber reiterates this teaching in numerous places. See, for instance, Ken Wilber, *The Integral Vision* (Boston: Shambala, 2007), 37–44.

30. I write this, mind you, as a member of a religious order and an ordained priest, not accusing "you" but asking *if* of "us."

Chapter 6   A New Asceticism

1. Wayne Teasdale, *The Mystic Heart: Discovering a Universal Spirituality in the World's Religions* (San Francisco: New World Library, 1999), 239–40.

2. Sam Keen, *To a Dancing God: Notes of a Spiritual Traveler* (San Francisco: HarperCollins, 1970), 148, 150, 155.

3. Bede Griffiths, *River of Compassion: A Christian Commentary on the Bhagavad Gita* (New York: Continuum, 1995), 114; *The New Creation in Christ: Christian Meditation and Community* (Springfield, IL: Templegate, 1992), 26–27.

4. William Johnston, *Mystical Theology: The Science of Love* (London: HarperCollins, 1995), 122.

5. *In Quest of the Absolute: The Life and Work of Jules Monchanin*, ed. and trans. J. G. Weber (Kalamazoo, MI: Cistercian, 1977), 114–15.

6. Sri Aurobindo, quoted in *All India Magazine* (December 2006), 19–20.

7. Griffiths, *New Creation in Christ*, 26.

8. Anselm Gruen, *Heaven Begins within You: Wisdom from the Desert Fathers* (New York: Crossroad, 1999), 76.

9. *Vita Antonii* #14 in *Athanasius: The Life of Antony and the Letter to Marcellinus*, trans. Robert C. Gregg (Mahwah, NJ: Paulist, 1980), 42.

10. Derwas Chitty, *The Desert a City* (Oxford: Basil Blackwell, 1966), 4–5. Chitty goes on to warn that Western Christians need to revise the ideas that we have inherited from Augustinianism, which he says "Augustine himself would have disowned," if we are really to understand the mind of the Greeks.

11. George A. Maloney, *The Breath of the Mystic* (Denville, NJ: Dimension, 1974), 130–31.

12. Spidlik, *The Spirituality of the Christian East* (Kalamazoo, MI: Cistercian, 1986), 63ff.

13. Simon Tugwell, *Ways of Imperfection* (Springfield, IL: Templegate, 1985), 28; see *Praktikos*, 56.

14. Maloney, *Breath of the Mystic*, 131.

15. John Paul II, Apostolic Letter *Amantissima Providentia*, AAS 72, April 1980. English translation published in *L'Osservatore Romano* weekly edition in English, June 23, 1980, 7.

16. Sri Aurobindo, *The Supramental Manifestation upon Earth* (Pondicherry: Sri Aurobindo Ashram, 1952, 2006), 10–11.

17. Sri Aurobindo, *The Synthesis of Yoga* (Pondicherry: Sri Aurobindo Ashram, 1957), 10.

18. Bede Griffiths, *Return to the Center* (Springfield, IL: Templegate, 1976), 93.

19. *Praktikos* 29 in *Praktikos, Chapters on Prayer*. Translated with an introduction and notes by John Eudes Bamberger, OCSO (Spencer, MA: Cistercian, 1970), 24.

20. *The Mother's Agenda*, vol. 2 (Paris: Istitut de Recherches Evolutive, 1961), 379–82.

Chapter 7 Sister Earth, Our Mother

1. *Sermo* 53, 1-2, 4: CCL 23, 214-16, quoted in *The Liturgy of the Hours*, vol. 2 (New York: Catholic Book Publishing, 1976), 816.

2. Olivier Clement, *The Roots of Christian Mysticism* (Hyde Park, NY: New City Press, 1995), 77, 80.

3. Amitav Ghosh, *The Glass Palace* (San Francisco: HarperCollins, 2000), 75.

4. Spidlik, *The Spirituality of the Christian East*, 188, see extensive footnote references.

5. There is no historically accurate version of this quote drawn from a letter allegedly written by Chief Seattle to the American government in 1854 in response to a request to buy the land of Suquamish tribe, but I find that the sentiments here are a very powerful and accurate assessment of our relationship to the Earth. (See, for example, http://www.barefootsworld.net/seattle.html.)

6. Sam Keen, *To a Dancing God: Notes of a Spiritual Traveler* (San Francisco: HarperCollins, 1970), 148.

7. Pir Zia Inayat Khan, *Saracen Chivalry* (New Lebanon, NY: Omega, 2012), 90.

8. Olivier Clement, *The Roots of Christian Mysticism* (Hyde Park, NY: New City Press, 1995), 78.

9. Ewert H. Cousins, *Christ of the 21st Century* (New York: Continuum, 1998), 132.

10. Huston Smith, *The World's Religions: Our Great Wisdom Traditions* (San Francsico: HarperSanFrancisco, 1991), 377.

11. Brian Schmisek, *Resurrection of the Flesh or Resurrection from the Dead: Implications for Theology* (Collegeville, MN: Liturgical Press, 2013), 104.

12. Carter Phipps, *Evolutionaries: Unlocking the Spiritual and Cultural Potential of Science's Greatest Idea* (New York: Harper Perennial, 2012), 68–69.

13. Ibid., 84–85.

14. From *Heart of the Matter*, quoted in *Pierre Teilhard de Chardin: Writings Selected with an Introduction* by Ursula King (Maryknoll, NY: Orbis, 1999), 41–42.

15. Ibid.

16. "Cosmic Life," quoted in *Pierre Teilhard de Chardin*, 49.

17. Pierre Teilhard de Chardin, "The Road of the West" in *Toward the Future* (New York: Mariner, 1975), 54; citing 1 Cor 15:28, "God will be all in all."

18. Pierre Teilhard de Chardin, *The Phenomenon of Man* (New York: HarperCollins, 1959), 293–94.

19. Clement, *The Roots of Christian Mysticism*, 54–55.

20. Bede Griffiths, "A Meditation on the Mystery of the Trinity," *Monastic Studies* 17 (1986), quoted in *The One Light* (Springfield, IL: Templegate, 2001), 380.

21. William Johnston, *Arise My Love: Mysticism for a New Era* (Maryknoll, NY: Orbis, 2000), 163–64.

22. Bede Griffiths, *The One Light*, 381.

23. Ilia Delio, *The Humility of God: A Franciscan Perspective* (Cincinnati: St. Anthony Messenger Press, 2005), 147.

24. Pope Benedict XVI, Message for the Celebration of the World Day of Peace, January 1, 2010.

Chapter 8   Awaken and Surrender!

1. "Dakhnī Oṁkār," in *Selections from the Sacred Writings of the Sikhs*, ed. George Fraser (New York: Macmillan, 1960), 98.

2. Bede Griffiths, *The One Light* (Springfield, IL: Templegate, 2001), 381.

3. Jean Bastaire, *Eros Redento: Amore e ascesi* (Torino: Qiquijon, 1991), 24.

4. Bede Griffiths, *The Marriage of East and West* (Springfield, IL: Templegate, 1982), 8.

5. Quoted in Shirley du Boulay, *Beyond the Darkness: A Biography of Bede Griffiths* (New York: Doubleday, 2003), 224.

6. Du Boulay, *Beyond the Darkness*, 225.

7. James Hollis, *Under Saturn's Shadow: The Wounding and Healing of Men* (Toronto: Inner City, 1991), 28.

8. Du Boulay, *Beyond the Darkness*, 225.

9. James Hillman, *The Myth of Analysis*, quoted in *Blue Fire: Selected Writings by James Hillman*, introduced and edited by Thomas Moore (New York: HarperPerennial, 1989), 269–70.

10. Du Boulay, *Beyond the Darkness*, 225.

11. Bede Griffiths, *The New Creation in Christ: Christian Meditation and Community* (Springfield, IL: Templegate, 1992), 42.

12. Bede Griffiths, *New Vision of Reality* (Springfield, IL: Templegate, 1989), 66–77.

13. Swami Satyananda Saraswati, *Kundalini Tantra* (Bihar, India: Bihar School of Yoga, 1996), 164.

14. Ibid.

15. Griffiths, *New Creation in Christ*, 42.

16. Du Boulay, *Beyond the Darkness*, 225.

17. This from the *Meditations on the Tarot* is worthy of further elucidation and study as well: "The vow of chastity means to say the putting into practice of the resolution to live according to solar law. . . . The heart lives only when it loves. It is then like the sun. And chastity is the state of the human heart in which the heart, having become solar, is the center of gravity. In other words, chastity is the state of the human being where the centre named in occidental esotericism as the twelve-petalled lotus (*anahata*) is awakened and becomes the sun of the microcosmic planetary system. The three lotus centres situated below it (the ten petalled, the six petalled, and the four petalled) begin then to function in conformity with the life of the heart; i.e., according to solar law. When they do this, the person is chaste, no matter whether he or she is celibate or married. Thus there are 'virgins' who are married and mothers of children, and there are physical virgins who are not so in reality. The ideal of the Virgin Mother that the traditional church puts forward is truly worthy of reverence." *Meditations on the Tarot: A Journey Into Christian Hermeticism*, Anonymous (Amity, NY: Amity House, 1985), 113.

18. *Wild Ways: Zen Poems of Ikkyu*, trans. John Stevens (Boston: Shambala, 1995), 58. (Thanks to Shanti Das for this.)

19. Griffiths, *New Vision of Reality*, 75.

20. Ibid., 77.

21. Unfortunately, as we have seen, Tantric practices have been abused since their earliest conception until today and often the true spirit of Yoga disappears from it. Instead, as Kôgen Mizuno writes about Tantric Buddhism, "a vulgar, often lascivious, hedonism substituted itself for it, of that which is indicated as Tantrism of the left." Kôgen Mizuno, *i concetti fondamentali del buddhismo* (Assisi: Cittadella Editrice, 1990), 40-41. Again, Bede's point—"Eros without agape is equally disastrous. It leaves us to the compulsion of human and sexual love."

22. Griffiths, 43.

23. Hillman, *The Myth of Analysis*, 65.

24. Quoted in Olivier Clement, *The Roots of Christian Mysticism* (Hyde Park, NY: New City Press, 1995), 22.

25. Quoted in Joseph Chu-Cong, *The Contemplative Experience: Erotic Love and Spiritual Union* (New York: Crossroad, 1999), 18.

26. Quoted in Bernard McGinn, *The Foundations of Mysticism* (London: SCM, 1992), 120. (*Comm. on Song* prol. [ed. 70.32–71.1, 71.22-25, Lawson 34–35].) I am taking some liberty here in only using the Greek terms to make my point. Origen uses the Latin *amor* along with *eros*, translated (at least by Lawson) as "passionate love," and *caritas* with *agape*, translated as "charity."

27. Ronald Rolheiser, *The Holy Longing* (New York: Doubleday, 1999), 4.

28. Ibid., 7.

29. Ibid., 193

30. Hollis, *Saturn's Shadow*, 28.

31. Richard Rohr, *Adam's Return: The Five Promises of Male Initiation* (New York: Crossroad, 2004), 131.

32. Anselm Gruen, *Heaven Begins within You* (New York: Crossroad, 1999), 76.

33. Christopher West, *Theology of the Body Explained: A Commentary on John Paul II's "Gospel of the Body"* (Boston: Pauline Books and Media, 1997), 3.

34. Ibid., 5.

35. Benedict XVI, Encyclical Letter on God Is Love (*Deus Caritas Est*), December 25, 2005, 8.

36. Ibid., 7–8.

37. Stuart Sovatsky, *Passions of Innocence: Tantric Celibacy and the Mysteries of Eros* (Rochester, VT: Destiny, 1994). Its reissued title is *Eros and Kundalini Consciousness*, which I find much less satisfying.

38. Du Boulay, *Beyond the Darkness*, 225.

39. "Back to the Beginning: An Interview with Andrew Olendzki," *Tricycle* (Winter 2003), 47.

Chapter 9   Map of the Inscape, the Soul

1. Quoted in Michael Strassfeld, *A Book of Life: Embracing Judaism as a Spiritual Practice* (Woodstock, VT: Jewish Lights, 2002), 10.

2. Though James Hillman prefers to refer to the soul and *anima* "becoming" psyche.

3. See especially *Care of the Soul,* the marvellous book by Thomas Moore, psychologist and student of James Hillman, for more on this.

4. Russell Shorto, *Saints and Madmen: Psychiatry Opens Its Doors to Religion* (New York: Henry Holt and Company, 1999), 15.

5. John O'Donohue, *Anam Cara: A Book of Celtic Wisdom* (New York: HarperCollins, 1997), 98.

6. Pierre Teilhard de Chardin, *The Phenomenon of Man* (New York: HarperCollins, 1959), 57.

7. Sri Aurobindo, *The Synthesis of Yoga* (Pondicherry: Sri Aurobindo Ashram, 1957), 511.

8. Katha Upanishad I.iii.10-11 (my own conflation from various translations).

9. *How to Know God: The Yoga Aphorisms of Patanjali,* trans. with a commentary by Swami Prabhavananda and Christopher Isherwood (Hollywood, CA: Vedanta Press, 1953), 16.

10. Lawrence Jaffe, *Liberating the Heart: Spirituality and Jungian Psychology* (Toronto: Inner City, 1990), 23 (citing "Letter to Pere Lachat," in *The Symbolic Life, Collected Works* 18, par. 1554).

11. Ruth Burrows, *Ascent to Love: The Spiritual Teachings of St. John of the Cross* (Denville, NJ: Dimension, 1987), 71.

12. Ilia Delio, *The Humility of God: A Franciscan Perspective* (Cincinnati: St. Anthony Messenger Press, 2005), 118. More on that: "It is not a direct vision of the Word; rather it is a steady look at the thing in itself—but at the thing seen precisely as sign, and so in the light of its relation to the Word. The Word is known in contuition only indirectly, as that by which and in the light of which the thing can be fully known. We might think of contuition as a type of intuition, a sense of 'something more' than what immediately strikes the eye. As Leonard Bowman writes, 'the awareness of the Word attained through contuition requires a capacity to perceive a paradox, to hold the mind in balance so the direct object can be perceived by way of an unseen light. To see only the object is

to miss its meaning; yet if it tries to see that light itself, it goes away.' " (Leonard J Bowman, "Bonaventure's 'Contuition' and Heidegger's 'Thinking': Some Parallels," *Franciscan Studies*, 37 [1977]: 24–25).

13. James Hollis, *Under Saturn's Shadow: The Wounding and Healing of Men* (Toronto: Inner City, 1991, 29.

14. Russell Shorto, *Saints and Madmen: How Science Got Religion* (New York: Henry Holt, 1999), 14–15.

15. Kabir Edmund Helminski, *Living Presence: A Sufi Way to Mindfulness and the Essential Self* (New York: Jeremy O. Tarcher, 1992), 64.

16. Oh that our spiritual communities could be those safe and healthy environments! They are often not, sadly.

17. Helminski, *Living Presence*, 64. More on that: "The ego is formed through trying to hold a place for ourselves in a world that has many contrary forces. As we grow into life, we face challenges and demands. We attempt to establish a position from which or through which to act."

18. Transcribed from unpublished video of Bede Griffiths lecturing in Australia in 1992.

19. O'Donohue, *Anam Cara*, 98.

20. *How to Know God*, 40; "*Mahat* in turn produces *ahamkara*, the ego principle" (The Oxford Dictionary of World Religions). It also adds that in Samkhya (and other nontheistic) philosophy, *mahat* is "the first evolution of *mulaprakriti*," and "synonymous with *buddhi* (intellect)," which is slightly different from how Bede understood it, or how Prabhvananda describes it above in footnote 2.

21. Swami Prabhavananda's commentary on the Yoga Sutras maps out a slightly different inscape than the Katha Upanishad, recalling Samkhya philosophy: "The first stage of evolution from undifferentiated Prakriti is called *mahat*, 'the great cause.' Mahat is the cosmic ego sense, the first dawning of differentiated consciousness. From mahat is evolved buddhi, the discriminating faculty. . . . From buddhi is evolved *ahamkar*, the individual ego-sense. From *ahamkar*, the lines of evolution branch off in three different directions—to produce manas, the recording faculty; the five powers of perception (sight, smell, hearing, taste, touch); the five organs of action (tongue, feet, hands, and the organs of evacuation and procreation); then the five *tanmatras*, which are the subtle inner essences of sound, feel, aspect, flavor and odor." *How to Know God*, 40.

22. Bede Griffiths, *Marriage of East and West* (Springfield, IL: Templegate, 1982), 76.

23. The 1989 Hibbert Lecture, AIM Monastic Bulletin no. 49 (1991), English edition, 51–58.

24. The book is in fact dedicated to Fr. Bede. As Shirley du Boulay recounts in her biography of Bede, Sheldrake discussed this book page by page with Bede, who gave him "remarkable insights into the philosophy of form, the scholastic understanding of the soul, and other metaphysical matters," while Sheldrake in turn introduced Bede to the thought of David Bohm and many other ideas from the realm of modern science. *Beyond the Darkness* (New York: Doubleday, 2003), 198.

25. "Wrong Turn: Biologist Rupert Sheldrake on How Science Lost Its Way," Mark Leviton, *The Sun*, February 2013, 7.

26. Ibid.

27. C. G. Jung, *The Archetypes and the Collective Unconscious* (London: Routledge & Kegan Paul, 1959), 43.

28. There is something resonant here also in the thought of the Australian philosopher David Chalmers. Whereas so many modern thinkers tend to see consciousness simply as an attribute of physicality and biology, Chalmers believes that consciousness is not physical at all, but actually one of the primitive fundamental entities of the universe, like mass, time, or space. The implications of this are astounding. If you distinguish consciousness from biology, if consciousness is a "primitive" like mass or space, then perhaps it is as universal as mass or space, and we could even refer to a sort of "panpsychism," the idea that "consciousness exists, in some very basic form, in all matter, even at the level of the atom." This is also very resonant with Teilhard's notion of psychism and cosmic embryogenesis, the idea that humans are "continuous with the rest of the world, even the inanimate parts of it, even stones and rivers, that consciousness penetrates very deep, perhaps all the way down into the natural order of things. See Larissa MacFarquhar, "Two Heads," *The New Yorker*, Feb. 12, 2007, 66–67.

29. Rupert Sheldrake, *A New Science of Life* (Los Angeles: Tarcher, 1981), 27.

30. Bede Griffiths, *New Vision of Reality* (Springfield, IL: Templegate, 1989), 53.

31. David Stacey, *The Pauline View of Man in Relation to its Judaic and Hellenistic Background* (New York: MacMillan: 1956), 74.

32. Plato, *Timaeus*, 30 b-c, trans. Francis Cornford (Indianapolis: Bobbs-Merrill, 1959).

33. Eric Voegelin, *Plato* (Baton Rouge, LA.: Louisiana State University Press, 1966), 196.

34. William Harmless, *Desert Christians: An Introduction to the Literature of Early Monasticism* (Oxford: Oxford University Press, 2004), 352.

35. *Kephalia gnostica* 4.90, quoted in ibid., 352.

36. Ibid.

37. *C. G. Jung, Emma Jung and Toni Wolff,* edited by Ferne Jensen (San Francisco: Analytical Club of San Francisco, 1982), 62, 65.

38. Jaffe, *Liberating the Heart,* 73.

39. Griffiths, *Marriage of East and West,* 72.

40. Lankavatara Sutra 154: 29-33, in Allen Watts, *The Way of Zen* (New York: Vintage, 1957), 74–75.

41. This is when the Bodhisattva awakens to *karuna,* or compassion: When we see into the true nature of reality, we feel compassion for all who are suffering because they are still in the bonds of ignorance. Out of that compassion, the Bodhisattva lets all the projections arise again, but now having become consciously identified with the *sunya,* the playful, purposeless *lila* of Ultimate Reality, the Void, the Divine Source.

42. In the Bhagavad Gita the *avyakta* is where souls dwell before and after death: "before birth beings are not manifest to our human senses; at death they return to the Unmanifest–*avyakta* again. They are manifest only in the interim between birth and death" (Bhagavad Gita 2:28). The Christian tradition, of course, does not hold to the preexistence of individual souls.

43. Bede Griffiths, "Dzogchen and Christian Contemplation," *A.I.M. (Alliance for International Monasticism),* 55 (1993), 122–25.

44. "In the early Upanishads, the inner part of a human being is often called *purusa,* 'man' or 'person,' rather than *atman.* Here the inner reality is pictured in almost physical form as a tiny being moving inside the body, a 'dwarf,' 'a thumb in length,' 'like a rice-grain or a barley-corn,' yet mysteriously as large as space. Some of the texts envisage a series of purusas or atmans, of increasingly subtle form, from the physical body to the inmost self." *The Upanishads,* Translation and Introduction by Valerie Roebuck (New Delhi, Penguin, 2000), xvii–xviii.

45. Lankavatara Sutra 154: 29-33, in Watts, 74–75.

46. Sogyal Rinpoche, *The Tibetan Book of Living and Dying* (San Francisco: HarperCollins, 1992), 46–47.

47. Ibid.

48. Ibid.

49. Ibid.

50. Griffiths, "Dzogchen and Christian Contemplation," 122–25.

51. Sogyal Rinpoche, *The Tibetan Book of Living and Dying,* 47.

52. Transcribed from unpublished video of Bede Griffiths lecturing in Australia in 1992.

53. *Peri logimon* 39, trans. William Harmless, in *Mystics* (New York: Oxford University Press, 2008), 152.

54. Chapter 5 of "The Book of Privy Counseling" in *The Cloud of Unknowing and the Book of Privy Counseling*, edited with an introduction by William Johnston (Garden City, NY: Image, 1973), 172.

55. See here again the admonition of "Letter to the Bishops of the Catholic Church on Some Aspects of Christian Meditation," issued by the Congregation for the Doctrine of the Faith in 1989, from chapter V on "Questions of Method": "The majority of the great religions which have sought union with God in prayer have also pointed out ways to achieve it. Just as 'the Catholic church rejects nothing of what is true and holy in these religions,' *neither should these ways be rejected out of hand simply because they are not Christian.* On the contrary, one can take from them what is useful so long as the Christian conception of prayer, its logic and requirements are never obscured. It is within the context of all of this that these bits and pieces should be taken up and expressed anew."

56. Ewert H. Cousins, *Christ of the 21st Century* (New York: Continuum, 1998), 32.

57. Origen, *Sermons on Joshua*, 22:4 (GCS 7:436); quoted in Olivier Clement, *The Roots of Christian Mysticism*, 176.

Chapter 10   Spirit: The Fine Point of the Soul

1. *Catechism of the Catholic Church* (Washington, DC: United States Conference of Catholic Bishops: 1994), no. 367.

2. Bede Griffiths, "Integration of Mind, Body, and Spirit," An Occasional Paper of the Fetzer Institute (Kalamazoo, MI: Fetzer Institute, 1994), 1.

3. Bede Griffiths, *Return to the Center* (Springfield, IL: Templegate, 1976), 108; *New Vision of Reality* (Springfield, IL: Templegate, 1989), 29, 60.

4. As we noted, Samkhya philosophy, on the other hand, uses this term for the conscious individual, equivalent to the *Purusha.*

5. Baldev Raj Sharma, *The Concept of Atman in the Principal Upanishads* (New Delhi: Dinesh Publications, 1972), 108–9.

6. *Svetashvatara Upanishad*, I.6–7.

7. This is the meaning given by Shankara, but Valerie Roebuck's literal translation is "It is thought of when it is realized by awakening to it."

8. *Kena Upanishad*, II.4-5.

9. Mircea Eleade, *Yoga: Immortality and Freedom* (Princeton, NJ: Princeton University Press, 1989), 14–15.

10. Bede Griffiths, *River of Compassion: A Christian Commentary on the Bhagavad Gita* (New York: Continuum, 1995), 108–9. Zaehner and Mascaró, whose texts Griffiths uses for his commentary on the Bhagavad Gita, agree with this interpretation.

11. *The Praktikos: Chapters on Prayer*, trans. with an introduction and notes by John Eudes Bamberger (Spencer, MA: Cistercian, 1970), no. 64.

12. William Harmless, *Desert Christians: An Introduction to the Literature of Early Monasticism* (Oxford: Oxford University Press, 2004), 353.

13. *Peri logimon* 39, trans. William Harmless, in *Mystics* (New York: Oxford University Press, 2008), 152.

14. Hans Urs von Balthasar, *Origen, Spirit and Fire: An Anthology of His Writings* (Washington, DC: Catholic University of America Press, 1984), 75.

15. Griffiths, *New Vision*, 222–23.

16. Aldous Huxley, Introduction to *Bhagavad-Gita: The Song of God*, trans. Swami Prabhavananda and Christopher Isherwood (Hollywood, CA: Vedanta Press, 1987), 10.

17. Bede Griffiths quoted in Rene Weber, *Dialogues with Saints and Sages* (London: Routledge & Kegan Paul, 1986), 171.

18. Weber, *Dialogues*, 172

19. Griffiths, *New Vision*, 168–69.

20. Transcribed from unpublished video footage of Bede Griffiths in Australia in 1992.

21. *How to Know God: The Yoga Aphorisms of Patanali*, trans. with a commentary by Swami Prabhavananda and Christopher Isherwood (Hollywood, CA: Vedanta Press, 1953, 1981), 182.

22. *Ascent of Mount Carmel*, 2, 29:5. *The Collected Works of John of the Cross*, trans. Kieran Kavanaugh and Otilio Rodriguez (Washington, DC: OCS Publications, 1991).

23. *Living Flame of Love* 1:12: "The soul's center is God." Kavanaugh and Rodriguez, *Collected Works.*

24. Weber, *Dialogues*, 173.

25. Bede Griffiths, "Dzogchen and Christian Contemplation," *A.I.M. (Alliance for International Monasticsm)* 55 (1993), 122–25.

26. John Main, "The Door to Silence," quoted in *Silence and Stillness in Every Season: Daily Readings with John Main* (New York: Continuum, 1997), 156.

27. Paul Evdokimov, *Woman and the Salvation of the World: A Christian Anthropology on the Charisms of Woman* (Crestwood, NY: St. Vladmir's Seminary Press, 1994), 43.

28. Abhishiktananda, *The Further Shore* (Delhi: ISPCK, 1975), 1.

29. *Against Akindynos*, IV, 22 *Coisl*. 98; quoted in John Meyendorff, *A Study of Gregory Palamas*, trans. by George Lawrence (London: The Faith Press, 1964), 175.

30. Griffiths, *River of Compassion*, 109.

31. Jean Mouroux, *The Meaning of Man* (New York: Sheed & Ward, 1948), 140.

32. Ibid., 141.

33. Ibid., 141–42.

34. Ibid., 142.

35. Ibid.

36. William Johnston, *Mystical Theology: The Science of Love* (London: HarperCollins, 1995), 248.

37. Tr. II, 3, 31. Meyendorff, *Study*, 172.

38. Meyendorff, *Study*, 173.

39. Ibid.

40. Ibid., 176–77.

41. Ibid., 175.

42. Johnston, *Mystical Theology*, 81.

43. *On the Creation of Man*, 11 (PG 44, 155), quoted in Olivier Clement, *The Roots of Christian Mysticism* (Hyde Park, NY: New City Press, 1995), 78

44. Ibid.

45. Cap. 9, 22-23: PG 32, 107-10, *Liturgy of the Hours*, vol. 2 (New York: Catholic Book Publishing, 1976), 976.

Conclusion   The End Is Not the End

1. *Hom. de croce et latrone* 1, 1-2: PG 49, 400.

2. Note, I am using the word "ascetical" in the pre-Christian Greek sense of practice or training, especially that of athletes, and in the Christian Patristic sense: "study, the practice of piety, spiritual exercise or training, an austere life." Eventually the term becomes mainly associated with the eremitical or monastic life. See *RB 1980: The Rule of St. Benedict in Latin and English with Notes*, edited by Timothy Fry (Collegeville, MN: Liturgical Press, 1981), 4.

3. Sri Aurobindo, *The Synthesis of Yoga* (Pondicherry: Sri Aurobindo Ashram, 1957), 396–97.

4. Bede Griffiths, *"Monaschesimo-indu-cristiano,"* in *Vita Monastica* XXIX (1975), 157.

5. Aldous Huxley, *The Perennial Philosophy* (New York: Harper & Brothers, 1945), 115, 299.

6. Ibid., 300–301.

7. Pierre Teilhard de Chardin, *Christianity and Evolution* (New York: Harcourt Brace Jovanovich, 1971), 11–12.

8. Bede Griffiths, *New Vision of Reality* (Springfield, IL: Templegate, 1989), 175.

Seth Godwin

V is for vunerable: Life outside
the comfort zone

Debbie Millman

| pre cynical